Access to Justice for Small Businesses

International Studies in Procedural Law

Series Editors

Fernando Gascón Inchausti (*Complutense University of Madrid, Spain*)
Burkhard Hess (*University of Vienna, Austria*)
Eduardo Oteiza (*National University of La Plata, Argentina*)

VOLUME 1

The titles published in this series are listed at *brill.com/ispl*

Access to Justice for Small Businesses

European and Comparative Perspectives

Edited by

Anna Nylund and Camilla Bernt

BRILL | NIJHOFF

ISSN 3117-9800
ISBN 978-90-04-77922-8
ISBN 978-90-04-77923-5 (PDF)
DOI https://doi.org/10.1163/9789004779235

Library of Congress Control Number: 2026948210

Brill Nijhoff and Koninklijke Brill BV are part of De Gruyter Brill.
www.degruyterbrill.com

Questions about General Product Safety Regulation: productsafety@degruyterbrill.com

Contents

PART 3
Pathways for Improving Access to Justice for Small Businesses

Acknowledgements

A book concerned with access to justice is necessarily the result of shared effort, and this book is the result of the hard work, insight, and commitment of many. We would like to extend our sincere gratitude to all the contributors to this volume. Most of the authors travelled from across Europe to join us in Bergen for a dedicated workshop, where insightful discussions and the generous sharing of ideas played a crucial role in shaping the direction of this book. We are equally grateful for the valuable contributions included here, each of which substantially enhances our understanding of the complex challenges surrounding access to justice for small businesses.

We also wish to express our appreciation for the support of the Research Council of Norway, whose funding of the project *Tvisteløsning på grunnplanet* (Primary Dispute Resolution) made this book possible. Finally, we thank the Faculty of Law at the University of Bergen for providing an excellent research environment and for facilitating the work that underpins this volume.

Anna Nylund and Camilla Bernt
Bergen, 30 January 2026

Abbreviations

ADR	Alternative Dispute Resolution
BeckRS	Beck-Rechtsprechung
BTE	Before-the-event
B2B	Business-to-business
B2C	Business-to-consumer
CDR	Consumer Dispute Resolution
CJC	Civil Justice Council
CMS	Consumer Mediation Services
CPR	Civil Procedure Rules
CREA	German Consumer Rights Enforcement Act
CSDDD	Corporate Sustainability Due Diligence Directive
ECHR	European Convention on Human Rights
ECtHR	European Court of Human Rights
ECJ	European Court of Justice
EESC	European Economic and Social Committee
EU	European Union
EWCA	England and Wales Court of Appeal
FOD	Federal Public Service Economy
GPaP	General Pre-action Protocol
GRUR-RS	Gewerblicher Rechtsschutz und Urheberrecht-Rechtsprechung
IF	Inclusion framework
LG	Landgerich
NCP	National contact point
NGO	Non-governmental organisation
NJW	Neue Juristische Wochenschrift
OCMC	Online Civil Money Claims
ODR	Online dispute resolution
OECD	Organisation for Economic Co-operation and Development
PaM	Pre-action Model
SBC	Small Business Commissioner
SCC	Stockholm Chamber of Commerce
SME	Small and medium enterprise
SNBCD	Swedish National Board for Consumer Disputes
SPV	Special purpose vehicle
VDuG	Verbraucherrechtedurchsetzungsgesetz
ZR	Zivilrecht

Notes on Contributors

Masood Ahmed
is Associate Professor of Law at the University of Leicester. His research focuses on civil procedure, the reform of civil justice, alternative dispute resolution, and international commercial arbitration. As a past member of the Civil Procedure Rule Committee, he has been involved in a number of major civil justice reform projects and has advised the Ministry of Justice, Civil Justice Council, and the Law Society of England and Wales.

Camilla Bernt
is Professor of Law at the University of Bergen and the co-chair of the research group for civil procedure and dispute resolution, and chair of the Mediation course. She has been a main lecturer in civil procedure since 2005. Her research interests and publications include civil procedure, mediation, and child law.

Alex Geert Castermans
is Full Professor of Civil Law at Leiden University and, at the time of writing the contribution, visiting fellow of the Robert Schuman Centre for Advanced Studies at the European University Institute in Florence, Italy. His research and teaching concern various topics of substantive private law as well as matters of corporate social responsibility.

Anna W. Ghavanini
is Full Professor of Procedural Law at the Department of Law, University of Gothenburg. She has previously held positions at the European University Institute and the University of Zurich. Her research interests include civil procedure, judicial decision-making, and EU constitutional law.

Bart Krans
is Full Professor of Civil Law and Civil Procedure Law at Leiden University. His research and teaching concern civil procedure law and various topics of substantive private law. He is a member of several editorial boards and has published numerous books and articles on civil procedure and substantive private law.

Anna Nylund
is Professor of Law at the University of Bergen and the co-chair of the research group for civil procedure and dispute resolution, and chair of the Commercial Dispute Resolution and Child Law courses. She has directed more than 10 research projects and has numerous publications in national, European, and comparative civil procedure; alternative dispute resolution; and child rights.

Silke Onraedt
is an academic assistant and PhD candidate at Ghent University (Belgium). Her research focuses on alternative dispute resolution, with particular attention to the conciliatory role of the judge. She studied law at Ghent University, where she obtained her Master of Laws *magna cum laude.*

Astrid Stadler
holds the Chair of Private Law, Civil Procedure, Private International Law and Comparative Law at the University of Konstanz, Germany. Her main research focus is collective redress. From 2011 to 2015, she held a part-time chair on comparative mass litigation at Erasmus University, Rotterdam. She has published more than 80 articles on collective redress and third-party litigation funding, and has edited several books with international teams of authors on the topic.

Magne Strandberg
is Professor of Law at the Faculty of Law at the University of Bergen. Civil procedure law is his main field of interest, and he has been chairing the mandatory procedural law course for many years. He is currently the vice dean of education.

Wannes Vandenbussche
is a civil procedure professor at Ghent University (Belgium). His main research interests include domestic, comparative, European procedure, evidence, and ADR. His teaching covers the same topics. He studied law at KU Leuven (Belgium), the Université Paris 1 Panthéon-Sorbonne (France), and Tilburg University (the Netherlands). He was an associate research scholar at Yale Law School (B.A.E.F. and Fulbright fellow). He is also an attorney-at-law at the Brussels Bar and an accredited mediator in civil and commercial matters.

CHAPTER 1

Access to Justice for Small Businesses: Small Businesses as the Invisible Stakeholders in the Justice System

Anna Nylund

1 Introduction to Small Businesses and Their Justice Needs

Small businesses are the backbone of European economies and societies; 98% of all businesses in Europe are small.[1] Small businesses are vital to the economy and local communities through employment opportunities and value creation: they employ 50% of the workers and generate 36% of total value added.[2] When the economic effects of sole proprietors are taken into account, the impact on employment and value creation is even greater. While many small businesses remain small throughout their lifespans and their owners might not seek to grow them significantly, some small companies develop into medium- and large-sized businesses.[3] Only some will eventually blossom into unicorns that generate huge profits; most small businesses simply fade away within the first few years of their lifespan. Nevertheless, thriving small businesses are a sine qua non for unicorns that develop into engines of the European economy but also provide services locally and Europe-wide.

Despite their importance, they are often invisible in discussions on the justice system.[4] Discussions on consumer law are one example. In consumer cases (business-to-consumer, B2C), businesses are imagined as powerful parties and consumers as weak parties, as if all businesses were relatively large and had

1 Eurostat, '2021: EU micro & small businesses employed 75.8 million' 9 November 2023 https://ec.europa.eu/eurostat/web/products-eurostat-news/w/ddn-20231109-2 (accessed 17 August 2026).

2 European Commission, *Annual Report on European SMEs 2023/2024* (GROW and JRC. SME Performance Review 2023/2024) 13.

3 Neil C Churchill and Virginia L Lewis, 'The five stages of small business growth' (2002) 3 *Entrepreneurship: Critical Perspectives on Business and Management* 83; Tim Mazzarol and Sophie Reboud, *Small Business Management: Theory and Practice* (4th edn, Springer 2019) 193–225.

4 See below, Section 3.

access to ample legal advice,[5] and as if courts should attempt to level the playing field by assisting consumers.[6] This probably reflects the leverage of medium and large businesses in shaping policies, but disputes might also be perceived differently depending on whether the parties are 'faceless' large companies or local small businesses personified by the owner and employees. When attorneys or dentists buy home cleaning services from a local cleaning company with six employees, the attorneys and dentists – the consumers – probably have better economic and other resources. Similarly, in business-to-business (B2B) disputes, the parties are presumed to have relatively equal power, and courts should consequently remain passive and refrain from levelling the playing field. Nevertheless, this is not the case when a local cleaning company with six employees has a dispute with a multinational company over cleaning services. Moreover, not all legal relationships (small) businesses have are within their core area. In addition to entering into contracts with customers and purchasing cleaning equipment from suppliers, the local cleaning business might rent office space and need office equipment and accounting services, among other things. The company's most common justice need could be unpaid bills, yet it could also be implicated in the Dieselgate scandal if it had bought Volkswagen diesel cars to drive from one customer to another. Although most disputes are ordinary, relatively simple, and low-value claims related to their core business, other disputes small businesses encounter are high-value, extraordinary cases involving peripheral aspects of their activities. Sometimes the other party is much more powerful than the business, sometimes weaker, and sometimes approximately equal in power.

5 Eg, recital of Council Directive 93/13/EEC of 5 April 1993 on unfair terms in consumer contracts (Unfair Terms Directive) [1993] OJ L95/29.

6 See extensive case law of the ECJ on the obligations of courts to enforce EU consumer law inter alia by raising issues on their own motion, encouraging the consumer to provide evidence, disapplying procedural and substantive rules, see eg, Case C-497/13 *Froukje Faber v Autobedrijf Hazet Ochten BV* [2015] EU:C:2015:357, Case C-83/22 *RTG v Tuk Tuk Travel SL* [2023] EU: C:2023:664; Case C-321/22 *ZL, KU, KM v Provident Polska S.A.* [2023] EU:C:2023:911. See also, eg, Stephanie Law, 'The transformation of consumer law in times of crisis: the ex officio control of unfair contract terms' in Alan Uzelac and Cornelis Hendrik (Remco) van Rhee (eds), *Transformation of Civil Justice: Unity and Diversity* (Springer International Publishing 2018); Jarich Werbrouck and Elise Dauw, 'The national courts' obligation to gather and establish the necessary information for the application of consumer law: the endgame?' (2021) 46 *European Law Review* 225; Alain Ancery and Bart Krans, 'Ex Officio Application of Procedural Agreements in Consumer Contracts?' in Anna Nylund and Antonio Cabral (eds), *Shaping Civil Proceedings Using Procedural Agreements* (Eleven 2024).

The lack of access to justice for small businesses likely reduces their profitability and prospects.[7] Procedural rules and the costs and delays associated with court proceedings probably disadvantage smaller businesses, either by increasing their risk of losing the case or by allowing larger businesses – and even powerful consumers – to force small businesses into unfavourable settlements. Small businesses' justice challenges have ramifications beyond their contribution to the local and European economies and employment. First, their owners have often invested most or all of their assets in their businesses. Thus, the company's economic problems could result in financial difficulties for its owners. Second, because the owner is personally deeply involved in the business, the business's problems could affect the owner's well-being by causing stress and overly long hours, and even have repercussions for the owner's close family.[8]

What is more, access to justice for small businesses also has implications for the legal system as a whole. When individuals and businesses are unable to enforce their legal rights effectively, rogue traders are, in practice, allowed to continue their business practices, whether by 'stealing' customers and giving specific sectors a bad reputation or by directly exploiting small businesses. Sometimes, access to dispute resolution can shift a business's negotiating position: the threat of a legal action can bring the other party to the negotiating table and induce the parties to make legally tenable claims and offers. Thus, effective enforcement of laws and the underpinning policy goals require access to justice for small businesses. Moreover, incorporating the perspectives of small businesses is likely to provide broader and novel views on the justice system, its potential and shortcomings. Doing so is likely to enable societies to improve the efficiency, quality, and legitimacy of the justice system for all.

This introductory chapter first defines small businesses and identifies their commonalities and differences (Section 2). The definition of small businesses provides a foundation for discussing their justice needs and the justice gaps they experience, as well as for analysing the policies and mechanisms that sustain these gaps and those designed to close them. Section 3 presents findings from studies that corroborate the premise that small businesses are often lauded as vital to economies and societies in Europe and beyond, yet are often forgotten when policies are shaped and implemented.

---

7 See Eurochambres, *Business Survey: The state of the Single Market: Barriers and Solutions*. December 2019, 6 and 25.

8 Eg, Mazzarol and Reboud (n 3) 9–20, 31–64, and 511–543.

Section 4 explains the aims and structure of this book. Section 5 discusses the contents of each chapter, their key issues, perspectives, and insights; the legal needs of small businesses and the influence of party constellations; selected procedural, substantive, and structural hindrances; and potential solutions. Then, Section 6 draws conclusions for policy and research on small and micro businesses' access to justice.

2 Small Businesses and Their Commonalities and Differences

Defining small businesses is a prerequisite for accurately analysing their justice needs. The most common ways to define small businesses are by number of employees, annual turnover, balance sheet total, or any combination of these. This book uses the same definition as the European Commission: small businesses are those with fewer than 50 employees and an annual turnover or balance sheet total of up to 10 million euros.[9] This definition covers 98% of all businesses in the EU; only 1% are medium-sized (50–250 employees) and 1% are large. Micro businesses have less than 10 employees and a turnover or balance sheet total of up to 2 million euros. In this book, the term 'small businesses' encompasses both small and micro businesses, unless the authors specifically refer to micro businesses. For the purposes of conceptual clarity, this book also includes sole proprietors and the self-employed in the category of micro businesses.[10]

Small businesses are not a coherent group.[11] They vary in size and in factors such as capital invested, profit margins, and corporate structure. Some small businesses have ample economic resources because they operate in high-profit markets or have access to other resources such as valuable machinery. Other businesses operate in markets with low profit margins and limited economic resources. There are also tangible differences among these businesses in the extent to which they depend on one or a few customers or suppliers, or on a broad base of customers or suppliers, and in whether they are dependent on a franchisor. Some businesses invest heavily in expensive machinery; others rely almost exclusively on human capital. Some sell niche services requiring extensive education; others rely on unskilled workers. Some operate in highly regulated domains; others in domains with limited regulation. More-

9 European Commission, 'SME definition' https://single-market-economy.ec.europa.eu/smes/sme-fundamentals/sme-definition_en (accessed 17 August 2026).

10 Mazzarol and Reboud (n 3) 8–9.

11 Mazzarol and Reboud (n 3) 2–10.

over, the availability of financial, legal, and other resources varies with the size of the business, the types of services it provides, the markets it operates in, the qualifications of the owner and employees, and other factors. Some businesses have highly qualified employees and owners who can easily assess legal risks and negotiate favourable contract terms, eg, law firms and accountants, while others have very limited access to legal information. In contrast, although the owners of the smallest micro businesses are acting in a business capacity, they can be in a position comparable to consumers given their legal, financial, and other resources.

Despite their differences, small businesses share many commonalities. Many small businesses operate with limited resources, and managers handle a wide range of tasks, which results in challenges with government compliance.[12] They tend to have high levels of external dependencies such as dependence on a single or a few customers and financial institutions. However, this could also entail advantages such as closer relationships with customers. Many operate in price-sensitive, local markets with low wages and are therefore vulnerable to economic downturns.[13]

These differences result in profound variations in the extent to which businesses turn to the justice system to resolve their disputes and in the types of situations in which they do so. It also engenders differences in the types of dispute resolution processes businesses use and would need to use.

3 Small Businesses: An Overlooked Stakeholder in the Justice System

The justice needs of small businesses are largely uncharted terrain. One reason could be the diversity of the businesses and the markets they operate in: the needs of a small law firm are probably very different from those of a plumber, a freelance journalist, and a café owner. Another reason is that the definition of small businesses varies, and that small and medium businesses are often lumped together without recognising the tangible differences between businesses with 250 employees, 25 employees, and just a few (part-time) employees, if any at all. Moreover, the policies targeting small businesses are fragmented and incoherent, comprising multiple layers that are

12 Mazzarol and Reboud (n 3) 9–14.
13 Mazzarol and Reboud (n 3) 9–14.

sometimes contradictory.[14] Given the heterogeneity of small businesses and their markets, the lack of coherence is not surprising. However, a study of UK business policies unravelled the role of 'institutional entrepreneurs' who push their agenda to advance their interests, which might not align with those of most small businesses.[15] The combined effect of institutional entrepreneurs and politicians who wish to appear efficient is policies based on poor data gathering, superficial policy announcements lacking substance, and ineffective implementation. Large businesses have ample opportunities to influence policymakers in diverse ways, including through the design of private dispute resolution systems. Commercial arbitration, which serves the needs of medium and large businesses, is the paradigmatic example of such a system. It also reflects how commercial disputes and dispute resolution are often implicitly viewed through the lens of larger businesses rather than small businesses, especially micro businesses.

Some of the specific justice barriers small businesses face likely arise from tacit assumptions about businesses and their legal (and financial) capabilities. More precisely, some problems seem to stem from policymakers' tendency to consider only medium-to-large businesses when designing procedural rules and the justice system as a whole. Consumers are depicted as 'vulnerable' and traders as those having resources, even if the consumer might have ample financial and personal resources. In contrast, the trader might be a micro business operating in a low-skill, low-margin sector and competing with large multinational corporations (eg, a local furniture dealer operating on thin margins, competing with IKEA). Similarly, in a business-to-business case, one party could be a micro business, whereas the other could be a highly profitable global company. Similarly, the threshold that distinguishes high- and low-value claims might not align with how businesses perceive low value: what is a low-value claim for one business might be a matter of life and death (bankruptcy) for another. Although the value of a claim is low, it could raise profound legal questions in need of clarification; thus, it could be far more important than the value of the claim itself suggests.

---

14 Anders Lundström and Lois A Stevenson, *Entrepreneurship Policy: Theory and Practice* (Springer 2005) 220 et seq.; Norin Arshed, Sara Carter and Colin Mason, 'The ineffectiveness of entrepreneurship policy: is policy formulation to blame?' (2014) 43 Small Business Economy 639; David Smallbone, 'Entrepreneurship policy: issues and challenges' (2016) 23 Small Enterprise Research 201; Oliver Mallett and Robert Wapshott, *A History of Enterprise Policy: Government, Small Businesses and Entrepreneurship* (Taylor & Francis Group 2020) 5–7.

15 Arshed et al (n 14) 651–653.

Given that policies for small and micro businesses have engendered widespread criticism for their ineffectiveness, it is hardly surprising that the justice needs of small businesses are largely uncharted territory. For example, the EU 2023 SME Relief Package mentions the word 'dispute' three times: once to declare that 'SMEs affected by breaches of EU law can rely on SOLVIT[16] to resolve disputes'[17] and twice in the context of simplifying reporting obligations related to consumer dispute resolution (CDR).[18] The word 'justice' is not mentioned once. In fact, the Commission uses the term 'small' to refer to businesses with 250–499 employees, which, in other contexts, would be considered medium-sized businesses.[19] Another example is the SME Strategy for a sustainable and digital Europe.[20] It mentions the word 'dispute' only twice and the word 'justice' not at all. The word 'dispute' is mentioned in the context of payment delays, unfair payment practices, and 'exploring the feasibility of alternative resolution/mediation mechanisms for SMEs for fast resolution of payment disputes in commercial transactions.'[21] The second occasion is when the Commission cites the Eurochambres 2019 Business Survey, which found that 62% of SMEs considered concerns about resolving commercial (and administrative disputes) to be a significant obstacle to operating in the Single Market.[22] The SME strategy does not define SMEs, nor distinguish between medium and small businesses, and mentions micro businesses only once.[23]

These examples suggest that EU policies do not adequately separate between medium and small businesses. It also indicates insufficient attention to access to justice. The Eurochambres Business Survey uncovered a gap in how smaller (ie, under 250 employees) and larger businesses (over 250 employees) viewed dispute resolution as an obstacle to operating in the Sin-

16 European Commission, 'What is SOLVIT?' https://ec.europa.eu/solvit/what-is-solvit/index_en.htm (accessed 17 August 2026); in March 2023, the Commission proposed a benchmark for SOLVIT to solve a minimum of 90% of the cases within 12 months in each Member State.

17 European Commission, *SME Relief Packages* (Communication from the Commission to the European Parliament, the Council, the European Economica and Social Committee and the Committee of the Regions, Strasbourg, 12.9.2023, COM(2023) 535 final) 9.

18 European Commission, *SME Relief Packages* (n 17) 10.

19 European Commission, *SME Relief Packages* (n 17) 19.

20 European Commission, *An SME Strategy for a sustainable and digital Europe* (Communication from the Commission to the European Parliament, the Council, the European Economica and Social Committee and the Committee of the Regions, Brussels, 10.3.2020, COM(2020) 103 final).

21 European Commission, *An SME Strategy* (n 20) 11.

22 European Commission, *An SME Strategy* (n 20) 7.

23 European Commission, *An SME Strategy* (n 20).

gle Market.[24] The concern was more pronounced among micro businesses (one to nine employees).[25] The Eurochambre study also suggests that many harmonisation measures have failed to achieve the goal of limiting fragmentation among the Member States' justice systems.[26]

However, investigating justice concerns related to litigation and other court procedures is likely to be underinclusive and to distort perceptions of small businesses' justice needs. For example, access to efficient debt collection processes is vital for many small businesses to ensure they are paid and maintain consistent cash flow. However, it could be equally crucial for them to be able to file collective actions, whether by pooling claims, pursuing group litigation, or bringing representative actions.

Still, focusing solely on formal legal proceedings is insufficient and not user-centric enough. While lawyers tend to emphasise legal aspects, small businesses might prioritise their long-term economic needs, which may entail maintaining working relationships with their suppliers and customers. Winning the legal battle in the case at hand could jeopardise long-term business relations and thus be unprofitable. This, in turn, is likely to influence which dispute resolution processes businesses prefer and which processes should be incorporated into the civil justice system. Highly adversarial processes oriented towards formal legal norms, such as litigation, may not meet the dispute resolution needs of small businesses. Additionally, a third-party resolution of a single issue, such as the value of the damage or the goods, rather than all issues, could suffice to meet businesses' justice needs. Consequently, no single form of dispute resolution provides an omnibus method for granting small businesses access to justice.

4 The Structure and Aim of This Book

This book endeavours to map the hindrances to real access to justice small businesses face and to explore avenues to increase access to justice in present-day Europe. The starting point is that the justice concerns of small businesses are likely to differ from those of medium and large businesses. Exploring those

24 Eurochambres (n 7) 10. The 2024 Eurochambres survey suggests a similar outcome but does not explore the topic in the same depth as the 2019 survey, see Eurochambres, *2024 Eurochambres Single Market Survey: Overcoming Obstacles*, https://www.eurochambres.eu/wp-content/uploads/2024/01/2024-Eurochambres-Single-Market-Survey-Full-Report.pdf (accessed 17 August 2026) 5.

25 Eurochambres (n 7) 28.

26 Eurochambres (n 7) 25.

concerns is pivotal to improving access to justice for small businesses and increasing understanding of contemporary civil justice systems more broadly.

It does so along three lines of inquiry. The first line interrogates the justice needs and justice gaps that small businesses face. In particular, it seeks to identify perspectives that are currently absent or receive limited attention in policy debates on promoting business in Europe and improving the efficiency and accessibility of justice systems. The second line of inquiry investigates selected features and developments of contemporary justice systems that could pose particular problems for small businesses. The third line of inquiry examines selected procedures that harbour the potential to enhance access to justice for small businesses. Three of the procedures discussed take place outside courts, and one is intended to facilitate the pooling of mass claims.

5 Access to Justice for Small Businesses: Needs, Barriers, and Solutions

5.1 Access to Justice Needs of Small Businesses

In Chapter 2, 'Empirical Studies on Small Businesses' Justice Needs', *Anna Nylund* explores the justice needs of small businesses, drawing on two empirical studies: one conducted in England and Wales, the other in the Netherlands. The studies showed a variety of justice needs and the ways businesses choose to address these disputes. In addition to providing quantitative data on the prevalence and nature of disputes, the two studies reveal the shortcomings of the court-centric and even lawyer-centric approach to access to justice. Small businesses turn relatively seldom to a lawyer, and court cases are just the tip of the iceberg. Instead, they seek advice primarily from other professionals, such as accountants, tax advisers, and public notaries, and prefer to handle disputes on their own or simply do nothing.[27] To those familiar with conflict resolution and access to justice research, this is unsurprising.[28] Given that small business owners have invested their financial and intellectual resources in their businesses and that the businesses probably rely heavily

27 Nylund, Chapter 2, Sections 3 and 5.

28 Eg, Alice Woolley and Trevor Farrow, 'Addressing Access to Justice Through New Legal Service Providers: Opportunities and Challenges' (2015) 3 Texas A&M Law Review 549; Hugh McDonald, 'Assessing Access to Justice: How Much "Legal" Do People Need and How Can We Know?' (2020) 11 UC Irvine Law Review 693; Rebecca L Sandefur and Emily Denne, 'Access to justice and legal services regulatory reform' (2022) 18 Annual Review of Law and Social Science 27.

on the owner's legal knowledge and experience, it is not surprising that they behave similarly, whether acting in their capacity as individuals or as business owners.

The other key insight is the value of theoretical concepts developed in access to justice scholarship, notably legal capability and legal confidence. Internal legal capability refers to the legal knowledge the business has access to through its owner and employees, based on their training and experience. The stronger the internal legal capability, the more likely the business is to assess the options at hand and select the most suitable pathway to justice. It is more likely to handle the dispute effectively on its own, seek appropriate external assistance when necessary, and thus arrive at a satisfactory and just outcome. Legal capability correlates with business size but may also correlate with the business sector. Legal confidence measures the extent to which businesses believe they can effectively resolve disputes and pursue their rights. This concept is essential because perceptions, rather than realities, often shape the course of action, including whether and how businesses respond to disputes. However, such perceptions could also influence the propensity to start a business, expand into new markets, and so forth. Moreover, legal confidence could also indicate general trust in the justice system, its accessibility and fairness, which, in turn, has ramifications for the legitimacy of democracy and the rule of law.

These findings have clear implications for policymakers and scholars: making court proceedings and court-connected proceedings more accessible and efficient does not suffice. Improving access to justice requires broadening the horizon to general capacity-building and self-help mechanisms, as well as a broad range of legal service providers beyond law firms and 'upstream', user-friendly, agile, informal dispute resolution processes, and complaints mechanisms, instead of 'downstream', costly, lengthy (and often adversarial or at least law-focused) formal proceedings.

In Chapter 3, 'Party Constellations and Access to Justice for Small Businesses: From Lilliput to Brobdingnag', *Anna Ghavanini* discusses the party constellation as an overlooked aspect of disputes and court cases, and how the assumption that businesses are stronger parties permeates policy- and law-making. First, Ghavanini questions the foundational dogma that consumers and employees are in a manifestly weaker position than their counterparts, ie, traders and employers.[29] The case law under the Unfair Terms

29 Ghavanini, Chapter 3, Section 2.

Directive[30] risks disproportionately disadvantaging small businesses vis-à-vis consumers. In cross-border relations, the combined effects of case law on forum agreements and consumer protection under the Brussels I bis Regulation[31] could be highly chilling for small businesses. Employment disputes challenge the notion of 'vulnerable' litigants due to the involvement of labour unions. If the employee receives legal aid, perhaps even including low-cost or free legal counsel, the balance tips in the employee's favour when the employer is a small business. Given that employment disputes likely play out differently when a single employee represents a tangible portion of the business's workforce, rules based on a strong presumption that the employer is the far more powerful party could negatively impact hiring practices and the growth of small businesses.

Anna Ghavanini also questions the assumptions underlying business-to-business disputes, both when the party constellation is a large business against a small or micro one and when both parties are small or micro businesses.[32] She gives several examples of how the doctrine of the 'weaker' parties applies only to situations in which an individual acts in their private capacity and is not extended to sole proprietors or micro businesses. The disadvantage the doctrine entails manifests in a variety of situations, in many of which small businesses are, in practice, in a position similar to that of consumers vis-à-vis their more powerful opponents such as financial services and social media. Moreover, systemic factors, notably the relatively low monetary threshold for small claims tracks, also disadvantage small businesses that are likely to be involved in low-value disputes and would benefit from a simplified, less costly process that is often geared towards self-represented litigants.

Finally, administrative procedure, although often overlooked in procedural law, is essential to access to justice for businesses as they operate in a society permeated by administrative rules and regulations.[33] Small businesses may need to appeal a tax or other administrative fee decision, obtain administrative permissions, such as building permits, and challenge sanctions imposed following inspections such as food safety inspections. In all these situations, the small business is clearly the weaker party, most likely with less subject-matter knowledge, access to information, and financial resources. Yet the pro-

30 Council Directive 93/13/EEC on unfair terms in consumer contracts (Unfair Terms Directive) [1993] OJ L95/29.

31 Regulation (EU) No 1215/2012 on jurisdiction and the recognition and enforcement of judgments in civil and commercial matters (recast) (Brussels I Regulation) [2012] OJ L351/1.

32 Ghavanini, Chapter 3, Section 3.

33 Ghavanini, Chapter 3, Section 4.

cedural rules do not adequately reflect the power discrepancy in this party constellation.

These two chapters demonstrate how small businesses, especially micro businesses, constitute an unseen demographic within the civil justice system. Their justice needs are consistently neglected in the formulation of procedural regulations and policies by the legislature and the judiciary. A more nuanced view of power differences among litigants would likely increase access to justice, especially for small businesses.

5.2 Barriers to Justice for Small Businesses

Chapters 4, 5, and 6 address legal mechanisms that affect small businesses' access to justice. Chapter 4, which discusses litigation costs, echoes some of the topics in Chapter 2 on the justice needs of small businesses, namely that a narrow legal approach is insufficient because it focuses only on the direct, tangible costs of dispute resolution. The following two chapters, Chapters 5 and 6, discuss how efforts to pursue per se legitimate goals, such as sustainability and diverse dispute resolution processes, can tangibly diminish access to justice for small businesses – and other groups. These chapters illustrate how small businesses are almost invisible stakeholders in the justice system, and the implications on their access to justice of their dependence on a single or a few powerful suppliers or customers.

In Chapter 4, 'Litigation Cost Regimes, Litigation Risks, and Access to Justice for Small Businesses: Insights from Norwegian Law', *Anna Nylund* and *Camilla Bernt* note that the quality of the discussion on litigation costs and their impact on access to justice is hampered by an underinclusive definition of legal costs and a lack of high-quality comparative data. Only direct, tangible costs, such as court fees and lawyers' fees, are included, while indirect costs, such as the owner of the business devoting time to dispute resolution instead of production and sales, and intangible costs, such as stress and deterioration of business relationships and reputation, are often not included.[34] Similarly, the implications of risks, such as uncertainty about how much compensation the losing party will have to pay, are frequently not adequately considered, even when there is reason to believe they will be important to many prospective litigants. Moreover, studies on litigation costs often do not, for example, mention enforcement costs, even though they often are an unavoidable part of the path to justice.

34 Nylund and Bernt, Chapter 4, Section 2.

Comparing the Nordic countries, the authors discuss court fees, evidence costs, lawyers' fees, and other costs, and how the structure and organisation of proceedings, access to evidence, and the types and amounts of evidence allowed influence total litigation costs.[35] For instance, when court fees are fixed, ie, they do not depend on the amount in dispute, they may be disproportionately high when the amount in dispute is relatively low, but above the threshold for small claims. Access to evidence and expert knowledge could be necessary to prove one's case, yet it could also be prohibitively expensive. Thus, it is paramount to strive to strike a balance between access and costs.

Lawyers' fees are usually the largest post and, thus, potentially the most significant source of litigation costs.[36] The regime for determining lawyers' fees, notably fixed fees or billing per hour, and the regime for cost-shifting (very limited, in accordance with a fixed schedule, or full shifting of necessary costs) could either render costs predictable, or very unpredictable, or something in between. The authors argue that a regime without cost-shifting delivers less justice than one with cost-shifting because pursuing one's rights is costly. For a small business, it might be better not to bring an action if the victory is pyrrhic. Full cost-shifting also entails problems because it is unforeseeable – and thus increases the risks.

In Chapter 5, 'The Corporate Sustainability Due Diligence Directive and Access to Justice for Small Businesses', *Alex Geert Castermans* and *Bart Krans* discuss how good intentions could be detrimental to small businesses. The authors recognise the importance of corporate responsibility for sustainability but argue that the EU Corporate Sustainability Due Diligence Directive (CSDDD) does not adequately account for the interests of small businesses, which serve as suppliers and business partners to large businesses.[37] Although the responsibilities lie with large (multinational) businesses, which have certain duties to assist their smaller business partners and bear the costs of verification, the CSDDD seems to disregard business reality. Many small businesses depend on a single large business, and likely try to avoid 'biting the hand that feeds them' by pursuing their rights under the CSDDD. Reporting the large company to national authorities is probably an equally risky course of action. The authors argue that the mechanisms under the Directive are insufficient for small businesses. This insight echoes Anna Ghavanini's message that power differences matter in litigation.

35 Nylund and Bernt, Chapter 4, Sections 3 and 5.

36 Nylund and Bernt, Chapter 4, Section 4.

37 Castermans and Krans, Chapter 5, Sections 2 and 3.

The authors point out beyond the specific design issues of the CSDDD, general factors that disadvantage small businesses vis-à-vis their larger counterparts, notably unequal access to costly, specialised legal services, and the willingness to protract court proceedings.[38] Large companies have the financial resources to prolong proceedings, particularly if they face the risk of losing the case. By extending and complicating the proceedings, they might induce the small business to yield or go out of business. Furthermore, the complex causal links that must be proven are problematic in themselves, as they increase the costs of evidence and litigation risks. The argument is essentially the same as for litigation costs: not only do direct, tangible costs matter but risks and indirect and intangible costs matter, too. In fact, the latter could far outweigh the direct costs.

Alex Geert Castermans and Bart Krans suggest two avenues for overcoming these justice gaps, drawing on Dutch experience. One avenue is through special courts or tracks serving small businesses, which would lower the direct and indirect costs and risks of litigation while also maintaining access to quality procedure and outcome.[39] The second avenue is public enforcement through public agencies, in which OECD (Organisation for Economic Co-operation and Development) national contact points could play a transformative role in promoting access to justice for small businesses.[40]

Chapter 6, 'The Complex Nordic Dispute Resolution Landscape and Access to Justice for Small Businesses', critically examines the potential drawbacks of a complex justice system for small businesses. *Anna Nylund* argues that the quality, cost, and duration of alternatives to court proceedings should be considered alongside those of court proceedings. Put differently, processes need to be regarded in combination, rather than in isolation.

She starts by investigating the extent to which small businesses have access to regular court proceedings in Finland, Norway, and Sweden, comparing the number of small claims cases and the costs and durations of those cases.[41] Despite having similar legal systems, there are tangible differences in this regard. Although the data do not specifically cover small businesses, they indicate that the justice gap they face varies substantially across the three countries, and that this, in turn, influences their access to many alternatives to court proceedings.

---

38 Castermans and Krans, Chapter 5, Sections 4 and 5.

39 Castermans and Krans, Chapter 5, Section 7.

40 Castermans and Krans, Chapter 5, Section 6.

41 Nylund, Chapter 6, Section 2.

Then she moves to test her main propositions, ie, the need to analyse justice systems as a whole, not just individual processes, and the need for access to efficient, high-quality proceedings, which is paramount for access to justice even when alternatives exist. The case studies are debt collection proceedings, such as payment order proceedings, initially uncontested claims which become contested in business-to-business and business-to-consumer cases.[42] The argument is that the more costly and time-consuming the regular proceedings are, the greater the risks simplified proceedings entail, especially when one party is more powerful. This proposition is similar to the one that Alex Geert Castermans and Bart Krans forward in their chapter.[43] Power differences matter and often disadvantage small businesses.

Anna Nylund also challenges the advantages of CDR, at least as it is found in the Nordic countries. Depending on the design of the process, notably restrictions in evidence, cost-shifting, and the legal effects of the outcome, and the facts of the case, CDR could either decrease or increase the justice gap that small businesses face.[44] The prolonged process is likely to make the pathway to justice lengthy and cumbersome. Thereafter, she investigates whether mediation, which harbours the potential to increase access to justice for small businesses by cutting direct and indirect, tangible and intangible costs, could close the justice gap.[45] The comparison of the mediation regimes in the three jurisdictions studied reveals that the traditional private, individualised approach to mediation is unlikely to serve small businesses well or meet their justice needs.

The conclusion is that small businesses need a justice system with quality processes, high-quality linkages, and guidance on selecting and sequencing processes. However, in practice, a complex justice system is likely to reduce, not increase, access to justice for small businesses.

All three chapters identify the costs, duration, and risks of regular court proceedings as a challenge to small businesses' access to justice. Moreover, accessibility of regular court proceedings carries over to their alternatives: the value of the alternatives, whether simplified processes or processes that promote amicable outcomes, depends on whether the parties have real, not just theoretical, access to regular court proceedings. While alternatives could be faster and cheaper, many processes are either costly or very slow, and the need to engage in several processes to effectively pursue one's rights often

42 Nylund, Chapter 6, Section 3.

43 Castermans and Krans, Chapter 5, Section 2.

44 Nylund, Chapter 6, Section 3.3.

45 Nylund, Chapter 6, Section 4. See also Ahmed, Chapter 9.

renders alternative dispute resolution (ADR) a barrier to access to justice. The authors also emphasise the role of indirect, intangible costs of dispute resolution, notably the need to maintain the business relationship with a supplier or customer on whom the business depends. For businesses, the logic of doing business, rather than the law, is often the dominant lens for businesses. This should be reflected in the dispute resolution landscape.

5.3 Pathways to Improving Access to Justice for Small Businesses

The final four chapters discuss solutions to increase access to justice for small (and medium) businesses, both in- and out-of-court, through both institutionalised and loosely regulated mechanisms. It is noteworthy that many of the solutions are highly sector-specific, even though similar solutions are often found across sectors.

In Chapter 7, 'Contract-Based Mechanisms as a Pathway to Access to Justice for Small Businesses: Examples from Norway', *Magne Strandberg* discusses contract-based forms of alternative dispute resolution commonly used by small businesses in Norwegian law. Civil procedure rules are general rather than tailored to specific cases, and judges are generalists who lack expert knowledge in most areas of life. Arbitration is very expensive and perhaps also overly complicated for everyday business disputes, which often have a relatively low value.

To remedy this problem, several business sectors in Norway have developed their own dispute resolution mechanisms, which are incorporated into standard business contracts.[46] Magne Strandberg discusses two examples: Insurance Claim Valuation, in which a third party is appointed to determine how much the insurance company will pay the insured, and Decision by Assessor, which is used in construction contracts. Although these are not specifically designed for small businesses, often, at least one party is a small business. The processes are akin to arbitration, but they do not fall under arbitration law; the Norwegian Arbitration Act applies only mutatis mutandis. The same applies to judicial valuation rules. Typically, these contract-based processes differ from arbitration and judicial valuation in that only part of the dispute, usually the level of compensation or only one issue, is handed over to the third party. Because the third party decides only part of the dispute, this is not arbitration or judicial valuation. Consequently, the process and outcome lack the procedural effects of arbitration and judicial valuation, not-

46 Strandberg, Chapter 7, Sections 1 and 2.1.

ably estoppel effects and direct enforceability. However, the obligations are binding as contractual obligations.

In many ways, these processes are comparable to Dispute Boards, which are usually permanent panels but can also be ad hoc bodies or consist of a single member, 'set up to accompany the performance of a contract' to assist the parties in overcoming (and avoiding) disagreements and disputes.[47] The typical constellation is a single-member or three-member board with technical, rather than legal, expertise.

Magne Strandberg concludes by commending these simpler, cheaper, faster, and expert-conducted processes for increasing access to justice for small businesses.[48] Yet, he also makes important points of criticism that echo those Wannes Vandenbussche and Silke Onraedt present in Chapter 8,[49] namely, the lack of a coherent regulatory, institutional, and policy approach.[50] In contrast to CDR, these contract-based mechanisms are found across disparate sectors, with limited, if any, cross-sectoral interaction. Therefore, there are a few opportunities for cross-fertilisation. Moreover, in many cases, disparate division of resources between the parties could have tangible implications for the procedure and outcome. In construction disputes, the extent to which sub-subcontractor small businesses have adequate participation rights is even more pressing because the outcome may affect them directly.

In Chapter 8, 'Small Businesses and Consumer Dispute Resolution', *Wannes Vandenbussche* and *Silke Onraedt* discuss a second avenue to increased access to justice for small businesses, namely, allowing them to use CDR processes, particularly when the other party is a large (or even medium-sized) business. Small businesses, especially micro businesses, often have very limited legal capabilities and financial resources, comparable to those of the average consumer. The problem of limited knowledge and highly uneven power relations is particularly pertinent outside their core business area, where it is dominated by a few large companies, as Anna Ghavanini notes in Chapter 3. When the small business engages the local electrician, there is no pronounced power imbalance; in contrast, this is not the case with the electricity itself because the seller is likely a large power company.

47 International Chamber of Commerce, Dispute Boards, https://iccwbo.org/dispute-resolution/dispute-resolution-services/adr/dispute-boards/ (accessed 17 August 2026). See also, eg, Anna Nylund, 'Agreements related to Alternative Dispute Resolution' in Anna Nylund and Antonio Cabral (eds), *Contractualisation of Civil Litigation* (Intersentia 2023) 90–92.

48 Strandberg, Chapter 7, Section 4.

49 Onraedt and Vandenbussche, Chapter 8.

50 Strandberg, Chapter 7, Section 4.

Vandenbussche and Onraedt analyse EU policies regarding whether and when small businesses, particularly micro businesses, are treated as consumers.[51] They note the absence of a clear policy: EU consumer legislation varies considerably in whether and how it explicitly addresses the issue. Although the EU seems to recognise the value of allowing small businesses to use CDR processes to promote access to justice and, in turn, their business opportunities, it does not do so coherently. The absence of a coherent approach means that EU law does not prohibit national laws allowing small businesses to use CDR. There is limited active encouragement to do so, and even less of a coherent policy on using CDR in this way and under which circumstances small businesses should be allowed to do so. For instance, which definition of a small business should be applied, and whether these should be omnibus rules, or limited to specific sectors (eg, starting with sectors with a few dominant actors, the services of which are indispensable for all or most businesses such as telecommunication and energy). A more coherent approach would likely make this avenue more accessible and better known among small businesses.

Wannes Vandenbussche and Silke Onraedt then discuss the Belgian experience with allowing small businesses to use CDR processes. Many of the Belgian CDR bodies have been available to small businesses for quite some time, predating EU law in this area. BELMED, a digital portal designed as a 'front door' for Belgian CDR processes, allows disputants to access information on available dispute resolution methods and identify the applicable bodies and independent mediators with relevant competence near their domicile.[52] Yet, there is limited evidence that small businesses use the processes.[53] Based on the Belgian experience, Onraedt and Vandenbussche conclude that making CDR available only to small businesses is insufficient. Despite the existence of a single, digital 'front door', they attribute some of the limited use of CDR to small businesses' limited awareness of available dispute resolution processes. The absence of a coherent terminology for who may use the CDR processes, and perhaps also the nature of those processes, contributes to rendering the dispute resolution landscape opaque.[54] Moreover, there are many other alternatives available to small businesses, such as the Chambers for Amicable Settlement, which operate free of charge in Belgian civil and commercial courts, and independent mediators whose services might be as effective as

51 Vandenbussche and Onraedt, Chapter 8, Section 2.
52 Vandenbussche and Onraedt, Chapter 8, Section 3.1.
53 Vandenbussche and Onraedt, Chapter 8, Section 3.2.
54 Vandenbussche and Onraedt, Chapter 8, Section 4.

CDR mechanisms. Read together with Astrid Stadler's observations on how including small businesses in German representative actions has failed,[55] it seems that letting small businesses use CDR mechanisms is more challenging than often thought.

In Chapter 9, 'Pre-action Protocols: Increasing Access to Justice for Small Businesses in England and Wales?', *Masood Ahmed* explores how pre-action protocols, a common place mechanism for expediting access to justice in English law, could influence access to justice for small businesses. Pre-action protocols mandate disputants to seek to resolve their disputes through ADR before bringing an action, making the courts a last resort. For small businesses, the General Pre-action Protocol (GPaP) is the most relevant one. It requires the parties to exchange relevant information regarding the legal and factual basis of the claim and the remedies they seek. Thereafter, the parties must engage with an ADR process, such as mediation, early neutral evaluation, or an ombudsman scheme. If the ADR process does not result in resolution, the parties must complete a joint stocktake report, in which they review their positions and prepare a joint report.

The primary advantages of GPaP are its potential to reduce direct and indirect litigation costs through early resolution and concentrating the case on key issues. The collaborative and clarificatory elements of the process are likely to narrow the scope of the case, thereby expediting resolution and reducing costs.[56] By explicitly naming several forms of ADR, it introduces small businesses to the manifold dispute resolution processes available, allowing them to select an appropriate process for their dispute, such as engaging an expert to provide an assessment or valuation, or obtaining a suggestion or recommendation on how to resolve their dispute, which they can then use to negotiate an outcome. It could also reduce the need for obtaining extensive legal or other specialist advice at an early stage. An early, amicable resolution seems to be consistent with small businesses' justice needs and preferences.[57] Efforts to make the justice system, in a broad sense, more accessible to disputants through simple language and a single, digital portal for accessing the system, and also, to some extent, managing the dispute resolution procedure and materials related to the dispute.[58]

However, the GPaP has also been criticised for front-loading the costs of dispute resolution: if the parties are mandated to undergo extensive pre-action

55 Stadler, Chapter 19, Section 2.
56 Ahmed, Chapter 9, Section 3.
57 Nylund, Chapter 2, Section 3.
58 Ahmed, Chapter 9, Section 5.

procedures, they risk depleting their resources long before they have the opportunity to bring an action.[59] The relationship between court-mandated mediation and access to court has been the subject of extensive debate in English law, such as whether courts have the power to mandate the parties to mediation (or use other forms of ADR), how non-compliance should be sanctioned, and whether courts may order the parties to take part in ADR multiple times (eg, try another process, if the first one did not result in the case being settled).[60] Critics have argued that mandatory ADR poses a risk for weaker litigants. New case law and the GPaP are built on the belief that an obligation to use an ADR process before bringing an action is consistent with access to justice and will ultimately benefit all stakeholders, including small businesses.[61]

In the final chapter, 'Special Purpose Vehicles in German Law: Improving Access to Justice for Small Businesses?', *Astrid Stadler* discusses special purpose vehicles (SPVs) that allow small businesses to claim their rights by pooling their claims, particularly in antitrust cases. SPVs could be regarded as a variant of collective redress or collective action. Stadler commences by noting that laws enabling small or micro businesses to participate in consumer collective redress have had minimal practical implications.[62] As mentioned above, she attributes part of this failure to differences in the law and contract terms in B2B and B2C contracts. Due to these differences, which are likely exacerbated by the ECJ case law on courts' obligation to enforce EU consumer law on their own motion, the legal differences between B2B and B2C cases are often sufficient to render combining such claims impracticable. Second, German consumer organisations, which bring the representative actions, have not been very keen to cooperate with traders' organisations, which are often their adversaries in other disputes. Third, the German Consumer Rights Enforcement Act (Verbraucherrechtsdurchsetzungsgesetz), which implements the Representative Actions Directive[63] into German law, probably contains an error that further weakens the possibilities for small businesses in relying on it to enforce their rights.[64]

---

59 Ahmed, Chapter 9, Section 3.

60 Ahmed, Chapter 9, Section 4.

61 Ahmed, Chapter 9, Section 5.

62 Stadler, Chapter 10, Sections 1 and 2.1.

63 European Parliament and of the Council Directive (EU) 2020/1828 on representative actions for the protection of the collective interests of consumers and repealing Directive 2009/22/EC (Representative Actions Directive) [2020] OJ L104/1.

64 Stadler, Chapter 10, Section 2.2.

According to Astrid Stadler, German small businesses are willing to pay for the enforcement of their antitrust rights as long as they do not need to be involved in the litigation themselves. Therefore, they use SPVs in which small businesses assign their claims to a debt collection company through a fiduciary assignment, akin to the model used to enforce compensation for delayed flights. This has the advantage of increasing the claimants' bargaining power while requiring limited resources from them and limiting the resources needed to prove the damage. Because the claims are assigned to a debt collection company rather than a lawyer, the restrictions on contingency fees do not apply. Consequently, the debt collection company may also find a third party to fund the litigation, thereby mitigating the high initial costs of obtaining evidence and so forth. The third-party funder also guarantees reimbursement of the defendant's costs if the defendant prevails.[65]

Despite their potential to substantially increase access to justice for small businesses in antitrust cases, SPVs have come under attack. Understandably, large businesses accused of cartel activity do everything in their power to avoid liability for damages and to act accordingly. The SPVs contest the prevailing principles governing the provision of legal services by allowing claimants to pool their claims and by opening the door to third-party litigation funding.[66] Moreover, allowing claimants to pool their claims through the SPV increases the workload of courts because it brings a new category of cases, cases which would otherwise not have been brought. Antitrust cases are highly complex legally, factually, and procedurally; therefore, creating a vehicle for bringing such cases, even if the total number of cases would be low due to pooling, increases the workload. Hence, not only prospective defendants and their lawyers but also the judiciary could oppose this kind of innovation, which, in turn, has resulted in many cases being dismissed. In this regard, even the ECJ has been surprisingly cautious considering its record of championing access to justice in competition law and effective judicial protection.[67]

Astrid Stadler's chapter illustrates the potential of procedural innovations and novel models to provide legal services and reduce the justice gap for small businesses. However, it also demonstrates the resistance to such advancements, particularly when the interests of large businesses, lawyers, and the judiciary coincide.

65 Stadler, Chapter 10, Section 3.1.
66 Stadler, Chapter 10, Sections 3.2.
67 Stadler, Chapter 10, Section 3.3.

Together, the four chapters demonstrate both the possibilities and pitfalls of alternatives to courts and alternative models for pursuing litigation. The pre-action protocols differ from contract-based dispute resolution processes and from small businesses using CDR in the comprehensive policy approach underlying them, resulting in more coherent regulatory and organisational frameworks. The German SPVs are the result of legal entrepreneurialism but also illustrate the difficulties such entrepreneurs face when they challenge prevalent models for providing legal services and litigation. The Norwegian contractual processes show how stakeholders within a specific business area can drive innovation in dispute resolution. While allowing small, particularly micro businesses, use of CDR processes seems like an easy solution; it entails many challenges, including differences in procedural rules.

6 Conclusions regarding Policies and Research Promoting Access to Justice for Small Businesses

Small businesses seem to be the invisible stakeholders in the civil justice system, whose voices and views are only intermittently taken into account. The absence of comprehensive, effective policies for bridging the justice gap for small businesses is striking. This could easily be attributed to the limited lobbying and bargaining power of small businesses; the ability to influence policies does not necessarily depend on the number of businesses or their total contribution to the economy but on the resources and capabilities that businesses, individually and collectively, can devote to lobbying. Moreover, small businesses are a diverse group operating in a variety of legal landscapes: they vary in terms of inter alia, legal capability, financial means, the composition of their suppliers and customers (eg, whether they rely on a single large business, or operate in consumer markets), and availability of sector-specific legal services and dispute resolution processes. Therefore, they have different justice needs. The chapters in this book and the research on small businesses' justice needs and the justice gap they experience, suggest that meeting those needs challenges existing models for providing legal services and dispute resolution.

Firstly, many small businesses prefer self-help and retaining business relationships over lawyers and vindicating legal rights.[68] Thus, what small busi-

68 Castermans and Krans, Chapter 5, Section 4; Nylund, Chapter 2; Stadler, Chapter 10, Section 1; Vandenbussche and Onraedt, Chapter 8, Section 3.2. See also Ahmed, Chapter 9, Section 2.

nesses need is help to self-help. Small businesses also need alternative legal services models. Therefore, the resistance from the legal profession to the German SPVs offered by debt collection companies is problematic.[69] While some resistance is understandable, lawyers and the judiciary should acknowledge that such innovative ways of providing legal services are indispensable to ensuring access to justice for small businesses and, probably, other groups of disputants as well. As Astrid Stadler notes, the debt collection company must engage a lawyer when they bring an action.[70] Therefore, novel models of dispute resolution services probably do not constitute a threat to the legal profession by reducing the need for legal counsel; they only change how clients enter the system.

Self-help should also be a guiding principle for the justice system. Small businesses need access to early (up-stream) negotiation-based dispute resolution processes that allow them to maintain business relationships while also vindicating their rights. Moreover, access to efficient debt collection procedures is essential for maintaining cash flow, and levelling the playing field between small businesses and their large-business counterparts, particularly when there is a pronounced power imbalance such as is the case in many franchising and licensing agreements.[71]

A second observation is that small businesses might prefer 'justice without law' or at least justice in which the law is just one concern. Many small businesses probably value outcomes based on their soundness from technical and business perspectives rather than a legal one, because the former could be more consequential for their prospects.[72] Thus, it may be advantageous to engage an expert in the relevant field rather than a lawyer. The Decision by Assessor and Insurance Claim Valuation in Norwegian law serve as examples, as Magne Strandberg illustrates.[73] This idea is one of the foundations of the English GPaP:[74] no single dispute resolution method fits all needs, and sometimes non-legal expertise is key to resolving disputes. In fact, legal knowledge could even be redundant.

---

69 Stadler, Chapter 10.

70 Stadler, Chapter 10, Section 2.

71 Ghavanini, Chapter 3, Section 2.

72 Castermans and Krans, Chapter 5, Section 4; Nylund, Chapter 6; Nylund and Bernt, Chapter 4, Section 2.

73 Strandberg, Chapter 7.

74 Ahmed, Chapter 10.

Thirdly, while small businesses clearly prefer consensual dispute resolution, they do not appear to use the available processes.[75] As Wannes Vandenbussche and Silke Onraedt note regarding Belgian CDR processes, one reason appears to be that small businesses may not be aware of the option to resort to CDR when the other party is a large business. Masood Ahmed argues that the coherent approach of the GPaP in English law, with simple language and a single digital portal for all kinds of disputes, is likely to improve awareness.[76] Another challenge could be the direct and indirect cost of alternative processes, as the parties must bear the costs of the proceedings.[77]

Fourthly, it is not surprising that the prohibitive cost and high risks of court proceedings are addressed almost unequivocally throughout this book. As Anna Nylund and Camilla Bernt explain, while discussions of legal costs are often limited to direct legal costs, indirect and intangible costs and risks are probably paramount for small businesses and tangibly influence their choices.[78] The assignment of claims through SPVs in German law also corroborates this finding: Astrid Stadler stresses that small businesses are willing to engage in litigation if their indirect costs are cut by limiting their direct involvement in the proceedings.[79] Thus, improving access to justice for small businesses requires broadening the discussions on legal costs. Alex Geert Castermans and Bart Krans illustrate how complex proceedings pre-empt good intentions of promoting small businesses' rights.[80] However, high costs are not inevitable; they depend on how court proceedings are designed, including the balance between written and oral elements, the availability and nature of the evidence presented, and the expertise brought to the proceedings, as Anna Nylund and Camilla Bernt note.[81] Simplified processes could be even riskier than regular proceedings due to their limited scope and the need to use several consecutive processes, as Anna Nylund argues.[82]

A fifth observation is that the strategy to allow small businesses, particularly micro businesses, to use CDR has proven far more complicated than expected. There are numerous differences between B2B and B2C contracts; consumer organisations may not view such developments favourably, and it

75 Castermans and Krans, Chapter 5; Nylund, Chapter 2; Stadler, Chapter 10; Vandenbussche and Onraedt, Chapter 8.
76 Ahmed, Chapter 9.
77 Nylund, Chapter 6.
78 Nylund and Bernt, Chapter 4.
79 Stadler, Chapter 10.
80 Castermans and Krans, Chapter 5.
81 Nylund and Bernt, Chapter 4.
82 Nylund, Chapter 6.

is not easy to develop a coherent approach as to when a small business shall be treated as a consumer.[83] Many of the disputes small businesses are involved in concern issues that never arise in consumer cases such as damages for antitrust violations or a lack of support in fulfilling certification requirements.[84] Moreover, as both Anna Ghavanini and Anna Nylund maintain,[85] CDR processes could disproportionately disadvantage small businesses by failing to properly recognise their limited legal capabilities and resources.

A final observation, addressed by all chapters in this book, is the lack of coherent policies on small businesses in many jurisdictions and the EU. While the justice needs of small businesses are recognised, as are some of the justice barriers they face, these insights seldom translate into coherent, effective policies. On the contrary, the policies are highly fragmented and haphazard, and thus ineffective, as several chapters in this book exemplify.[86]

These observations lead to two overarching conclusions regarding policy development on small businesses' access to justice.

Firstly, policies must be firmly grounded in recognition of the tangible differences between small and large businesses in their ability to pursue their legal rights. As Anna Ghavanini argues, the tacit assumptions underpinning B2B, B2C, and B2A (business-to-administration) disputes must be questioned because they rest on untenable arguments for small businesses, particularly micro businesses. Instead, policies should rest on the recognition that small businesses, especially micro businesses, have limited resources and legal capabilities, and that there are often tangible power imbalances between small and large businesses. Small businesses, especially micro businesses, can thus be compared to consumers. Therefore, it is necessary to distinguish among different party constellations while also developing coherent policies across case types. However, the policies should also be mindful of the substantive law differences between B2B and B2C contracts.

Secondly, coherent policies to promote access to justice for small businesses in general, and micro businesses in particular, are urgently needed. A comprehensive analysis of the sources and implications of the justice gap for small businesses, followed by policy development targeted at closing the gap, is needed. Based on the contributions in this book, no single solution will suffice to secure access to justice for small businesses; rather, a combination

83 Stadler, Chapter 10; Vandenbussche and Onraedt, Chapter 8.

84 Castermans and Krans, Chapter 5; Stadler, Chapter 10.

85 Ghavanini, Chapter 3; Nylund, Chapter 6, Sections 3.3 and 4.2.

86 Castermans and Krans, Chapter 5, Section 5; Ghavanini, Chapter 3; Stadler, Chapter 10; Vandenbussche and Onraedt, Chapter 8.

of solutions is needed. It is easy to support Alex Geert Castermans and Bart Krans in advocating innovation through pilot projects with special proceedings tailored to the needs of small businesses and their justice needs. This should include new forms of collective actions. However, alternative dispute resolution beyond regular court proceedings, particularly assignment of claims, ombudspersons, and similar institutions, is also needed.[87]

Specifically, development is needed in the following domains:

- Accessible, low-cost, high-quality legal services for small businesses beyond the current high-cost model for providing legal services through law firms
- Early, consensual dispute resolution mechanisms tailored for self-represented small businesses, aiming for interest-based outcomes
- Pilot projects for small commercial dispute proceedings
- User-friendly, high-quality debt collection proceedings to encourage timely payment
- Continued efforts to lower the costs and risks associated with regular and small claims proceedings
- Make the power imbalances between small and large businesses (and public bodies) and the limited power imbalances between small businesses and consumers (and employees) an integral starting point for all policies and law-making regarding the civil justice system

Small businesses also deserve to be explicitly and visibly included in research on civil procedure and alternative dispute resolution. Researchers should be mindful that B2B disputes often involve small businesses whose justice needs and legal capabilities differ from those of large businesses. They should also consider how different party constellations shape equality of arms, procedural fairness, and the ability to carry the costs and risks of legal proceedings. More research on access to justice for small and micro businesses is needed: their justice needs, the justice gap they face, their preferences regarding access to justice, and accessible mechanisms for delivering justice to them. This includes identifying the key shortcomings of current mechanisms for delivering justice, including legal services, ADR, and court proceedings, and ways to overcome the barriers to justice.

Policymakers and legislators should encourage experimentation and innovation and refrain from impeding efforts to rethink how legal services and dispute resolution, in all their forms, are delivered. Small businesses are too important to European economies and societies to allow us to perpetuate the current justice gap by adhering to existing practices, policies, and regulation.

---

87 Ahmed, Chapter 9; Castermans and Krans, Chapter 5, Nylund, Chapter 6; Nylund and Bernt, Chapter 4; Stadler, Chapter 10; Strandberg, Chapter 7; Vandenbussche and Onraedt, Chapter 8.

References

Ancery A and Krans B, 'Ex Officio Application of Procedural Agreements in Consumer Contracts?' in A Nylund and A Cabral, *Shaping Civil Proceedings Using Procedural Agreements* (Eleven 2024).

Arshed N, Carter S and Mason C, 'The ineffectiveness of entrepreneurship policy: is policy formulation to blame?' (2014) 43 Small Business Economy 639.

Churchill NC and Lewis VL, 'The five stages of small business growth' (2002) 3 Entrepreneurship: Critical Perspectives on Business and Management 83.

Eurochambres, *Business Survey: The state of the Single Market: Barriers and Solutions*. December 2019.

European Commission, *SME Relief Packages* (Communication from the Commission to the European Parliament, the Council, the European Economic and Social Committee and the Committee of the Regions, Strasbourg, 12.9.2023, COM(2023) 535 final).

European Commission, *Annual Report on European SMEs 2023/2024* (GROW and JRC. SME Performance Review 2023/2024).

Lundström A and Stevenson LA, *Entrepreneurship Policy: Theory and Practice* (Springer 2005).

Mallett O and Wapshott R, *A History of Enterprise Policy: Government, Small Businesses and Entrepreneurship* (Taylor & Francis Group 2020).

Mazzarol T and Reboud S, *Small Business Management: Theory and Practice* (4th edn, Springer 2019).

McDonald H, 'Assessing Access to Justice: How Much "Legal" Do People Need and How Can We Know?' (2020) 11 UC Irvine Law Review 693.

Nylund A, 'Agreements related to Alternative Dispute Resolution' in A Nylund and A Cabral (eds), *Contractualisation of Civil Litigation* (Intersentia 2023).

Sandefur RL and Denne E, 'Access to justice and legal services regulatory reform' (2022) 18 Annual Review of Law and Social Science 27.

Smallbone D, 'Entrepreneurship policy: issues and challenges' (2016) 23 Small Enterprise Research 201.

Werbrouck J and Dauw E, 'The national courts' obligation to gather and establish the necessary information for the application of consumer law: the endgame?' (2021) 46 European Law Review 225.

Woolley A and Farrow T, 'Addressing Access to Justice Through New Legal Service Providers: Opportunities and Challenges' (2015) 3 Texas A&M Law Review 549.

PART 1

Access to Justice Needs of Small Businesses

CHAPTER 2

Empirical Studies on Small Businesses' Justice Needs

Anna Nylund

1 Introduction

Despite the vast body of empirical, sociolegal literature on the justice gaps and needs individuals face,[1] relatively few studies have been done on access to justice for small businesses. The research focuses overwhelmingly on low-income and disadvantaged individuals and groups rather than on businesses. Given that particularly micro business owners are often in roughly the same position as individuals and that their private financial situation is closely linked to that of their business, they are likely to face similar justice needs and gaps. The consequences of the justice gaps are also likely to resemble those for individuals. However, businesses often have long-term relationships or repeated transactions with suppliers and buyers, which could influence their justice needs, and the magnitude of the outcome's impact could consequently be greater. Empirical studies on small businesses' justice needs are therefore paramount for informed policies for the civil justice system.

The sociolegal research corpus provides not only empirical evidence but also a rich theoretical and conceptual framework for discussing and assessing access to justice. While the focal point of civil procedure is court procedures, notably regular procedures, ie, the pinnacle of formalised, professionalised legal procedures, many contemporary sociolegal approaches to access to justice investigate access to justice from the perspective of ordinary, and often disadvantaged, individuals, and the use of less formalised, simplified procedures. These two perspectives are not mutually exclusive; on the contrary, they are complementary. Although access to a formal court procedure is a vital right under the rule of law, and courts are paramount institutions, such pro-

1 See eg, Deborah L Rhode and Scott L Cummings, 'Access to justice: Looking back, thinking ahead' (2017) 30 Georgetown Journal of Legal Ethics 485; Rebecca L Sandefur, 'Access to Justice' in Shauhin Talesh, Elizabeth Mertz and Heinz Klug (eds), *Research Handbook on Modern Legal Realism* (Edward Elgar 2021) 324–335; Naomi Creutzfeldt, Arabella Kyprianides, Ben Bradford and Jonathan Jackson, *Access to Justice, Digitalization and Vulnerability* (Bristol University Press 2024).

 | HTTPS://DOI.ORG/10.1163/9789004779235-003

cesses might not be the ideal pathway to an appropriate remedy in all situations. Therefore, it is paramount to understand when and which court procedures are suitable avenues to justice, and to develop high-quality out-of-court pathways to justice. Moreover, it is vital to understand not only the immediate factors that hinder access to courts and justice, but also, from the perspective of courts, the more peripheral factors. By flipping the point of view from courts to individuals and businesses, such factors could become the most proximate and pressing to resolve.

This chapter examines access to justice for small businesses, drawing on insights from sociolegal studies. The main sources of information are two surveys on access to justice for small businesses. One was conducted in England and Wales in 2021, surveying 10,000 small businesses with up to 49 employees.[2] The other was conducted in the Netherlands in 2018, and encompassed Dutch businesses with up to 10 employees, ie, only micro businesses.[3] Both studies include sole proprietors as businesses. Despite differences in the period surveyed and the inclusion criteria (the Dutch study included only micro businesses), the results are still comparable, and much of the survey data on English and Welsh businesses is reported by business size. Although the two studies do not provide a sufficient basis for robust conclusions about the justice gaps and needs faced by European small businesses, they still offer some indications.

First, in Section 2, the conceptual and theoretical foundations of sociolegal access to justice studies are laid out. These are helpful for analysing survey results. Then, Section 3 provides background on the legal issues small businesses encounter and on whether and how they proceed to address them. Sections 4 and 5 present and discuss the findings on the justice barriers small businesses face. Section 4 investigates psychological issues: how access to justice relates to businesses' perceptions of their ability to identify and act on legal issues, and how they regard their chances of obtaining a favourable outcome. Section 5 discusses the role of knowledge and experience in finding an appropriate legal service provider, be it an accountant, lawyer, or other professional, and an appropriate procedure, as well as costs and similar factors. It also examines how satisfied small businesses are with the services they receive. The perception of the outcome and repercussions of unresolved legal issues or poor results is discussed in Section 6. Finally, Section 7 discusses

2 Legal Services Board, *Small business legal needs: wave four survey 2021* (April 2022).

3 T Geurts and MJ ter Voert, *Geschillen in het MKB.* English summary. Cahier 2019–11 (Wetenschappelijk Onderzoek- en Documentatiecentrum 2019).

avenues to improve access to justice for small businesses, drawing on the findings of the empirical studies.

2 Access to Justice Needs, Gaps, and Capabilities

Although the number of incoming cases in courts represents only the tip of the iceberg of the legal issues individuals and businesses face, discussions of access to justice, particularly in the field of civil procedure, tend to be court-centric.[4] Even in sociolegal studies, access to justice is often framed from the perspective of the law and lawyers, rather than from the user's perspective. The main question, then, is whether individuals have access to a formal legal process. Rebecca Sandefur notes how lawyers often conflate access to legal services with justice.[5] For them, access to justice is a matter of getting access to a formal process or legal services (provided by a lawyer), not whether individuals obtain a just outcome. Moreover, even if access to justice were framed in terms of the outcome, researchers note that justice through the law might not serve the goals and interests of individuals (and businesses).[6] Individuals' and businesses' perception of what is just may not reflect what the law is, either because their understanding of the law is erroneous (which is surprisingly common)[7] or because the law's outcome does not correspond to what they believe to be a just and equitable, or practicable and reasonable, outcome.[8]

Over the past decades, access to justice research has shifted from measuring primarily the gap between the number of justiciable legal problems and

4 Katherine S Wallat, 'Reconceptualizing access to justice' (2019) 103 Marquette Law Review 581; Sandefur, 'Access to Justice' (n 1).

5 Rebecca L Sandefur, 'Access to what?' (2019) 148 *Daedalus* 49.

6 Eg, Jacqueline M Nolan-Haley 'Court mediation and the search for justice through law.' (1996) 74 Washington University Law Quarterly 47; Jacqueline M Nolan-Haley, 'Revisiting Deals and Justice in Court-Connected Mediation' in Art Hinshaw, Andrea Kupfer Schneider and Sarah R Cole '*Discussions in Dispute Resolution: The Coming of Age* (2000–2009) 2 (Oxford University Press 2025).

7 Eg, Donna Shestowsky, 'When ignorance is not bliss: An empirical study of litigant's awareness of court-sponsored alternative dispute resolution programs' (2016) 22 Harvard Negotiation Law Review 189; Pascoe Pleasence, Nigel J Balmer and Catrina Denvir, 'Wrong about rights: Public knowledge of key areas of consumer, housing and employment law in England and Wales' (2017) 80 The Modern Law Review 836.

8 Jonathan M Hyman and Lela P Love, 'If Portia were a mediator: an inquiry into justice in mediation' (2002) 9 *Clinical Law Review* 157; Charlie Irvine, 'What do "lay" people know about justice? An empirical enquiry' (2020) 16 International Journal of Law in Context 146.

the number of cases in which those involved have sought legal assistance through legal services or procedures to investigating broader measures.[9] This builds on the insight that the gap between justiciable issues and cases taken to a lawyer or a legal procedure is not only a matter of resources, but also of correctly 'naming' the issues as a legal problem and finding someone to blame.[10] Knowing how to claim one's rights and considering formal claims worthwhile are also essential factors influencing access to justice.

In this regard, the concepts of legal capabilities and legal confidence are interesting. Pascoe Pleasance and associates have defined legal capabilities as the capabilities 'required for [a business] to have an effective opportunity to make a decision about whether and how to make use of the justice system to try to resolve a problem.'[11] Legal capability requires legal knowledge, literacy, and skills.[12] This includes the ability to recognise and frame an issue as legal (naming), assess the severity of the problem (assessing), seek legal assistance (seeking), and pursue an appropriate remedy (claiming). It is also a matter of attitudes, including confidence in the legal system that provides them with access to justice. Finally, capabilities are also a matter of resources, particularly financial resources, and personal resources, such as not being held back by health conditions. The legal capabilities approach offers an interesting lens for understanding barriers to access to justice for small businesses, as they are, in many ways, similar to individuals and because it is multifaceted.[13]

The self-reported level of legal capabilities is often reflected in legal confidence. According to Pasco Pleasence and Nigel Balmer, legal confidence consists of three main factors.[14] The first factor is one's confidence in achieving a fair and satisfactory outcome in disputes in general. The second is legal self-efficacy and anxiety related to the law and dispute resolution. Thirdly, one's

9 Eg, Hazel Genn, *Paths to Justice* (Bloomsbury 2009) 249 ff.

10 William LF Felstiner, Richard L Abel and Austin Sarat, 'The emergence and transformation of disputes: Naming, blaming, claiming…' (1980) 15 Law and Society Review 631.

11 Pascoe Pleasence, Christine Coumarelos, Suzie Forell and Hugh M McDonald, *Reshaping legal assistance services: building on the evidence base. A discussion paper* (Law and Justice Foundation 2014), 123–124. See also Martin Gramatikov and Robert B Porter, 'Yes, I can: Subjective legal empowerment' (2011) 18 Georgetown Journal of Poverty Law and Policy 169; Ann-Katrin Habbig and Ingrid Robeyns, 'Legal Capabilities' (2022) 23 Journal of Human Development and Capabilities 611.

12 Pleasence et al (n 11) 130–138.

13 See Nylund, Chapter 1.

14 Pascoe Pleasence and Nigel Balmer, *Legal Confidence and Attitudes to Law. Developing Standardised Measures of Legal Capability.* (PPSR 2018). The scale builds on Gramatikov and Porter (n 11).

perception of the accessibility and equality of justice influences one's legal confidence. The higher the confidence, the higher the likelihood that one pursues one's rights. Building legal capabilities and confidence is, therefore, key to improving access to justice.

The concepts of legal capability and legal confidence are essential tools for understanding why many small businesses do not claim their rights. They also point to measures to increase access to justice that go beyond measures already taken.

3 Legal Issues Small Businesses Face and Their Resolution

This section provides background on the prevalence, sources, and nature of the legal issues that Dutch, English, and Welsh small businesses report facing. The survey of English and Welsh small businesses found that 32% of respondents had faced a legal issue in the previous 12 months.[15] As expected, the prevalence of legal issues increases with company size: only 24% of those with one employee had faced a legal issue, compared with 67% of those with 10 to 49 employees. Trading issues were the most common category experienced (21%), followed by regulation (9%), employees (8%), and tax (7%).

This corresponds relatively well with the Dutch study, which found that 35% of Dutch micro businesses had experienced one or more conflicts in the previous 12 months.[16] The most common subject matter was related to purchases and sales (30%), followed by employment issues (7%) and environmental issues (1%). The most common type of counterpart is another business (56%), followed by private persons, including employees (25%) and government entities (13%).

Only 12% of businesses in England and Wales that had experienced a legal issue identified it as such.[17] This reflects research on whether individuals can name an issue as legal correctly,[18] and it is not surprising, considering that the legal capabilities of particularly micro businesses are more comparable to those of individuals than to those of large businesses. This indicates a relatively low legal capability. The most common characterisation of the issue was bureaucratic or a private business matter. Other commonly used characterisations were 'bad luck' and 'moral'. Unsurprisingly, businesses with internal legal cap-

15 Legal Services Board (n 2) 2–11.
16 Geurts and Voert (n 3) 2–4.
17 Legal Services Board (n 2) 12–13.
18 Eg, Genn (n 9) 5–9.

abilities, such as a lawyer or other employee with at least some legal training, are more likely to describe the issue as legal than those without.

Turning to the outcome of the legal disputes, the most common outcome in the English and Welsh study was an agreement between the parties (30%), followed by the business acting independently of the other side to sort out the problem (12%), the problem sorting itself out (10%), and putting up with or moving away from the problem (10%). Only 3% reached an agreement through a solicitor or similar acting on behalf of the business, and another 3% through a decision of a commercial dispute resolution service, such as eBay and PayPal. Decisions or actions by regulators, ombudsmen, and similar accounted for only 1% of the outcomes, as did court (tribunal) decisions and independently hosted conciliation, mediation, and arbitration processes.[19]

In contrast, the Dutch micro businesses surveyed were more likely than their English and Welsh counterparts to resort to court services (12%), administrative complaints boards (2%), and consumer complaints boards (2%).[20] Dutch businesses also used private online services and arbitration.

The English study found that only 6% of the small businesses surveyed had internal legal capacity, that is, the owner or one or more employees had some training or experience with legal issues. This group includes accountants and similar professions. Despite this, half of the businesses had not engaged any professional services in the past 12 months. Of those who had used external legal services, 40% had used accountants, 12% had used membership services of their trade body, 11% had sought assistance from a tax or financial adviser, and 8% had engaged a lawyer.[21] For all services, except for accountants, businesses with 10 to 49 employees used services the most, and sole proprietors used them the least. Businesses with 2 to 9 employees had slightly higher accountant usage (65%) than businesses with 10 to 49 employees (63%).[22]

The Dutch survey yielded partly different results regarding the use of external help. One difference was that more Dutch businesses than English businesses (62% versus 49%) had engaged external help, and 24% of those Dutch businesses had engaged a lawyer. Other external capacities used in the Netherlands were accountants (24%), tax and financial advisers (16%), debt collection agencies (14%), legal expenses insurers (10%), and bailiffs (6%).

---

19 Legal Services Board (n 2) 16. See also Castermans and Krans, Chapter 5, Section 5; Stadler, Chapter 10, Section 1; Vandenbussche and Onraedt, Chapter 8, Section 3.2.

20 Geurts and ter Voert (n 3) 2–3.

21 Legal Services Board (n 2) 21.

22 Legal Services Board (n 2) 22.

These studies uncover many similarities between the two jurisdictions. The prevalence and nature of legal issues seem to be approximately the same. It is also notable that small businesses turn primarily to other professionals, rather than lawyers, such as accountants and tax and financial advisers, when seeking external advice. This is perhaps not so surprising, as many problems relate to payments, whether private law – such as paying for goods and services – or public law – such as taxes and administrative fees. Moreover, contracts have financial and tax-related aspects, on which accountants or tax advisers can provide advice. Small businesses are likely to have ongoing client relationships with an accountant or tax/financial adviser, which probably lowers the threshold for seeking advice. This should be considered when developing the civil justice system by including processes in which advice from accountants and similar professions suffices.

Nonetheless, there are notable differences between the two countries: Dutch businesses are more likely to seek external assistance when facing legal issues than their English and Welsh counterparts. This is especially true regarding the decision to engage a lawyer and to choose the dispute resolution process, particularly the tendency to prefer third-party processes. Since these are not comparative studies, the reasons behind these differences remain unclear. One possible explanation is that such services are more expensive in England and Wales than in the Netherlands. Another is that assistance is more accessible in the Netherlands, and there are more early intervention options, which businesses learn to use and thus come to value external expertise. Whether these factors explain the differences requires further research.

Of course, one could also argue that learning to resolve disputes through direct negotiations is often the most efficient approach. Furthermore, many disputes resolve themselves over time, and when one party is not reliant on the other, avoidance could be a better strategy than spending resources on resolution. This could explain why disputes are more common when a small business depends on a single supplier or customer: dispute avoidance is not feasible, and investing resources to resolve issues to prevent future conflicts may be worthwhile. Consequently, many dispute resolution methods might be a waste of resources.

4 Legal Confidence as a Potential Justice Barrier for Small Businesses

The English and Welsh report estimated how small businesses' perceptions, notably their legal confidence, influence their choices of strategies to resolve disputes.[23] Of the small businesses surveyed, about a fifth (20%) reported low legal confidence, another fifth (22%) reported high legal confidence, and the majority (58%) reported medium legal confidence.[24] The larger the business, the more likely it is to report high levels of legal confidence, and businesses with internal legal capacity reported higher levels than those without. These findings are not very surprising, considering that the larger the business, the more likely it is to have internal legal capacity and to be familiar with how the law and the justice system work. Put differently, knowledge and experience breed legal confidence. Moreover, the larger the business, the more resources it has and, thus, it probably also perceives itself as having more leverage.

Turning to the confidence in gaining access to justice, small businesses in England and Wales consider the justice system to be unaffordable, with 77% disagreeing that the justice system provides good value for money, 71% disagreeing that their business can afford legal services, and 90% agreeing that legal services are too expensive for most small businesses. Similarly, 61% disagreed that taking cases to court is easy, and 85% agreed that taking a case to court is generally more trouble than it is worth. The respondents also tend to regard the justice system as somewhat inequitable, with 87% agreeing that those with less money generally get a worse outcome and 92% agreeing that the law is like a game in which the skilful and resourceful are more likely to get what they want. However, views were split on whether issues like those they faced are usually resolved promptly and efficiently, and whether large businesses' lawyers have better access to good lawyers than small businesses. In other words, this reflects low confidence in the justice system, in the ability to seek assistance and to successfully claim one's rights, rather than in one's capability to name the legal issue and to address it without involving external legal expertise. The results correlated with business size and internal legal capacity: businesses with 10–49 employees and those with internal legal capacity had the least pessimistic views of the justice system and access to lawyers.[25] Businesses with higher trust in their legal capabilities and in the accessibility and equality of the justice system were more likely to shop around for legal assistance, seek professional advice, and perceive the process and outcome as fair.[26] Higher digital skills and the use of digital resources (eg, creating and maintaining a website, using online services, and communicating online)

23 Legal Services Board (n 2) 22.
24 Legal Services Board (n 2) 23–24.
25 Legal Services Board (n 2) 25–27.
26 Legal Services Board (n 2) 28.

were also associated with higher trust in legal capabilities and access to justice.[27]

Although the Dutch study did not measure legal capability or legal confidence, it too suggests that many small businesses score relatively low on legal confidence. The Dutch respondents were relatively sceptical about their prospects of getting justice.[28] Only 6% of the micro businesses surveyed believed that they had access to justice. More than a third (36%) considered it difficult for a business like theirs to get justice. The majority consider the legal processes to be too complex (55%), costly (59%), and time-consuming (73%).[29] Around 10% reported having no faith in courts making fair decisions or their lawyer providing quality legal services. Experience with legal issues was associated with more negative views regarding access to justice and trust in the legal system.

5 Hurdles for Small Businesses to Seek Legal Advice

Surveys of how businesses acted when facing a legal issue and how they perceived the procedure and outcome corroborate the findings on legal capacity and business size: the more substantial the internal legal capacity and the larger the business, the more likely the business is to seek assistance.[30] Put differently, internal legal capacity provides the knowledge of when and how to seek assistance, and its size is likely to correlate with prior experience in this regard.

In the Dutch study, about a quarter of businesses reported difficulty finding a qualified legal service provider.[31] A fifth of the businesses thought that there were insufficient facilities for advice or assistance for micro businesses. Dutch micro businesses reported that they did not engage a professional because they thought it would be too expensive, take too much time or effort or be of limited help.[32] Instead, a third reported handling the situation on their own, one in six asked a friend for help or advice, and one in ten did nothing. These findings are consistent with those from England and Wales.[33] The Dutch study found that the more severe the consequences of the dispute or issue and the

27 Legal Services Board (n 2) 32.
28 Geurts and ter Voert (n 3) 2.
29 Geurts and ter Voert (n 3) 8.
30 Legal Services Board (n 2) 42–43.
31 Geurts and ter Voert (n 3) 2.
32 Geurts and ter Voert (n 3) 5.
33 Legal Services Board (n 2) 34–35.

longer it had been present, the more likely the business was to engage a professional. Businesses with an existing contract with a legal service provider were more likely to seek advice than those without one.[34]

However, English and Welsh businesses that dealt with the issue without assistance were more satisfied with the result than those that had sought advice.[35] Perhaps the reason is that the issue is so simple that they can handle it themselves and that doing so allows businesses to retain control over the process and outcome. Businesses seeking advice from friends and family could indicate that the problem is relatively simple and common. This, in turn, suggests that self-help is fundamental to increasing access to justice, enabling small businesses to address their problems efficiently. It also seems to support the idea that when disputants collaborate, they often achieve outcomes superior to those they would obtain in a legal process.

English and Welsh small businesses reported selecting professionals primarily based on prior use of the professional and their expertise and reputation.[36] However, only 28% of the businesses surveyed had shopped around for a provider. The majority (54%) wanted to do so but did not know how. Some thought it was unnecessary, too time-consuming, or difficult. Those businesses that had shopped around placed greater emphasis on reputation, expertise, and cost than those who had not, who, in turn, placed greater emphasis on prior use and recommendations from accountants and trade bodies. In the Dutch study, a third of respondents found it challenging to find good legal advice and a good service provider.[37]

This indicates that many small businesses just use the same professional(s) without considering whether the assistance they provide is suitable for the issue at hand. Many find it difficult to locate information on available legal services and service providers, their suitability, and competence for the case at hand. This indicates that access to justice needs to be addressed at the front end, even before the business considers seeking legal advice, not just in court proceedings.

Of those who had sought assistance from a legal service provider in England and Wales, 70% were satisfied with the service and 9% were dissatisfied.[38] The Dutch study found similar results: most businesses (67%) were satisfied, and a minority (11%) were dissatisfied with the service provider.[39] In the English and

34 Geurts and ter Voert (n 3) 5.
35 Legal Services Board (n 2).
36 Legal Services Board (n 2) 44–50.
37 Geurts and ter Voert (n 3) 8.
38 Legal Services Board (n 2) 50–55.
39 Geurts and ter Voert (n 3) 7.

Welsh study, the primary sources of dissatisfaction were efficiency and quality, ie, the process took too long and/or was too costly, and the service quality was not satisfactory.[40] In contrast, the Dutch respondents were predominantly dissatisfied with the costs.[41] Dissatisfaction with efficiency could indicate problems with the management of expectations: small businesses have too little and inaccurate information about the cost and duration of the process. The perception of poor quality could reflect low quality, miscommunication, poor expectation management, or the selection of a less suitable professional.

6 Small Businesses' Perceptions of Getting Justice and the Repercussions of Unmet Justice Needs

Turning to perceptions of the process and outcome, the survey of English and Welsh businesses indicates that the majority of small businesses perceive the process as fair. However, the experience of procedural justice correlated with business size, with smaller businesses reporting lower satisfaction.[42] The Dutch study had similar findings, with a quarter of respondents involved in judicial and non-judicial formal processes being dissatisfied with procedural justice, for example, because they did not feel they had received adequate information, received equal treatment, or had been heard.[43] A third of the Dutch respondents who had received a decision from a court or other (quasi-)adjudicative body were dissatisfied with it, and another third reported that the decision was to their disadvantage.[44] Businesses that sorted out the issue on their own were slightly more satisfied with the outcome. Interestingly, some Dutch small businesses did not consider the dispute settled despite receiving a decision.

These findings indicate that even if formal justice is delivered, small businesses sometimes perceive that justice has not been done. It underscores the importance of procedural justice, of courts and other bodies being user-friendly and communicating effectively with users.

About half of businesses in England and Wales reported no negative consequences arising from their legal issue.[45] The other half had experienced eco-

40 Legal Services Board (n 2) 50–55.
41 Geurts and ter Voert (n 3) 7.
42 Legal Services Board (n 2) 50–52.
43 Geurts and ter Voert (n 3) 7.
44 Geurts and ter Voert (n 3) 8.
45 Legal Services Board (n 2) 55–56.

nomic consequences, most commonly loss of income and additional costs. Others reported lost opportunities and indirect costs, such as the inability to complete scheduled work, loss of a customer or contract, and inability to take on new work. Furthermore, some reported intangible damages, notably reputational damage and damage to business relationships. Sole proprietors were the most vulnerable. Low legal capability and confidence were also associated with negative consequences.[46] The Dutch study had similar findings.[47]

7 Avenues for Improving Access to Justice for Small Businesses

The findings on the legal issues small businesses face, their perceptions of their legal capability and legal confidence, how they decide to handle the issues, and the outcomes indicate that access to court proceedings might not be the key issue. Instead, capability-building appears paramount. Small businesses need easily accessible information on their rights, how to pursue them, and when and where to seek advice. They would benefit from greater legal literacy and a better understanding of the roles of different professionals and processes in the legal system. This could be through education tailored to small businesses facing specific issues, such as commercial leases, employment, or value-added tax, as well as readily available resources they can consult, including information on legal rules and procedures and guidance on finding a suitable professional. Given that addressing the issues without external assistance was associated with greater satisfaction with the outcome, this should also include advice on how to negotiate outcomes. In other words, they need help to self-help through their business and professional organisations and public bodies.

The two studies also highlight the role of professions other than lawyers as key actors in the civil justice system and providers of legal services. These groups include accountants, tax advisers, and public notaries, among others. Easy access to these professionals, through sufficient availability, clear roles, and affordable pricing, probably suffices to meet much of the justice needs of small businesses.

This does not preclude making dispute resolution processes more accessible and creating mechanisms to level the playing field within them. On the contrary, accessible, efficient, and user-friendly dispute resolution processes

46 Legal Services Board (n 2) 57–58.

47 Geurts and ter Voert (n 3) 3–4.

are also crucial for building confidence in the legal and justice systems among small businesses. Small businesses prosper when they have adequate access to justice through both processes that promote formal justice through the law and those that promote negotiated, interest-based justice. Some of these challenges – and possible solutions – are examined in the following chapters.

Above all, it is important to recognise the specific justice challenges, needs, and gaps that small businesses – micro businesses in particular – face, and to address them. In many ways, these businesses resemble individuals rather than large businesses. The civil justice system needs to recognise this by operating with a more fine-grained distinction between disputants, which includes small (and micro) businesses as a distinct category.

References

Creutzfeldt N, Kyprianides A, Bradford B and Jackson J, *Access to Justice, Digitalization and Vulnerability* (Bristol University Press 2024).

Felstiner WL, Abel RL and Sarat A, 'The emergence and transformation of disputes: Naming, blaming, claiming…' (1980) 15 Law and Society Review 631.

Genn H, *Paths to Justice* (Bloomsbury 2009).

Geurts T and ter Voert MJ, *Geschillen in het MKB.* English summary. Cahier 2019–11. Wetenschappelijk Onderzoek- en Documentatiecentrum 2019.

Gramatikov, Martin and Robert B Porter, 'Yes, I can: Subjective legal empowerment' (2011) 18 Georgetown Journal of Poverty Law and Policy 169.

Habbig A-K and Robeyns I, 'Legal Capabilities' (2022) 23 Journal of Human Development and Capabilities 611.

Hyman JM and Love LP, 'If Portia were a mediator: an inquiry into justice in mediation' (2002) 9 Clinical Law Review 157.

Irvine C, 'What do "lay" people know about justice? An empirical enquiry' (2020) 16 International Journal of Law in Context 146.

Legal Services Board, *Small business legal needs. Wave four survey 2021* (Legal Service Board, April 2022).

Nolan-Haley JM, 'Court mediation and the search for justice through law' (1996) 74 Washington University Law Quarterly 47.

Nolan-Haley J, 'Revisiting Deals and Justice in Court-Connected Mediation' in Art Hinshaw, A Kupfer Schneider and SR Cole (eds), *Discussions in Dispute Resolution: The Coming of Age* (2000–2009) (Oxford University Press 2025).

Pleasence P and Balmer N, *Legal Confidence & Attitudes to Law. Developing Standardised Measures of Legal Capability.* (PPSR 2018).

Pleasence P, Balmer NJ and Denvir C, 'Wrong about rights: Public knowledge of key areas of consumer, housing and employment law in England and Wales' (2017) 80 The Modern Law Review 836.

Pleasence P, Coumarelos C, Forell S and McDonald HM, *Reshaping legal assistance services: building on the evidence base. A discussion paper* (Law and Justice Foundation 2014).

Rhode DL and Cummings SL, 'Access to justice: Looking back, thinking ahead' (2017) 30 Georgetown Journal of Legal Ethics 485.

Sandefur RL, 'Access to what?' (2019) 148 Daedalus 49.

Sandefur RL, 'Access to Justice' in S Talesh, E Mertz and H Klug (eds), *Research Handbook on Modern Legal Realism* (Edward Elgar 2021).

Shestowsky D, 'When ignorance is not bliss: An empirical study of litigant's awareness of court-sponsored alternative dispute resolution programs' (2016) 22 Harvard Negotiation Law Review 189.

Wallat KS, 'Reconceptualizing access to justice' (2019) 103 Marquette Law Review 581.

CHAPTER 3

Party Constellations and Access to Justice for Small Businesses: From Lilliput to Brobdingnag

Anna W Ghavanini

1 Introduction

The principle of equality of arms is a fundamental component of the right to a fair trial under Article 6(1) of the European Convention on Human Rights (ECHR). According to the Grand Chamber of the European Court of Human Rights, this principle requires 'fair balance' between the parties and specifically that 'each party must be afforded a reasonable opportunity to present his case under *conditions that do not place him at a substantial disadvantage* vis-à-vis his opponent or opponents'.[1] In disputes where one of the parties is a small or micro business, this becomes particularly challenging, as a substantial disadvantage may follow immediately from traits of the parties themselves. The question is then: How can or indeed must procedural rules provide conditions that compensate for the disadvantage in which the party already finds itself?

Broadly speaking, civil procedure is conceived of as governing disputes between equals, each able to defend their own interest. In some instances where this is patently untrue, such as in consumer or employment cases, special provision has been made to empower the systemically weaker actor, thus securing, or at least attempting to secure, a level playing field.[2] The case of small businesses presents, however, two distinctive difficulties. First, the category is not homogeneous. As has been observed in the introduction to this volume, the term 'small businesses' is typically given a broad definition and

---

1 *Avotiņš v Latvia* App no 17502/07 (ECtHR, 23 May 2016), para 119; *Regner v Czech Republic* App no 35289/11 (ECtHR, 19 September 2017) para 146. Emphasis added.

2 See, for instance, sections 3–5 of Regulation (EU) No 1215/2012 on jurisdiction and the recognition and enforcement of judgments in civil and commercial matters (recast) (Brussels I Regulation) [2012] OJ L 351/1. The EU Court of Justice (CJEU), as well as the Union legislature, have been particularly vigilant concerning the procedural protection of the consumer, see eg, Verica Trstenjak and Erwin Beysen, 'European consumer protection law: *Curia semper dabit remedium?*' (2011) Common Market Law Review 95; Christine Riefa and Mateusz Grochowski, 'The enforcement of EU consumer law' in Miroslava Scholten (ed), *Research Handbook on the Enforcement of EU Law* (Edward Elgar 2023).

 HTTPS://DOI.ORG/10.1163/9789004779235-004

thus encompasses businesses with very different procedural 'armoury' and consequently very different needs. This suggests that a 'one size' procedural regime for small businesses will, in fact, not fit all, or even most.

Second, even adopting the narrower definition employed here,[3] protecting small businesses is a more complex matter than protecting consumers or employees. The consumer and the employee are not merely the designations of a legal subject, but of a person in a particular legal relationship. While any natural person can be a consumer, we are only consumers when, for personal purposes, we enter into a contract for the sale of goods or services with a business acting within its trade.[4] And we are only employees in relation to our employers. The 'small business' label, on the other hand, designates a business of a certain size and is independent of the legal relationships it engages in. Thus, any measure offering protection to small businesses will have to take into account the wide variety of situations in which that protection may be needed. Like the hero of Jonathan Swift's *Gulliver's Travels*, a small business may, depending on the company in which it finds itself, come across as both very small and very big. No doubt, the small business will most often indeed be the smaller party, feeling as inconsiderable as Gulliver would have felt upon reaching the shores of the land of the giants, Brobdingnag. However, like Gulliver in Lilliput, even the small business may itself become the giant, compared to the (even) smaller and less resourceful parties with whom it may find itself in disagreement, for instance, in its capacity as employer or retailer.

This chapter will explore the various relationships within which a small business may find itself having to defend its interests in court. It will analyse the relative position of the small business in each, demonstrating the difficulties arising in different constellations and discussing how equality of arms can be achieved. Section 2 examines disputes where the small business will be appearing against a natural person: consumers and employees, most commonly. Section 3 then deals with business-to-business disputes, distinguishing between those where there is no inherent imbalance between the parties (i.e., the counterpart may be either another small business or a larger business) and those where the small business will regularly or systemically find itself at a disadvantage vis-à-vis a larger and/or multinational business. Finally, section 4 considers the particular challenges presented by disputes between small businesses and public authorities. Section 5 summarises and concludes.

---

3 As proposed by the editors of this volume, the term 'small business' is used here to designate businesses with less than ten employees and a relatively limited turnover, as well as sole proprietors and self-employed persons (see Nylund, Chapter 1).

4 This definition is found in Council Directive 93/13/EEC on unfair terms in consumer contracts (Unfair Terms Directive) [1993] OJ L 95/29 Article 2.

2 Small Businesses v Natural Persons

When getting into a dispute with a natural person, the small business finds itself in the position of Gulliver in Lilliput – not in possession of any more strength or resources than usual, but still relatively speaking the bigger party. Yet, as we shall see, it is not a given that the small business has the upper hand in court. In particular, disputes of this kind are often governed by substantive legislation designed to protect the weaker party; a protection that at least partly carries over to the judicial setting.

The two most common types of dispute in this constellation are likely those with consumers and those with employees. In consumer disputes, the business – whether small or large – has the benefit of being a repeat player acting within its trade, thus possessing experience and expertise. This advantage is, however, relative to the size of the business. A small business will often have fewer customers and less experience with dispute resolution than a larger one, and many small businesses will not have in-house legal expertise. While acting in a professional capacity will likely induce a more circumspect outlook, a single-person business may have little more expertise in matters of dispute resolution and particularly in the intricacies of ordinary civil procedure than an average consumer.

Acting as claimant – which is probably the most common party constellation in consumer disputes – the business typically has a simple monetary claim upon the consumer, which will be relatively easy to prove. Many jurisdictions provide for various forms of simplified or summary proceedings for these types of claims;[5] at the EU level, the Small Claims Procedure[6] and the European Payment Order[7] provide for simplified access to justice in cross-border cases. Where the small business appears as defendant, on the other hand, these benefits do not materialise (with the exception of small claims procedures, which may still be available); disputes are typically more legally complex, mandating a fuller trial and thus more demanding in both substance and procedure. At the same time, consumer claimants can benefit from the

5 See eg, Torbjörn Andersson, 'Ex Officio Application of the Unfair Terms Directive Cases against Consumers: A Swedish Perspective' in Anna Nylund and Magne Strandberg (eds), *Civil Procedure and Harmonisation of Law* (Intersentia 2019). A comparative overview is compiled by the EU Commission is available here: https://e-justice.europa.eu/topics/money-monetary-claims/small-claims_en (accessed 17 August 2026).

6 Regulation (EC) NO 861/2007 establishing a European Small Claims Procedure (Small Claims Regulation) [2007] OJ L199/1.

7 Regulation (EC) NO 1896/2006 creating a European order for payment procedure (Order for Payment Regulation), [2006] OJ L399/1.

right to sue in the court of their own domicile according to Article 18 of the Brussels I Regulation and also have the possibility, at least under certain circumstances, to bring collective actions, as guaranteed by the Representative Actions Directive.[8] In particular, the latter mechanism may – if effectively designed and used[9] – significantly shift the balance between a large group of claimants and a small business acting as defendant.

More broadly, and regardless of which party appears as claimant or defendant, recognition of the disadvantages that consumers face in disputes with traders has led legislatures to adopt a broad range of consumer protection mechanisms intended to level the playing field in consumer disputes. Within European Union law, these include the prohibition of prorogation of jurisdiction in standard or other pre-dispute agreements under the Unfair Terms Directive[10] and the extensive duties of national courts to act ex officio to protect the consumer's interests during the course of litigation.[11] Such measures, while well-intentioned and in many cases necessary to ensure effective judicial protection for consumers, will, however, affect the balance between the parties differently depending on the resources available to the trader. While the benefit of having the case heard in their own court of domicile may be key to effective access to justice for a consumer, the result is that the trader may be forced to conduct parallel proceedings before different courts with limited opportunities for coordinating its defence. This may prove prohibitively expensive for a small business. Similarly, the court's duty to examine of its own motion that the rights of the consumer are adequately protected is justified by the assumption that the trader is capable of effectively protecting theirs; where that active approach is followed in a dispute against a small trader, this may create, rather than even out, an information inequality. At least in the case of micro businesses (including, in particular, sole proprietors

8 Directive (EU) 2020/1828 on representative actions for the protection of the collective interests of consumers (Representative Actions Directive) [2020] OJ L409/1. See also Vandenbussche and Onraedt, Chapter 8; and Stadler, Chapter 10, Section 2.

9 Cf eg, Beate Gsell, 'The new European Directive on representative actions for the protection of the collective interests of consumers – a huge, but blurry step forward' (2021) Common Market Law Review 1365; Lena Hornkohl, 'Up- and downsides of the new EU Directive on representative actions for the protection of the collective interests of consumers – comments on key aspects' (2021) Journal of European Consumer and Market Law 189, who both caution that the Directive's general vagueness and exaggeration of the risk of abusive procedures may render it ineffective.

10 Article 3(3) compared to Annex 1(q).

11 See, eg, Joined Cases C-240/98 to C-244/98 *Océano Grupo* [2000] EU:C:2000:346; Case C-40/08 *Asturcom* [2009] EU:C:2009:615; Case C-137/08 *Pénzügyi Lízing* [2010] EU:C:2010:659; Case C-32/12 *Duarte Hueros* [2013] EU:C:2013:637.

and the self-employed), one might wonder whether it may not be reasonable to extend some consumer protection measures also to traders.

Similar concerns arise in employment disputes, which are often both legally and factually more complex than consumer cases and have higher financial stakes. Employment disputes are often heard in special proceedings before designated labour tribunals, catering to the particular needs of the labour market and the social partners.[12] However, the role of the social partners in adjudication varies significantly between jurisdictions. In Sweden, the social partners take centre stage, to the extent that actions are brought and defences are lodged by the organisations in their own names on behalf of organised members, with the members themselves enjoying only a secondary right to bring judicial actions if their trade union or employers' organisation refuses.[13] In Germany, trade unions have an important role to play as legal advisors and representatives before the labour courts, but have little opportunity to take action in their own name.[14] In Great Britain, there is virtually no role for the social partners within the judicial procedure, which is, in principle, enacted as a dispute between the individual employee vis-à-vis their employer.[15] It goes beyond the scope of this chapter to evaluate each system. Suffice it to observe that, where the employer is a small business, the imbalance inherent in the employment relationship is comparatively insignificant, meaning that a more individualistic procedural setting like the British one may provide for the equality of arms (or, differently put, an equal amount of obstacles). An organisation-centred procedure, such as the Swedish one, may work best in cases where both employer and employee are organised, meaning that each of the parties has access to resources and expertise at comparable or at least satisfactory levels. Where one party is unorganised, however, it will create significant imbalances, which will be particularly pronounced in the case of small business facing a trade union as a counterparty.

---

12 Kuan-Ling Shen, 'Labour proceedings in the judicial system: a comparative analysis' in Burkhard Hess et al (eds), *Comparative Procedural Law and Justice* (Part XII, chapter 4) <cplj.org/a/12–4> (accessed 17 August 2026).

13 Anna Wallerman Ghavanini, 'United we stand, divided we sue: Collective access to court for labour and social security claims in Sweden' (2021) European Labour Law Journal 492, 499.

14 Bernd Waas, 'Enforcement of Labour Law: The Case of Germany' (2021) 37 International Journal of Comparative Labour Law and Industrial Relations, 225, 236.

15 Susan Corby, 'Labour courts in Great Britain and Sweden: a self-service model v collective regulation' University of Greenwich Business School Working Paper WERU No 4, 2013.

3 Small Businesses v Other Businesses

Disputes between one business and another are, as a rule, regulated by private law and resolved through civil procedure. While some types of specialised disputes, including, for instance, those concerning intellectual property, will often be subject to the jurisdiction of specialised courts with their own procedural arrangements, the majority will be adjudicated through the ordinary civil litigation tracks: civil procedure before general courts as well as a range of alternative dispute resolution methods, with arbitration taking pride of place. Indeed, these cases are the very ones for which civil procedure is designed: private law disputes between economically active actors capable of rational decision-making.[16]

Many of the transactions undertaken by a small business will be with another trader, which in turn may be a small, medium-sized, or large one. To this category belong, for instance, the purchase of goods and materials, the purchase and lease of equipment, and intellectual property disputes. Depending on the line of business, some small firms may find themselves more regularly in contact with larger contracting parties. For instance, freelancers in the cultural and creative industries, as well as niche retailers and artisanal food producers, will likely conduct most of their transactions with consumers or other small or medium-sized actors, whereas small firms in the construction business will often enter into an agreement with large-scale property developers, and small-scale farmers may count large corporations among both their suppliers and their customers. Nevertheless, there is no imbalance inherent in these contractual relationships, and the small business may act as buyer or seller, applicant or defendant.

As there is no systemic imbalance between the parties in business-to-business disputes, civil procedure typically does not include special provisions made for the protection of a weak party. As the EU Court of Justice put in the 1997 judgment in *van Schijndel,* the disputes in question concern 'civil rights and obligations freely entered into by the parties', in which 'conceptions prevailing in most of the Member States as to the relations between the State and the individual' require that the judge takes a passive role, the parties being responsible for bringing any legal and factual claims that they find relevant as well as the evidence needed to prove them.[17] Yet, small businesses face obstacles related not only to their relative size vis-à-vis the other party but also to

16 See also Castermans and Krans, Chapter 5.

17 Joined Cases C-430/93 and C-431/93 *van Schijndel and van Veen* [1995] EU:C:1995:441, paras 20–21.

their absolute size, which may hinder their effective access to – and enjoyment of – civil justice.

Small claims procedures represent one widely adopted means of dealing with the problem that civil procedure tends to be inaccessible to all but the most resourceful, financially speaking. The relevance of small claims procedures as well as their impact on access to justice for small businesses will, however, vary widely between jurisdictions.[18] For instance, the European small claims procedure, which caps claims at EUR 5,000,[19] will likely be outside the scope for many commercial claims, even for small-sized traders; the same goes, *in forte,* for the Swedish small claims procedure, which is capped at about half that sum.[20] On the other hand, the small claims track under the English Civil Procedure Rules is the normal track for claims up to GBP 10,000 (approx. EUR 11,000),[21] and the Norwegian equivalent can be relied upon for claims as large as NOK 250,000 (approx. EUR 21,000),[22] making these procedures more relevant for commercial actors.

Small claims procedures, where available, often contain provisions limiting the court fees or the attorney fees that a party can be obliged to cover, or both. In ordinary civil procedure, by contrast, the English rule is predominant for the allocation of litigation costs,[23] meaning that the losing party must compensate the winner for their costs. The risk of incurring liability for exorbitant costs is widely recognised as a main obstacle to access to justice overall, and is, for obvious reasons, more acute for actors of limited means, including small businesses. In this regard, arbitration is particularly troublesome. While arbitration may well be a beneficial dispute resolution mechanism, including for small businesses, even the more summary forms of arbitration, such as the Expedited Rules provided by the Arbitration Institute of the Stockholm Chamber of Commerce,[24] are often prohibitively expensive, particularly for smaller claims. Unlike consumers, small businesses enjoy no protection against pre-

18 For a comparison between small claims regimes in France, Spain, and Italy, see Elisabetta Silvestri, 'Small Claims and Procedural Simplification: Evidence from Selected EU Legal Systems' (2018) Access to Justice in Eastern Europe 6. See also Nylund, Chapter 6.

19 the Small Claims Regulation Article 2.

20 Section 1:3d of the Swedish Code of Judicial Procedure (*Rättegångsbalken*).

21 English CPR rule 26.9.

22 Section 10-1 of the Norwegian Dispute Act (*Tvisteloven*).

23 George B Shepherd, 'The Impacts of the European Rule for Fee-Shifting on Litigation Behavior' in Hans-Eric Rasmussen-Bonne *et al* (eds), *Balancing of interests: liber amicorum Peter Hay zum 70. Geburtstag* (Recht und Wirtschaft 2005) 381.

24 Stockholm Chamber of Commerce Arbitration Institute https://sccarbitrationinstitute.se/en/scc-expedited-arbitration-rules-english-2023/ (accessed 17 August 2026).

dispute arbitration clauses and may not have the knowledge or bargaining power to oppose the inclusion of such a clause in a contract with a larger counterparty.

Furthermore, within the business-to-business category, there are types of disputes that place a small business firmly in the land of the giants. This may especially be the case for financing, loans, credits, and insurances, which are, with very few exceptions, provided by large-scale corporations; for social media accounts and other online services; and for franchising and licensing arrangements. These relationships all share some essential characteristics with consumer contracts, aside from the fundamental power imbalance between the parties.

As for financing contracts and social media accounts, the service provided to a small business is often of the same or a very similar kind to that provided to a consumer, and it would, from the perspective of the provider, not seem to make a radical difference whether the debtor is a natural person acting in their personal capacity or a micro business; it may even be difficult to distinguish between the two capacities.[25] Furthermore, the typical claim raised by the bank or another creditor will, like the trader's in a consumer case, be a legally simple claim of payment under the contract, for which most jurisdictions will provide summary procedures, whereas a claim arising on the debtor's side may be more complex, thus requiring a full trial. While insurance policy holders, whether natural or legal persons, are protected in European cross-border disputes by section 3 of the Brussels I Regulation, no special provision exists for small, non-consumer debtors when engaging in litigation.

Franchising and licensing agreements are of a more clear-cut commercial kind, differing from almost any contract a consumer may enter into.[26] Nevertheless, these, too, share some central traits with consumer disputes.[27] In particular, the franchisor regularly enters into similar contracts as part of its business model, and the 'product' is subject to limited customisation; since standardisation of the contract is core to protecting the brand, the franchisee must, in principle, accept the franchisor's terms or take their business else-

25 Cf Case C-498/16 *Schrems* [2018] EU:C:2018:37 paras 25–41.

26 The Court of Justice has rightly held that a franchisee cannot be considered a consumer in relation to the franchisor, even before the former has started trading (Case C-269/95 *Benincasa* [1997] EU:C:1997:337, paras 15–19).

27 Cf Christopher R Drahozal, 'Unfair arbitration clauses' (2001) University of Illinois Law Review 695, 696 n 9, who observes that consumer and franchise contracts are often treated as comparable in (North American) literature.

where.[28] Yet, in civil procedure, disputes between franchisors and franchisees are typically treated as being between equals. Thus, there is, for instance, no protection against arbitration clauses, despite such clauses being relatively common and tending to favour the franchisor, who benefits disproportionately from the confidentiality afforded by arbitration and can often dictate the choice of location and other specifics of the arbitration agreement.[29]

A possible access to justice avenue available to small businesses in these structurally uneven relationships is that of collective redress, which is particularly relevant in disputes where one (stronger) party has entered into a large number of similar contracts with (weaker) counterparties. The viability of this avenue depends, however, on how collective actions are construed. Following a criticised and largely ineffective recommendation on common principles for injunctive and compensatory collective redress mechanisms,[30] the EU legislature has focused its efforts concerning collective redress on consumer relationships in particular, through the Representative Actions Directive discussed above, leaving (small) businesses to fend for themselves under the highly diverse collective redress mechanisms available (or not) under national law.[31]

4 Small Businesses v Public Authorities

Small businesses – and not only those – will regularly come into contact with public authorities: applying for permits, paying their fees, submitting to inspections, and filing their tax reports. They may participate in public procurement procedures or apply for protection for their trademarks and other

28 Cf Robert W Emerson and Zachary R Hunt, 'Franchises, consumers, and employees: choice and arbitration' (2022) William and Mary Business Law Review 487, 540.

29 See, in the North American context, Emerson and Hunt (n 28) 544.

30 Commission Recommendation 2013/396/EU on common principles for injunctive and compensatory collective redress mechanisms in the Member States concerning violations of rights granted under Union Law [2013] OJ L201/60. The Commission itself, in a subsequent report, described the implementation of this recommendation as 'limited', Report COM(2018) 40 final on the implementation of the Commission Recommendation of 11 June 2013 on common principles for injunctive and compensatory collective redress mechanisms in the Member States concerning violations of rights granted under Union law (2013/396/EU) 20. For a critical assessment of the Recommendation, see eg, Christopher Hodges, 'Collective Redress: A Breakthrough or a *Damp Squib*?' (2014) Journal of Consumer Policy 67.

31 For a recent comparative overview, see Alan Uzelac and Stefaan Voet (eds), *Class Actions in Europe: Holy Grail or a Wrong Trail?* (Springer 2021).

intellectual property. While these rules are mostly the same for any business operator, the preponderance of red tape, particularly in the shape of permits to be obtained through lengthy, complex, and often obscure application procedures, is widely recognised as a major obstacle for small business operators across Europe. Unlike larger operators, these may not have the legal expertise required to deal effectively with such requirements nor the financial resources to weather a delay in the processing of their applications, including the time required to challenge a rejection in court.[32]

Unlike in civil litigation, imbalance is inherent in business-to-administration disputes. The applicable procedural rules are doubtlessly designed with this very situation in mind. However, as has already been observed, administrative complaints occur across a wide variety of cases, ranging from social benefits for the most vulnerable members of society to large-scale urban and regional planning projects. Although neither of these two extremes is of particular relevance for small businesses, their mention illustrates that administrative justice is not a uniform category and that the degree of imbalance shifts between different kinds of administrative proceedings. Natural persons normally do not pursue the same type of administrative claims as businesses do. The extreme imbalance encountered by small businesses arguing against a specialised public authority with extensive expertise within its field should not be underestimated.

The design of administrative procedure globally, as well as within Europe, has been described by one commentator as 'bewilderingly diverse'.[33] In most European states, appeals against administrative decisions will ultimately be decided by specifically designated administrative courts; however, in certain jurisdictions, including Denmark, Norway, and the United Kingdom, they are

32 The Draghi Report European Commission, *The future of European competitiveness – Part A: A competitiveness strategy for Europe,* (September 2024) https://commission.europa.eu/topics/competitiveness/draghi-report_en#paragraph_47059 (accessed 17 August 2026) observed that 55% of small and medium businesses consider 'regulatory obstacles and the administrative burden as their greatest challenge' (p 31) and argued that EU bureaucracy 'imposes a proportionally higher burden on SMEs' compared to larger companies (p 65). *Nota bene* that the definition of small businesses used in the report differs from that adopted in this volume. For an illustrative example of the administrative burdens facing small businesses, see Albertjan Tomljenaar and Ko de Ridder, 'Administrative justice from a continental European perspective' in Michael Adler (ed), *Administrative Justice in Context* (Hart 2010) 301–303.

33 Michael Asimow, 'Five Models of Administrative Adjudication' (2015) American Journal of Comparative Law, 3; Kieran Bradley, 'Tribunals and adjudication' in Peter Cane *et al* (eds), *The Oxford Handbook of Comparative Administrative Law* (OUP 2021) 747.

instead heard by the civil courts.[34] There is no agreement between European jurisdictions on the adversarial or inquisitorial nature of administrative proceedings,[35] nor on the degree of written and oral elements (although Article 6 ECHR contributes to harmonisation through the requirement of an oral hearing at least in those administrative cases that concern 'civil' rights). Furthermore, the above-mentioned diversity of cases coming before the administrative courts may necessitate adaptations and special rules not only between but also within jurisdictions. Against this background, it is almost impossible, and certainly beyond the scope of this chapter, to provide an overall assessment of the impact of administrative procedures on access to justice for small businesses in disputes with administrative authorities.

5 Conclusions

This chapter has demonstrated how small businesses in commercial or otherwise trade-related disputes can appear both as the stronger and – more often – as the weaker party. However, in the cases where the small business comes off as the more resourceful party, the counterparty can often rely on rather extensive mechanisms designed to level the playing field and compensate for the imbalance between the parties. When, conversely, the small business finds itself at a disadvantage compared to its counterparty, such protective procedural devices are typically not available. The result is that the small business appears to be at a constant disadvantage, whether as a result of economic realities or of legal provisions.

How can this be resolved? Arguably, in cases where a small business faces a factually or structurally stronger counterparty, justice is not necessarily best served by the passive court-as-referee approach. A generally available, low-effort solution would be to charge the courts to pay particular attention to the situation of small businesses, ensuring, where necessary, that their arguments are adequately substantiated. While the degree of permissible *ex officio* court activity varies from one jurisdiction to another, most jurisdictions will allow for some level of active involvement of the bench in the interests of substantive justice and/or procedural fairness. This solution also has the benefit of being adaptable to the actual power (im)balance of every individual dispute, with cases involving the smallest actors in either absolute (micro

34 See Li-Ann Thio, 'Courts and Judicial review' in Cane (n 33) 721.

35 See Asimow (n 33) concerning the administrative procedures of France, Germany, the United Kingdom, and the European Union.

businesses) or relative (small businesses in dispute with large, multinational businesses) terms, presumably justifying the most far-reaching judicial interventions.

As a matter of *lex ferenda*, one might question whether legislative measures may be warranted to ensure the effective judicial protection of small businesses. Two main avenues for such reforms deserve to be mentioned. First, a sectoral approach could address those relationships where the disadvantage of the small business appears to be structural, including financing, digital services, and franchising. Drawing on the rules of consumer protection, possible measures could involve special rules on pre-dispute choice of court and arbitration clauses, as well as the introduction of sector-specific collective action mechanisms. Second, a more universal approach might consist of a small claims – or perhaps, 'medium claims' – procedure specifically designed for business-to-business disputes, combining a higher claims threshold with limitations on cost awards and simplified and transparent rules on the course of proceedings. Future research should evaluate the appropriateness and elaborate on the possible design of both solutions.

References

Andersson T, 'Ex officio application of the Unfair Terms Directive cases against consumers: a Swedish perspective' in Nylund A and Strandberg M (eds), *Civil Procedure and Harmonisation of Law* (Intersentia 2019).

Asimow M, 'Five models of administrative adjudication' (2015) 63 American Journal of Comparative Law 3.

Bradley K, 'Tribunals and adjudication' in P Cane, H Hofmann, E Mak and P Lindseth (eds), *The Oxford Handbook of Comparative Administrative Law* (OUP 2021).

Corby S, 'Labour courts in Great Britain and Sweden: a self-service model v collective regulation' (University of Greenwich Business School Working Paper WERU No 4, 2013).

Drahozal CR, 'Unfair arbitration clauses' (2001) University of Illinois Law Review 695.

Emerson RW and Hunt ZR, 'Franchises, consumers, and employees: choice and arbitration' (2022) William and Mary Business Law Review 487.

European Commission, The Future of European Competitiveness – Part A: A Competitiveness Strategy for Europe (September 2024) https://commission.europa.eu/topics/competitiveness/draghi-report_en#paragraph_47059 (accessed 17 August 2026).

Gsell B, 'The new European Directive on representative actions for the protection of the collective interests of consumers – a huge, but blurry step forward' (2021) Common Market Law Review 1365.

Hodges C, 'Collective redress: a breakthrough or a damp squib?' (2014) Journal of Consumer Policy 67.

Hornkohl L, 'Up- and downsides of the new EU Directive on representative actions for the protection of the collective interests of consumers – comments on key aspects' (2021) Journal of European Consumer and Market Law 189.

Riefa C and Grochowski M, 'The enforcement of EU consumer law' in M Scholten (ed), *Research Handbook on the Enforcement of EU Law* (Edward Elgar 2023).

SCC Arbitration Institute, SCC Expedited Rules 2023 (English) https://commission.europa.eu/topics/competitiveness/draghi-report_en#paragraph_4705 (accessed 17 August 2026).

Shen KL, 'Labour proceedings in the judicial system: a comparative analysis' in B Hess et al (eds), *Comparative Procedural Law and Justice* (Part XII Chapter 4) https://cplj.org/a/12-4 (accessed 17 August 2026).

Shepherd GB, 'The impacts of the European rule for fee-shifting on litigation behavior' in HE Rasmussen-Bonne et al (eds), *Balancing of Interests: Liber Amicorum Peter Hay zum 70. Geburtstag* (Recht und Wirtschaft 2005).

Silvestri E, 'Small claims and procedural simplification: evidence from selected EU legal systems' (2018) Access to Justice in Eastern Europe 6.

Thio LA, 'Courts and judicial review' in P Cane, H Hofmann, E Mak and P Lindseth (eds), *The Oxford Handbook of Comparative Administrative Law* (OUP 2021) 721.

Tomljenaar A and de Ridder K, 'Administrative justice from a continental European perspective' in M Adler (ed), *Administrative Justice in Context* (Hart 2010).

Trstenjak V and Beysen E, 'European consumer protection law: Curia semper dabit remedium?' (2011) Common Market Law Review 95.

Uzelac A and Voet S (eds), *Class Actions in Europe: Holy Grail or a Wrong Trail?* (Springer 2021).

Wallerman Ghavanini A, 'United we stand, divided we sue…' (2021) European Labour Law Journal 492.

Waas B, 'Enforcement of labour law: the case of Germany' (2021) 37 International Journal of Comparative Labour Law and Industrial Relations 225.

PART 2

Barriers to Justice for Small Businesses

CHAPTER 4

Litigation Cost Regimes, Litigation Risks, and Access to Justice for Small Businesses: Insights from Norwegian Law

Anna Nylund and Camilla Bernt

1 Introduction

Litigation costs are perhaps the most critical hindrance to access to justice, also for small businesses.[1] Often, the list of costs is limited to direct costs, notably court fees, lawyers' fees, bailiff costs, witness compensation, experts' fees, and, particularly, in cross-border cases, translation, and interpretation costs.[2] However, this kind of list disregards many types of costs. It does not include indirect costs incurred by the party, such as travel expenses to attend hearings, and intangible costs, which are difficult to estimate and monetise. Cost-shifting rules obliging the loser to cover all necessary and proportionate costs of the prevailing party prevent pyrrhic victories in which the prevailing party must use a significant portion of the award to cover litigation costs. However, such rules increase litigation risks.[3] To adequately estimate litigation risks, parties must, before filing an action or a defence, not only estimate their own costs but they must also assess the other party's costs and the probability of prevailing. If the costs and risks are too high, relinquishing the claim could be the most prudent course of action. Thus, the ability to bear those costs and risks is likely to have a tangible impact on whether a business pursues litigation.

Small businesses are more likely than medium and large businesses to face difficulties bearing the costs and risks of litigation, as they have fewer

1 Christopher JS Hodges, Stefan Vogenauer and Magdalena Tulibacka, 'Introduction' in Christopher JS Hodges, Magdalena Tulibacka and Stefan Vogenauer (eds), *The costs and funding of civil litigation: a comparative perspective* (Hart 2010) 4.

2 European Commission, *Study on the Transparency of Costs of Civil Judicial Proceedings in the European Union*, (European Commission 2007), https://e-justice.europa.eu/37/EN/costs?init=true (accessed 19 August 2026).

3 Michaela Keet, Heather Heavin and John Lande, *Litigation Interests and Risk Assessment. Help Your Clients Make Good Litigation Decisions* (American Bar Association Publishing 2020) 29–64.

 | HTTPS://DOI.ORG/10.1163/9789004779235-005

resources. Because small businesses tend to be one-shot players with limited litigation experience and internal legal capacity, they are probably also less well-equipped to accurately estimate those costs and risks.[4] Costs may also be asymmetric if the other party is a large business that uses costly, specialised legal services, but the small business uses the less costly services of a 'high street' lawyer. Moreover, in cases involving highly specialised issues, the services of the 'high street lawyer' might not be adequate. Instead, the business may have to resort to a far more costly, highly specialised lawyer who is not only more expensive but also does not know the business well enough to meet its specific needs. This could increase costs and risks. For a small business, losing an average-sized court case could entail serious economic repercussions, including insolvency. The owner-manager is also likely to face higher intangible, stress-related costs arising from the dispute and its resolution.

This chapter discusses various types of litigation costs and risks in general, advocating broadening the category to include indirect and intangible costs and litigation risks as an essential element (Section 2). Then, it examines how the design of the cost rules and court proceedings influence access to justice for small businesses using Norway as a case study.[5] Because the cost schemes differ across proceedings, Norwegian law is well-suited to illustrate how different regimes influence the costs within a single jurisdiction. Norway also illustrates how pre-action obligations influence legal costs. Comparisons with other Nordic countries are made when the Norwegian regime alone is insufficient as a case study. Norway has long been grappling with prohibitively high litigation costs, which have continued to escalate despite reforms intended to reduce them.[6]

Section 3 investigates how specific categories of direct costs are incurred depending on the design of court fees, lawyers' fees, and the proceedings. Section 4 interrogates the impact of different cost-shifting regimes, and Section 5 discusses costs that are often excluded from litigation costs, even though they are unavoidable in many cases. In Section 6, the potential of novel technologies is briefly discussed. Finally, concluding observations are offered in Section 7.

---

4 See Nylund, Chapter 2.

5 Costs are a problem for small businesses in many jurisdictions, see eg, Ahmed, Chapter 9; Castermans and Krans, Chapter 5, Section 4; and Stadler, Chapter 10, Section 1; Vandenbussche and Onraedt, Chapter 8, Section 3.

6 NOU 2020: 11, *Den tredje statsmakt. Domstolene i endring*, 203 ff.; *Behandling av sivile saker.* Anbefalinger fra en arbeidsgruppe sammensatt av dommere fra tingrettene og lagmannsrettene, advokater oppnevnt av Den norske Advokatforeningen, og representanter fra Domstoladministrasjonen. 1. mai 2024, 7–10.

2 Direct and Indirect, Tangible and Intangible Costs

As mentioned, typically only direct, tangible costs are considered when discussing barriers to justice, while indirect and intangible costs are disregarded.[7] Direct, tangible costs typically arise as preparation for the court case before filing and during court proceedings. Indirect, tangible costs arise from management spending time on decision-making related to the forthcoming and ongoing litigation, such as reading documents, discussing them with legal counsel, preparing evidence, and attending court hearings.[8] These are resources that would otherwise be spent on management of the ongoing business, product development, sales, marketing, and so forth. In micro businesses, the time the owner spends on litigation or preparing for it is likely to reduce the time spent on production of services and products, marketing, and customer relations, resulting in a tangible loss of revenue.

The dispute may also entail intangible costs, such as loss of reputation, deterioration in the social environment within the business, and a reduced quality of life for the owner. The intangible losses could translate into tangible losses when loss of reputation and a lower-quality work environment result in fewer sales, lower productivity, lower prices, and, consequently, less revenue. The psychological strain resulting from the dispute could have serious repercussions for the owner. Disputes can be stressful, especially if the outcome could have tangible consequences for the business and its future, or even result in insolvency. These emotional costs are likely higher for small business owners who have made significant economic, intellectual, and personal investments in the business and whose personal financial situation might depend on the businesses. A quick, amicable resolution can therefore substantially reduce the intangible costs. When discussing litigation or dispute resolution costs, indirect and intangible costs should also be considered because they influence whether and when bringing an action is worthwhile and when parties should primarily use other forms of dispute resolution. These 'hidden' costs could also be higher for small businesses than for larger businesses due to, inter alia, the owner's personal involvement, the close working environment, and lower economic buffers.

---

7 Michaela Keet, Heather Heavin, and John Lande, Litigation Interests and Risk Assessment. Help your Clients Make Good Litigation Decisions (American Bar Association Publishing 2020).

8 Keet, Heavin and Lande (n 7); Maurits Barendrecht, José Mulder and Ivo Giesen, 'How to Measure the Price and Quality of Access to Justice?' (November 2006), SSRN: https://ssrn.com/abstract=949209 (accessed 19 August 2026).

Because cost-shifting normally only applies to direct, tangible costs, both parties must bear their own indirect and intangible costs. This, too, makes litigation costly and risky. Of course, the potential indirect and intangible costs could turn out to be gains, such as when the harm to reputation turns into an increase in reputation for the prevailing party, or when it turns out that the contested business practices and terms of the party are lawful, or those of the other party are manifestly unlawful.

3 Amount of Costs

3.1 Court Fees and Similar Costs

Court fees are relatively low in most European countries. In some countries, there is a lump-sum payment up front; in others, the system is pay-as-you-go, that is, each new step incurs a payment. In some countries, the sum is fixed regardless of the amount in dispute; in other countries, it varies.[9] Norway has a moderate pay-as-you-go system that uses a fixed fee schedule.[10] The general fee includes a main hearing of up to one day, with each additional day incurring additional costs. If the parties withdraw the case or settle, the fee is reduced, with a higher reduction the earlier the case is withdrawn or settled. The fee for small claims is lower than for regular civil cases.

The fixed-fee system could make court fees for small claims very high, which would probably disadvantage small businesses, as even relatively small claims are considerable from their perspective and their limited financial resources. In Norway, the court fee for a regular civil case with a one-day main hearing is NOK 6,725 (approximately EUR 570). For small claims, ie, when the amount in dispute is less than NOK 250,000 (approximately EUR 21,000), the fee is NOK 4,707 (EUR 395 in 2026, which is almost 2% of the amount in dispute. However, one must take into account that if the amount in dispute is below NOK 200,000 (approximately EUR 16,800), the case must first proceed to the Conciliation Board, a quasi-court with lay judges, or another dispute resolution board, for which the claimant must pay a court

---

9 Hodges, Vogenauer, and Tulibacka (n 1) 14.

10 The fees are set at a specific number of court fees 'R' (*rettsgebyr*) and the value of R is adjusted each year. The regular fee for cases with a one-day hearing is 5 R and 8 R for a two-day hearing, pursuant to the Court Fee Act (*Lov om rettsgebyr*) section 8. If the case is dismissed, the fee is 2 R, the same applies to cases withdrawn or settled earlier than 4 weeks before the main hearing. Cases in the small claims track are charged 3.5 R. In 2026, one R is NOK 1,345 (approximately EUR 110).

fee.[11] Thus, the court fees for a small claims case that has passed through the Conciliation Boards total NOK 6,778 (approximately EUR 570), which is roughly the same as for a regular case scheduled for a one-day hearing. However, one should note that when the case passes through the Conciliation Board, the delay is probably the key source of direct and indirect costs, not the court fees as such.

In comparison, Sweden has a flat, up-front fee, with a reduced fee for small claims.[12] Denmark, in turn, has sought to develop self-funding courts by using court fees consisting of a flat fee and an additional fee, which was initially set at 2% of the amount in dispute.[13] The amendment was implemented in 2000 without prior discussion of its impact on access to the courts, and it led to very high fees, especially in small-claims cases. The fees were lowered a few years later, now consisting of a basic fee and an additional fee for cases proceeding to the main hearing.[14] For small claims, there is a flat fee.

A comparison of court fees for a claim of EUR 5,000 and one of EUR 50,000 in the Nordic countries illustrates how different court fee schemes affect costs. The court fees for a claim of EUR 5,000 are DKK 750 (approximately EUR 100) in Denmark, NOK 4,707 (approximately EUR 395) in Norway, and SEK 2,800 (approximately EUR 250) in Sweden. As noted above, parties to a Norwegian lawsuit must also pay for the Conciliation Board (or another dispute resolution method) before filing their case, which effectively increases the fees to about EUR 570, which is more than 11% of the amount in dispute. In contrast, claimants in Danish courts only pay about 2% in fees. For a claim of EUR 50,000, the court fees range from SEK 2,800 (EUR 250 or 0.5% of the value)

11 The court fee for Conciliation Boards is 1.54 R, which is approximately EUR 170.

12 Swedish Decree on Fees in General Courts (*Förordning om avgifter vid de allmänna domstolarna*). In 2025, the fee was SEK 900 (approximately EUR 80) for small claims, ie claims below SEK 29,400 (approximately EUR 2,700), and SEK 2,800 (approximately EUR 250) for other claims.

13 Retsplejerådet, *Reform af den civile retspleje I: Instansordningen, byrettens sammensætning og almindelige regler om sagsbehandlingen i første instans*, Betænkning nr. 1401, 2001, 75–81.

14 Retsplejerådet, *Reform av den civile retspleje III: Adgang til domstolene, Betænkning nr. 1434, 2004*, 237 et seq. In 2025, the basic fee was DKK 750 or DKK 1,500 (approximately EUR 100 and EUR 200, respectively), depending on whether the amount in dispute was below or above DKK 100,000 (approximately EUR 13,400), and the additional fee started at DKK 3,000 when the amount in dispute was between DKK 100,000 and DKK 150,000. The maximum amount is DKK 160,000 (approximately EUR 21,400) when the amount in dispute exceeds DKK 6 million (approximately EUR 803,300), under the Danish Court Fee Act (*Retsafgiftsloven*).

in Sweden, NOK 4,707 (EUR 395 or 0.8% of the value) in Norway, to DKK 9,500 (approximately EUR 1,270, or 2.5% of the value) in Denmark.

In addition to court fees, the parties might have to pay separately for the service of documents and similar services. These costs depend on how the service is conducted, particularly on how the statement of claim is served and how witnesses are summoned. Electronic communication makes these costs negligible. In Norway, lawyers must use the digital case filing system to file the case.[15] Self-represented may do so but are not mandated to do so. Witnesses may be summoned in any way the parties find suitable, which makes the direct and indirect costs associated with summoning 'benign' witnesses negligible. However, if the services of a bailiff or similar professional are needed, the costs could be significantly higher due to bailiff fees. In cross-border cases, translation and interpretation services increase the costs and, therefore, also the risks.

3.2 Lawyers' Fees

Lawyers' fees are often the costliest part of court proceedings. In many countries, such as Germany, parties are obliged to have a lawyer, except in small claims proceedings.[16] Even when the parties are not mandated to have a lawyer, as is the case in the Nordic countries, the complexity of substantive and procedural rules often requires legal advice. Self-represented parties may risk having their case dismissed on formal grounds or losing because they invoke 'wrong' or less advantageous legal norms, or because they do not understand what evidence is required.

Lawyer's fees could be very high, depending on the nature of the proceedings, such as the number and length of court hearings, the need to produce and prepare evidence and other documents, access to potential evidence, and the complexity of the legal and factual issues at hand. The type of lawyer engaged will also influence costs, as specialised business lawyers employed by large law firms and niche 'boutique' law firms tend to charge palpably higher fees than lawyers working for smaller, often local, firms. Access to and the nature of appellate proceedings are also important factors influencing the potential costs.[17] Moreover, well-resourced parties, who can bear the extra

---

15 Decree on electronic communication with courts (*Forskrift om elektronisk kommunikasjon med domstolene*).

16 See German Civil Procedure Code section 78.

17 Magne Strandberg, 'Tilgang til andre instans som hinder for tilgang til første instans?' in Anna Wallerman Ghavanini and Sebastian Wejedal (eds), *Access to justice i Skandinavien* (Santérus Academic Press Sweden 2022).

costs, could also intentionally generate costs by invoking facts and norms that tangibly increase the workload of the legal counsel, or that require costly evidence.

The way in which lawyers' fees are determined influences the extent to which small businesses can calculate the approximate costs for proceedings: are fees quoted on an hourly basis, for individual steps of the proceedings (eg, preparing and writing the statement of claim, written and oral preparations, main hearing), or for the entire (first instance) proceedings? Are lawyers required or encouraged to give a quote or estimate of the total costs? There is considerable variation among jurisdictions,[18] yet there are only a few quantitative studies on actual litigation costs.[19] For example, to the authors' knowledge, costs have, with a few exceptions, not been subject to a comprehensive, rigorous empirical analysis in Norway or other Nordic countries.[20] This is surprising, particularly because Norwegian lawyers are typically paid by the hour, not on a fixed fee basis. Therefore, it is very difficult to estimate fees in advance, particularly for small businesses and others with limited internal legal capacity such as in-house lawyers. Assessing the necessity and proportionality of each step taken by the lawyer, and therefore the proportionality of the total fees, is also challenging. Hence, it is not surprising that a Dutch study found that clients tend to prefer fixed fees over hourly rates and a mix of the two.[21]

In small and simplified claims proceedings, exceptions to the requirement of having a lawyer, or to the rule that only lawyers may act as legal counsel, apply in many countries such as Germany. Pursuant to Section 79 of the German Code of Civil Procedure (*Zivilprozessordnung*), debt collection employ-

---

18 Matthias Reimann (ed), *Cost and Fee Allocation in Civil Procedure – A Comparative Study*, (Springer 2012); and Severine Menétrey, 'Cost Efficiency as a Guiding Principle in Civil Justice' in Burkhard Hess, Margaret Woo, Loic Cadiet, Séverine Menétrey and Enrique Vallines García (eds), *Comparative Procedural Law and Justice*, Part III Chapter 4, cplj.org/a/3-4 (accessed 22 December 2025), paras 16–24.

19 The reason is that many studies are conducted not as quantitative analyses of all cases or a representative selection of cases within a jurisdiction but as country reports in which the reporters estimate the costs based on their experience. Examples of such studies are *Study on the transparency* (n 2) and Reimann (n 18).

20 Kaijus Ervasti, *Riidat käräjäoikeuksissa – empiirinen tutkimus riita-asioista ja oikeudenkäyntikuluista.* (Oikeuspoliittisen tutkimuslaitoksen julkaisuja 217, Optula 2005); Kaijus Ervasti, 'Oikeudenkäyntikulujen kehitys alioikeusuudistuksen jälkeen' (2006) Defensor Legis 599; and NOU 2020: 11 (n 6) 307–316.

21 Flóra Felső, Sander Onderstal and Jo Seldeslachts, 'The Pricing Structure of Legal Services: Do Lawyers Offer What Clients Want?' (2002) 61 Review of Industrial Organization 123.

ees and employees may represent a party in debt collection proceedings under some circumstances.[22] A similar rule is found in the Norwegian Dispute Act (*tvisteloven*) Sections 6-7, which grants debt collection agencies and employees the right to act as representatives in small claims before the Conciliation Boards. This lowers the costs of debt collection proceedings while still allowing small businesses to seek assistance from experts in debt collection.

3.3 Costs for Evidence

The cost of evidence varies across jurisdictions depending, for instance, on whether there are a few or many restrictions on the type and amount of evidence allowed, as well as on the extent to which parties have access to evidence, eg, through disclosure.[23] This, in turn, influences not only the direct and indirect costs associated with evidence but also whether the parties can prove their case.

Some disputes faced by small businesses involve complex factual issues. For example, a company has ordered custom-made equipment or components that do not work as intended. Determining whether the problems result from a breach of contract may require expertise, firstly, to enable the business to assess whether to pursue the claim legally and, secondly, to inform negotiations with the other party. Another example is when the small business faces an allegation of trademark infringement accompanied with a claim for damages. Both, determining whether there is a trademark infringement and calculating damages, may require expertise. In both cases, expert evidence may be needed both for pre-filing negotiations and during the court proceedings, particularly if a court of general jurisdiction hears the case without involving expert judges.

In Norway, there is almost no specialisation in the court system; therefore, the need for expertise is normally met by party- or court-appointed experts, or both, which incurs costs for the parties. Usually, the court appoints the expert, which considerably reduces the costs as only one, not two, experts are needed (or two, not four, if the case requires expertise in multiple fields). Moreover, court-appointed experts are thought to be less biased because their loyalty lies with the court rather than with any of the parties.[24] If the lawsuit is successful,

22 See also Stadler, Chapter 10.

23 For an overview, see Menétrey (n 18) para 25 –40; and Magne Strandberg, 'Access to Evidence in the US, Germany, and Norway' in Margaret YK Woo and Cornelis Hendrik van Rhee (eds), *Comparative Civil Procedure* (Edward Elgar 2025).

24 Inge Lorange Backer, *Norsk sivilprosess* (3rd edn, Universitetsforlaget 2024) 330.

the costs may be shifted to the other party under the cost-shifting rules. This increases litigation risks considerably. Consequently, particularly for businesses with limited financial resources, even a poor settlement or not pursuing the claim at all could be the most rational solution.

Under Norwegian law, there is also the option of appointing two expert judges, ie, persons with relevant expertise beyond the law, when the proper administration of justice so requires.[25] Expert judges are appointed for an individual case, not on a long-term basis. The cost of the expert judges, however, must be borne by the parties. Furthermore, in the preparatory works of the Dispute Act, it is highlighted that the adversarial principle and proper presentation of evidence may indicate that a court-appointed expert may be preferable to expert judges particularly when there may be different opinions and assessments on significant points.[26] Relying on expert judges seems to entail greater risk, since the party will have far less knowledge of the experts' views and assessments before the judgment than in the case of a court-appointed expert, whom they may cross-examine. Thus, they also have fewer opportunities to challenge the views of the expert judge compared to a court-appointed expert. It could be argued that both the costs and the concerns highlighted in the preparatory works make the use of expert judges less attractive for small businesses in Norway than a court-appointed expert.

If the small business's counterpart is a larger business or other legal entity with considerably more financial resources and can bear the cost of experts or expert judges, this may compel the small business to consider waiving its claim or settling. This is particularly problematic for party-appointed experts because the parties typically appoint one each. However, under the Norwegian system, in which the parties bear the cost of expert judges, expert judges are probably as expensive as experts. As explained above, given that the parties may not cross-examine judges, expert judges are not only costly but may also undermine fair trial guarantees. From an access to justice point of view, where costs can be a notable barrier to pursuing valid claims or disputing ill-founded ones, it would be preferable to have a system in which the court has in-house, part-time, or on-call expert judges paid by the court. Of course, expert judges do not eliminate the need for experts entirely, but in many cases, they likely reduce it and potentially increase the quality of the outcome.

---

25 Cf Dispute Act Section 9–12 Subsection 2. See Magne Strandberg, 'Appointment of Experts in Norwegian Civil Proceedings' in Alan Uzelac and Stefaan Voet (eds), *The Heroes of the Judicial Periphery* (Bloomsbury 2025).

26 NOU 2001: 32 *Rett på sak Lov om tvisteløsning* (*tvisteloven*) 755–756.

The more extensive the access to evidence, the more likely the court is to have a robust basis for its ruling. However, greater access to evidence also entails a higher risk of prohibitive litigation costs. The way evidence is presented, such as the length and scope of witness examinations and the number of witnesses, influences litigation costs. Norwegian courts allow the parties to call many witnesses, and the examinations have a broad scope, making them lengthy and increasing litigation costs. According to a Norwegian government report, only 21% of civil cases had a main hearing lasting less than 5 hours, and in 46% of cases, the main hearing exceeded 10 hours, ie, they lasted at least two full days.[27] Moreover, in small claims cases, the main hearing is usually no more than 4 hours, with a maximum of 5 to 6 hours. Still, once the amount in dispute exceeds the small claims limit and the case is heard in regular proceedings, the main hearing typically runs 3 hours longer.[28] Costs are proportional to the length of the main hearing, which largely reflects the number and length of witness examinations.[29] Consequently, limiting the evidence leads to a shorter main hearing, which, in turn, reduces costs. This could be a challenge for small businesses because they might not understand this connection, and thus, inadvertently increase costs by invoking more evidence than needed or by conducting a lengthy examination of the evidence. Moreover, larger businesses with greater financial resources could increase costs by prolonging the main hearing.

In Norway, costs could be significantly reduced if courts carefully managed the volume of evidence and its presentation.[30] Standardising – and shortening – the length of main hearings is paramount for lowering the costs of civil proceedings.[31] Shortening the hearings would automatically force the legal counsel to limit their presentations to the most important issues, thus also contributing to narrowing the scope of the proceedings to core disputed issues.

4 Cost-Shifting and Litigation Risks

Cost-shifting rules are probably paramount for small businesses' access to justice. In most European jurisdictions, cost-shifting occurs under one of two

27 NOU 2020: 11 (n 6) 270.
28 NOU 2020: 11 (n 6) 271.
29 NOU 2020: 11 (n 6) 308.
30 NOU 2020: 11 (n 6) 277 –286.
31 *Behandling av sivile saker* (n 6) 14 ff.

models.[32] In the first model, costs are capped at a certain percentage of the amount in dispute or at a cost schedule. The limitation often applies to lawyers' fees and costs, not necessarily to the cost of evidence. In the second, the prevailing party is entitled to full compensation for all necessary and proportionate costs.

The first model, which applies in Norwegian small claims proceedings, has the advantage of predictability and probably also keeps costs proportional to the value of the claim, their main disadvantage is that the value of a claim and its complexity do not necessarily correlate. Some smaller claims are legally or factually complex. This means that the amount of legal advice needed to pursue the claim may be disproportionate to the claim's value. If lawyers charge by the hour, a rational party may decide not to pursue a claim because of its complexity. Larger companies could bear the costs of the case, where small businesses could not, and rational apathy is the best course of action for the latter. If this concerns only a few cases, it is not such a problem. However, when the real costs prevalently far exceed recoverable costs, it hinders access to court and becomes a systemic problem.

The second model, which applies in general civil cases in Norway, has the advantage of preventing pyrrhic victories, in which the cost award is so small that much of the payment the prevailing party receives goes to covering the costs for the proceedings. However, litigating can be very costly, and financially stronger parties can tangibly increase the economic risks by engaging costly lawyers, compelling weaker parties, often small businesses, to abandon their claims due to prohibitive financial exposure. This development has been observed in the Netherlands, where the increased cost risks following the implementation of full cost compensation under the Intellectual Property Rights Enforcement Directive led to fewer intellectual property cases.[33] This was the exact opposite of the Directive's aim.

A further challenge associated with 'full' cost-shifting is that 'full' is limited to necessary and proportionate costs.[34] While this levels the field between parties with limited resources and those with abundant resources, those using 'high street' lawyers and those choosing 'boutique' lawyers, it also creates what Christopher Hodges and associates refer to as 'the recoverability gap':[35] compensation for costs could be palpably lower than the actual costs incurred.

32 Hodges, Vogenauer, and Tulibacka (n 1) 17–20.

33 Paulien MM van der Grinten, 'Challenges for the creation of a European law of civil procedure' (2009) https://ssrn.com/abstract=1392006, 7 (accessed 19 August 2026).

34 Hodges, Vogenauer, and Tulibacka (n 1) 18.

35 Hodges, Vogenauer, and Tulibacka (n 1) 20.

Risk assessment is difficult because estimating both the number of billed hours and the cost per hour, as well as the extent to which costs will be shifted, could be challenging. A recent report from the Finnish Competition and Consumer Authority shows that, at times, the risk of high costs alone suffices to pressure less resourceful parties to relinquish their claims.[36] Rogue debt collection companies exploit consumers, and probably also small businesses, by filing weakly founded or even unfounded debt collection proceedings, knowing that if the debtor contests the debt, the case will be transferred to regular proceedings, for which the debt collection company can claim very high litigation costs. Even if the debt was unfounded, the risk of incurring high costs due to cost-shifting is, in itself, likely to pressure the alleged debtor to pay a debt with no or very weak legal foundations.

Under the Norwegian Dispute Act Sections 20-2 and 20-5, the losing party shall compensate the prevailing party for all necessary and proportionate costs. Necessary costs shall be evaluated based on the factual and legal complexity of the case and proportionality in relation to the amount in dispute and the importance of the case for the parties. For lawyers' fees, this means considering the total amount, not just the number of billed hours or the hourly rate. The cost of evidence shall also be considered, ie, whether the evidence was necessary to prove the case and whether the necessary proof could have been obtained in a less costly manner. Because the rules rely on general assessments without specific guidance on whether a cost is necessary and proportionate, predicting the extent to which costs can be shifted is difficult. A 2024 report noted that it is difficult to assess what constitutes necessary and proportionate costs, but that, as a rule, they should not exceed the amount in dispute.[37] In HR-2023–1268, the Norwegian Supreme Court rejected costs amounting to about 130% of the amount in dispute, but did not indicate the appropriate level of compensation. This increases litigation risk because one may not receive full compensation even if one prevails, and estimating how much one must pay the prevailing party is often very difficult.

In small claims cases, when the amount in dispute is below NOK 250,000 (approximately EUR 22,000), the costs for lawyers' fees, including travel costs, are capped at 20% of the amount in dispute.[38] This brings foreseeability, as the parties will know in advance how much they will have to pay to the other

36 Ari Luukinen, Juha Jokinen, Jari Suurla, Jarkko Vuorinen, Antti Sieppi, Matti Sipiläinen, Julia Sjöström, Lauri Wilenius and Netta Heiskanen, *Summaarisen menettelyn epäkohdat ja mahdollinen väärinkäyttö kuluttajien velkomusasioissa.* Kilpailu- ja kuluttajaviraston Tutkimusraportteja 4/2025 (Kilpailu- ja kuluttajavirasto 2025).

37 *Behandling av sivile saker* (n 6) 11.

38 Dispute Act section 10-5.

party and how much they will receive if they prevail. In combination with fixed fees, this gives full foreseeability. However, the compensation is very low and does not result in full compensation. Given that Norwegian lawyers charge around NOK 2,500 (approximately EUR 220) and upwards per hour, the 20% cap results in a maximum of NOK 50,000 for lawyers' fees when the amount in dispute is NOK 250,000, equivalent to no more than 15–20 hours. For more experienced lawyers, this would be fewer hours. If the amount in dispute is NOK 200,000, the maximum of NOK 40,000 would cover approximately 12–15 billed hours, of which five would be spent on the day of the hearing. In a simple case, this suffices, but if the case involves more complex legal or factual issues, this would probably be insufficient.

In 2018, the Norwegian Department of Justice suggested extending the cost-capping rules to disputes in which the amount in dispute was below a certain threshold, such as NOK 500,000, NOK 750,000, or NOK 1,000,000, with the cap set at 40% of that amount.[39] During the public consultation, both courts and the bar association opposed the suggested rule, inter alia, due to the high cap.[40] In 2024, a commission recommended a similar rule for cases in which the amount in dispute is below NOK 1.5 million (approximately EUR 130,000).[41] However, the cap would be 30% of the amount in dispute, and it would be a general norm from which the court would have discretion to deviate. The committee emphasised that this would be the maximum rate, a ceiling, not the normal rate. For small businesses, such a rule would likely increase access to justice by reducing litigation risk and, to some extent, litigation costs.

5 Additional Risks and Costs

Enforcement costs are a category of direct costs that are sometimes overlooked. Unless a party complies with the outcome, whether a court ruling or a settlement agreement, enforcement can lead to additional delays and expenses. The extent to which direct costs arise from enforcement depends on the nature of enforcement proceedings, such as whether the small business, as a creditor, needs legal advice. In Norway, enforcement costs NOK 928 (approximately EUR 80), which is not prohibitively high. However, the parties

39 *Høringsnotat. Forslag til endringer i tvisteloven – tvistelovevalueringen* (Lovavdelingen, juli 2018. Snr 18/3837) 40–45.

40 Høringsnotat (n 39).

41 *Behandling av sivile saker* (n 6) 32–33.

may need legal assistance, which would increase costs. In other jurisdictions, enforcement costs could be much higher in relation to litigation costs than in Norway.

Even if a party has prevailed and been awarded full compensation for legal costs, it may still be unable to recover its actual costs. One reason is that the other party could be insolvent or on the brink of insolvency. Consequently, it may be difficult to recover full costs, or recovery may take considerable time. In fact, even recovering the amount awarded for the substantive claims could be an insurmountable task. This risk is tangible when the opponent is also a small business with limited resources.

Business owners can also deliberately choose not to comply with court rulings. A small business owner could choose bankruptcy rather than paying their obligations, particularly if a court ruling would complicate the business's future. It could be easier to let the company go bankrupt and then start a new business. Larger businesses could transfer the disputed claims to an empty subsidiary and let that subsidiary go bankrupt to avoid paying.[42] Despite the potential recoverability gap, no studies on the topic exist to the authors' knowledge.

In cross-border cases, costs and risks tend to increase. The apparent reasons relate to the need to understand foreign legal systems, their substantive and procedural law, and the costs associated with translation and interpretation. However, differences in the level and distribution of legal costs increase the risks. Assessments based, erroneously, on one's own jurisdiction could lead to miscalculation. However, many small businesses are likely to rescind their claim or simply reduce cross-border business.

6 Technology as a Potential Solution to High Costs

Technology harbours great potential to facilitate self-representation and simplify proceedings. For instance, systems with easily understood, step-by-step instructions could simplify the filing and responding for self-represented parties in debt-collection processes, and information could reduce the need for engaging external legal capacity.[43] Online dispute resolution, in which technology is involved as a 'fourth party' rather than merely a means of communi-

42 Eg, Henrik Bellander, 'Procedural Agreements and Litigation Costs' in A Nylund and A Cabral (eds), *Shaping Civil Litigation Using Procedural Agreements* (Eleven 2023).

43 For an example from how this is envisaged in English law, see Ahmed, Chapter 9.

cation, could reduce direct and indirect costs.[44] However, technology could also reduce access to justice. It could be biased, eg, it could favour some types of parties, either by design or through biased learning materials.[45] It might not be user-friendly, eg, it could use 'legalese' instead of plain language, or clicking the wrong 'button' when the alternatives are unclear could have serious consequences. Also, using AI to simplify language could lead to overly simplistic or misleading language, hampering rather than easing access to justice for businesses with limited internal legal capacity.[46]

In cross-border cases, technological advancements, particularly AI, offer the potential to provide easy access to fast, affordable translations and even interpretation. However, this necessitates reliable, well-trained AI and, probably, keeping a trained lawyer or legal linguist in the loop.[47]

7 Conclusion

It is reasonable to conclude that costs are a substantial hindrance to access to justice for small businesses in Norway and beyond.[48] This is particularly true for lower-value claims and disputes that raise complex factual or legal issues.

44 See eg, Fernando Esteban de la Rosa and John Zeleznikow, 'Making intelligent online dispute resolution tools available to self-represented litigants in the public justice system: towards and ethical use of AI technology in the administration of justice' (2021) *Proceedings of the Eighteenth International Conference on Artificial Intelligence and Law*; Amy J Schmitz and John Zeleznikow. 'Intelligent legal tech to empower self-represented litigants' (2021) 23 Columbia Science and Technology Law Review 142; Amy J Schmitz, 'Foundational Considerations for Using Technology in Dispute Resolution and Application to the Civil Resolution Tribunal' (Ohio State Legal Studies Research Paper No 891, 17 December 2024) https://ssrn.com/abstract=5061992 (accessed 19 August 2026).

45 Fife Ogunde, 'Generative AI and access to justice in Canada: The case of Self-Represented Litigants [SRLs]' (2024) 40 Windsor Yearbook of Access to Justice 211.

46 Maria Zimina-Poirot, Christopher Gledhill and Manon Bouyé, 'Towards Clear, Simple, and Inclusive Legal Language: Exploring Generative Artificial Intelligence (GAI) Models as Content Rephrasing Assistants in Multilingual Settings' (2025) 14 International Journal of Language & Law 143.

47 Andrzej Greńczuk, Iwona Chomiak-Orsa and Katarzyna Tryczyńska, 'AI-Supported Translation Tools for Legal Texts: A Comparative Analysis' (2024) 246 Procedia Computer Science 5545; Abdel Rahman Mitib Altakhaineh, Ghazi Ayed Alghathian and Mashal Mufleh Jarrah 'A comparative study of accuracy in human vs. AI translation of legal documents into Arabic' (2025) International Journal of Language & Law (JLL) 1463; Patrizia Giampieri, 'The use of AI in the translation of legal documents' (2024) 17 Zeitschrift für Translationswissenschaft und Fachkommunikation 343.

48 Ahmed, Chapter 9; Castermans and Krans, Chapter 5; Stadler, Chapter 10; Vandenbussche and Onraedt, Chapter 8.

In these instances, court fees and the costs of legal counsel and obtaining evidence may become disproportionate to the value of the disputed claim. Furthermore, the cost risk increases when procedural rules allow extensive evidence and lengthy hearings.

Qualitative research on litigation costs, particularly comparative research on how different procedural regimes and cost-shifting rules influence the total litigation costs, their distribution, and the foreseeability of both total costs and recoverable costs, is sparse. Given that the subject matter and the value of the dispute impact the costs,[49] improving access to justice for small businesses requires understanding how these differences create unequal access to justice, particularly across different fields. Only by understanding the real cost of the dispute, for the prevailing and losing party, can the direct, tangible costs of disputing and their effects on litigation risks and thus also access to justice, be correctly assessed. These studies should employ a comprehensive approach that includes all direct, tangible costs, including pre-filing processes and enforcement, and, as far as possible, indirect and intangible costs. Of course, indirect and intangible costs are much more difficult to identify, estimate, and monetise than direct tangible costs. Despite the difficulties, these costs should be included because they could have a tangible impact on the profitability and longevity of small businesses, as well as the well-being of their owners and employees. While litigation will always cause stress and drain resources, justice systems can only be efficient and accessible if they seek to mitigate these negative externalities.

In addition to gross and net litigation costs, litigation risks need more attention from the legal community and policymakers. The ability to accurately estimate and bear litigation costs, and risks, is probably a key factor influencing real, not just formal, access to justice. The more financially strong a business is, the more likely it is to be able to bear the costs and risks, and the more unequal the financial situation of the parties to the dispute, the more leverage the financially stronger party has. This applies not only to consumers and similar groups but also to small businesses. Policymakers should therefore be mindful of how litigation costs affect small businesses, particularly micro businesses and those operating in low-margin markets.

49 Ervasti (n 20); Hodges, Vogenauer, and Tulibacka (n 1); and NOU 2020: 11 (n 6).

References

Altakhaineh, ARM, Alghathian GA and Jarrah MM, 'A comparative study of accuracy in human vs. AI translation of legal documents into Arabic' (2025) 14 International Journal of Language & Law 63.

Backer IL, *Norsk sivilprosess* (3rd edn, Universitetsforlaget 2024).

Barendrecht M, Mulder J and Giesen, I, 'How to Measure the Price and Quality of Access to Justice?' (November 2006) available at SSRN: https://ssrn.com/abstract=949209 (accessed 19 August 2026).

Behandling av sivile saker. Anbefalinger fra en arbeidsgruppe sammensatt av dommere fra tingrettene og lagmannsrettene, advokater oppnevnt av Den norske Advokatforeningen, og representanter fra Domstoladministrasjonen. 1. mai 2024.

Bellander H, 'Procedural Agreements and Litigation Costs' in A Nylund and A Cabral (eds), *Shaping Civil Litigation Using Procedural Agreements* (Eleven 2023).

de la Rosa FE and Zeleznikow J, 'Making intelligent online dispute resolution tools available to self-represented litigants in the public justice system: towards an ethical use of AI technology in the administration of justice' (2021) *Proceedings of the Eighteenth International Conference on Artificial Intelligence and Law.*

Ervasti K, *Riidat käräjäoikeuksissa – empiirinen tutkimus riita-asioista ja oikeudenkäyntikuluista.* (Oikeuspoliittisen tutkimuslaitoksen julkaisuja 217, Optula 2005).

Ervasti K, 'Oikeudenkäyntikulujen kehitys alioikeusuudistuksen jälkeen' (2006) Defensor Legis 599.

Felső F, Onderstal S and Seldeslachts J, 'The Pricing Structure of Legal Services: Do Lawyers Offer What Clients Want?' (2022) 61 Review of Industrial Organization 123.

Giampieri, Patrizia, 'The use of AI in the translation of legal documents' (2024) 17 Zeitschrift für Translationswissenschaft und Fachkommunikation 343.

Greńczuk A, Chomiak-Orsa I and Tryczyńska K, 'AI-Supported Translation Tools for Legal Texts: A Comparative Analysis' (2024) 246 Procedia Computer Science 5545.

Hodges, CJS, Tulibacka M and Vogenauer S, 'Introduction' in CJS Hodges, M Tulibacka, and S Vogenauer (eds), *The costs and funding of civil litigation: a comparative perspective* (Hart 2010).

Høringsnotat. Forslag til endringer i tvisteloven – tvistelovevalueringen. Lovavdelingen, juli 2018. Snr 18/3837.

Keet M, Heavin H and Lande J, *Litigation Interests and Risk Assessment. Help Your Clients Make Good Litigation Decisions* (ABA Publishing 2020).

Luukinen A, Jokinen J, Suurla J, Vuorinen J, Sieppi A, Sipiläinen M, Sjöström J, Wilenius L and Heiskanen N, *Summaarisen menettelyn epäkohdat ja mahdollinen väärinkäyttö kuluttajien velkomusasioissa.* Kilpailu- ja kuluttajaviraston Tutkimusraportteja 4/2025 (Kilpailu- ja kuluttajavirasto 2025).

Menétrey S, 'Cost Efficiency as a Guiding Principle in Civil Justice' in B Hess, M Woo, L Cadiet, S Menétrey and E Vallines García (eds), *Comparative Procedural Law and Justice* (Part III Chapter 4), cplj.org/a/3–4 (accessed 25 August 2026).

NOU 2001: 32 *Rett på sak Lov om tvisteløsning (tvisteloven)*.

NOU 2020: 11 *Den tredje statsmakt. Domstolene i endring.*

Ogunde F, 'Generative AI and access to justice in Canada: The case of Self-Represented Litigants [SRLs]' (2024) 40 Windsor Yearbook of Access to Justice 211.

Retsplejerådet, *Reform af den civile retspleje I: Instansordningen, byrettens sammensætning og almindelige regler om sagsbehandlingen i første instans*, Betænkning nr 1401, 2001.

Retsplejerådet, *Reform av den civile retspleje III: Adgang til domstolene*, Betænkning nr. 1434, 2004.

Schmitz AJ, 'Foundational Considerations for Using Technology in Dispute Resolution and Application to the Civil Resolution Tribunal' (December 17, 2024). Ohio State Legal Studies Research Paper No. 891, Available at SSRN: https://ssrn.com/abstract=5061992 (accessed 25 August 2026).

Schmitz AJ and Zeleznikow J, 'Intelligent legal tech to empower self-represented litigants' (2021) 23 Columbia Science & Technology Law Review 142.

Strandberg M, 'Tilgang til andre instans som hinder for tilgang til første instans?' in A Wallerman Ghavanini and S Wejedal (eds), *Access to justice i Skandinavien* (Santérus Academic Press Sweden 2022).

Strandberg M, 'Access to Evidence in the US, Germany, and Norway' in MYK Woo and CH Rhee (eds), Comparative Civil Procedure (Edward Elgar 2025).

Strandberg M, 'Appointment of Experts in Norwegian Law' in A Uzelac and S Voet (eds), Heroes of the Judicial Periphery (Bloomsbury 2025).

van der Grinten, PMM, 'Challenges for the creation of a European law of civil procedure' (2009) available at SSRN: https://ssrn.com/abstract=1392006 (accessed 19 August 2026).

Zimina-Poirot M, Gledhill C and Bouyé M, 'Towards Clear, Simple, and Inclusive Legal Language: Exploring Generative Artificial Intelligence (GAI) Models as Content Rephrasing Assistants in Multilingual Settings' (2025) 14 International Journal of Language & Law 14.

CHAPTER 5

The Corporate Sustainability Due Diligence Directive and Access to Justice for Small Businesses

Alex Geert Castermans and Bart Krans

1 Shifting the Burden of Responsible Business Conduct

The Corporate Sustainability Due Diligence Directive (CSDDD)[1] is aimed at (i) realising the European sustainability goals as articulated in the 'European Green Deal' following the 2015 Paris Climate Agreement, (ii) protecting human rights and (iii) improving the sustainability of the global supply chains of companies falling under the scope of the CSDDD. In short: companies falling under the scope of the Directive – large companies, see CSDDD Article 2 – must further sustainable production and distribution that is: environmentally friendly, respecting human rights and labour standards.

In order to promote responsible business conduct, large companies are, among other things, obliged to integrate due diligence into their policies and risk management systems.[2] They must have a code of conduct in place, committing their employees and their subsidiaries to prevent and mitigate possible negative impacts of their business decisions on the environment or human rights.[3] They are also obliged to seek contractual assurances from their direct business partners that they will ensure compliance with the company's code of conduct and, as necessary, a prevention action plan, including by establishing corresponding contractual assurances from their partners, to the extent that their activities are part of the company's chain of activities.[4] Where necessary, they may also seek contractual assurances from indirect business partners.[5] Furthermore, business partners should be committed to

1 European Parliament and Council Directive (EU) 2024/1760 on corporate sustainability due diligence and amending Directive (EU) 2019/1937 and Regulation (EU) 2023/2859 (CSDDD) OJ L2024/1760.

2 Directive on Corporate Sustainability Due Diligence (CSDDD) Articles 6–8.

3 CSDDD Article 7 (2) (b).

4 CSDDD Articles 7 (2) (b), 10 (2) (b) and 11 (3) (c).

5 CSDDD Articles 7 (2) (b), 10 (4) and 11 (5).

 | HTTPS://DOI.ORG/10.1163/9789004779235-006

a system of identifying and assessing actual and potential impacts, and to measures to verify compliance.[6]

Living up to the CSDDD comes at a cost, not only for the targeted large companies but also for their business partners. Depending on the code of conduct of the large companies and the contractual assurances, they too will have to have a due diligence framework in place. Moreover, they have to invest in new methods of production and distribution and pay for the costs of compliance and verification.

It is not considered reasonable to simply shift the burden to the business partner, for this would ignore the large company's own level of involvement in the potential and actual adverse impacts.[7] According to the CSDDD, large companies are supposed to share the burden, at least if their business partner is a small business.[8] Thus, small businesses can claim some support from their large business partners, in order to enable the latter to live up to their obligations under the CSDDD.

In this chapter, we will analyse whether the CSDDD and procedural law are fit for realising this support and protection of small businesses in court. First, we will explore the way the CSDDD protects small businesses and whether the directive orders access to justice for small businesses (Sections 2 and 3). Then, we will turn to the existing systems. Civil procedural law offers access to justice but is considered difficult, costly and time-consuming (Section 4). Whereas access to justice is not merely a matter of fact but a legal issue (Section 5); and an existing complaints mechanism cannot serve as an alternative (Section 6), we need to look into improving civil procedural law (paragraph 7). The matter needs urgent attention, for the CSDDD is supposed to be transposed into national law by mid-2027.

6 CSDDD Article 10 (5).

7 Sarah Dadush, Daniel Schönfelder and Michaela Strebelt, 'What does the EU CSDDD say about contracts?' (2024) New York University Journal of Law & Business 246, 268, referring to CSDDD Article 10 (1).

8 Definition of CSDDD Article 3 (1) (i). In fact, the CSDDD extends support to small and medium businesses (ie, SMEs). We will stick to this book's focus on small businesses.

2 An Obligation to Support Small Businesses

The CSDDD includes several safeguards for small businesses.[9] For instance, large companies must adapt their purchasing practices,[10] avoid unfair contract clauses and cover the cost of third-party verification for business partners that are small businesses.[11] They also need to provide proportionate support and invest in their value chain to help small businesses comply with the requirements. They shall be required to:

> provide targeted and proportionate support to an SME which is a business partner of the company, where necessary in light of the resources, knowledge and constraints of the SME, including by providing or enabling access to capacity-building, training or upgrading management systems, and, where compliance with the code of conduct or the prevention action plan would jeopardise the viability of the SME, by providing targeted and proportionate financial support, such as direct financing, low-interest loans, guarantees of continued sourcing, or assistance in securing financing.[12]

Whereas a small business is supposed to assure that it will live up to the code of conduct of the large company, in order to contribute to the fulfilment of the large company's due diligence obligations, it is in return entitled to support by the large company, to prevent that the small business's financial efforts would cause bankruptcy of the small business or put the small business in a situation where bankruptcy is imminent.[13]

Ideally, contracting parties will discuss these issues when entering into the agreement. In order to be able to conduct proper due diligence in which at least both parties' operations are involved, each party must strive for cooperation and transparency. For this reason, the agreement should set out a joint commitment to cooperate in carrying out due diligence in an ongoing fashion and throughout the life of the contract, as well as a clear allocation of tasks

---

9 See Commission staff working document accompanying the Proposal for a Directive of the European Parliament and of the Council amending Directives 2006/43/EC, 2013/34/EU, (EU) 2022/2464 and (EU) 2024/1760 as regards certain corporate sustainability reporting and due diligence requirements, SWD(2025) 80 final, 26 February 2025, 9. The Commission is proposing to restrict the obligations to tier-1 as the rule, with exceptions; see 36.

10 CSDDD Articles 10 (2) (d) and 11 (3) (e).

11 CSDDD Articles 10 (5) and 11 (6).

12 CSDDD Article 10 (2) (e) compared to Article 11 (3) (f).

13 CSDDD recital 46 and 54.

reflecting the shared responsibility to prevent or mitigate potential negative impacts. Whereas one of the parties is a small business, it may be more appropriate for them to commit to cooperating in the large company's due diligence framework, rather than setting up their own.[14]

Ideally, the large company will seek the prescribed contractual assurances, at which point the small business will make it clear that there is a need for support with a view to carrying out the requested assurances.

In practice, the purchase terms and conditions of large companies and the corresponding Codes of Conduct do not show any consideration for small business partners, nor do they provide for a lenient oversight mechanism and flanking policies for these business partners.[15] Although large companies seem to be willing to grant suppliers time to make improvements in the field of sustainability and to offer 'tips' for compliance or online training courses, they seem to demand compliance with their responsible business policy without distinguishing between small and large business partners. Take, for example, the way Unilever – according to *unilever.com,* one of the world's largest and most global consumer goods companies – deals with these issues. According to its responsible Partner Policy, Unilever endeavours to provide support and guidance and embraces the spirit of partnership in areas where it can 'collaborate in a pre-competitive environment to address endemic issues in our industries'.[16] Yet, Unilever – the Buyer – charges its supplier, small or large, without further ado, the cost of third-party monitoring and remedying:

> 6.3. Supplier shall undertake third-party Responsible Business audits required by Buyer at its own cost and rectify any non-compliance identified in such audits within a reasonable timeframe stipulated by Buyer.[17]

So, what will happen if a small business invokes a provision of national law, transposing Article 10 (5) CSDDD, which orders large companies like Unilever

---

14 Dadush et al (n 7) 268.

15 Jaap Baaij and Alex Geert Castermans, 'The potential of contractual assurances to advance supply chain due diligence' in Elbert de Jong (ed), *Corporate Accountability and Liability for Climate Change* (Edward Elgar 2024) 109, 133–136.

16 Unilever, *Responsible Partner policy* (2022) 7, https://www.unilever.com/files/56455dcf-0f8f-41cb-a3a9-2f77bf8a6291/unilever-responsible-partner-policy.pdf (accessed 17 August 2026).

17 Unilever, *General Terms and Conditions for the Purchase of Products and Services* (December 2024) https://www.unilever.com/files/global-purchasing-gtcs-english.pdf (accessed 17 August 2026).

to bear the cost of the independent third-party verification, where measures to verify compliance are carried out in relation to small businesses? What will happen, in general, if parties disagree about the needs of the small business and the entitlement to support? What will happen if an impact on human rights or the environment arises during the execution of the agreement, and the parties disagree on how this should be addressed? What if the large company simply passes on the burden to the small business?

3 A Claim to Support Small Businesses

To a certain extent, the CSDDD offers answers to these questions. The EU Member States must designate one or more supervisory authorities to supervise compliance with the obligations laid down in the provisions of national law adopted pursuant to the Directive's due diligence framework.[18] Natural and legal persons must be entitled to submit 'substantiated concerns', through 'easily accessible channels', to this supervisory authority, when they have reasons to believe, on the basis of objective circumstances, that a company is failing to comply with the provisions of national law adopted pursuant to this Directive.[19] Apparently, they may also request to take action against the large business in order to ensure that the large business fulfils its obligation to support its small business partners.[20] This mechanism should be free of charge or with a fee limited to covering administrative costs only.[21] The authority may then initiate an investigation.[22]

Thus, if a large company and its small business partner do not agree on the support the company should provide, the small business partner may turn to the relevant authority to express its concerns regarding the support that the large company is obliged to give. The result of the investigation should be expected in due time:

> Member States shall ensure that supervisory authorities assess the substantiated concerns in an appropriate period of time and, where appropriate, exercise their powers as referred to in Article 25.[23]

18 CSDDD Article 24 (1).
19 CSDDD Article 26 (1).
20 See CSDDD Article 26 (5), referring to the authority's decision to accept of refuse any request for action.
21 CSDDD recital 75.
22 CSDDD Article 25 (2).
23 CSDDD Article 26 (4).

The authority has the power to order compliance – for example, to cease infringements or to provide remediation – and to impose penalties.[24] The penalties provided for shall be effective, proportionate and dissuasive, taking into account, for example, any investment made and any targeted support provided pursuant to the due diligence obligations (CSDDD Articles 10 and 11).[25] The authority shall inform the persons who expressed their concerns of the result of the assessment and of its decision to accept or refuse any request for action, as well as of a description of the further steps and measures, and practical information on access to administrative and judicial review procedures.[26]

Up to this stage, the mechanism seems to be promising for small businesses. Then the focus of the CSDDD explicitly turns to access to court. Surprisingly, the subject is not a claim against the large company but a claim against the authority:

> Member States shall ensure that persons submitting substantiated concerns in accordance with this Article and having, in accordance with national law, a legitimate interest in the matter, have access to a court or other independent and impartial public body competent to review the procedural and substantive legality of the decisions, acts or failure to act of the supervisory authority.[27]

Going to court to assess the actions of the authority detracts from the low-threshold nature of the mechanism, assuming that the small business is waiting for a speedy assessment of the claim to support, instead of an assessment of the authority's decisions and acts. If the small business must go to court anyway, then it is better to have a claim on the large company assessed immediately.

This raises the question of whether procedural law will effectively provide the support and protection that the CSDDD provides to small businesses.

---

24 CSDDD Article 25 (5) (a) (i) and (iii).
25 CSDDD Article 27 (2) (b).
26 CSDDD Article 26 (5).
27 CSDDD Article 26 (6).

4 Small Businesses' 'Suffering' in the Court System: A Dutch Report from 2019

In 2019, the Dutch Research and Data Centre[28] published a report on disputes and the sector of small and medium-sized businesses.[29] The report is based on the presumption that to promote a supportive environment in which small businesses can thrive, the quality and accessibility of the legal system play an important role.[30] Within this context, the report aims to provide a quantitative and representative overview of the disputes that small and medium-sized businesses experience, how they deal with them and how they evaluate existing legal provisions. The so-called 'landscape of disputes' is evaluated from the perspective of Dutch businesses.[31] Here, we will present the report as it is, followed by some reflections on how it has been received and some additional thoughts with regard to the difficulty and costs.

The research questions were:

- How many businesses have experienced civil-law and administrative-law conflicts in the past year? What is the nature of these conflicts?
- How many businesses have turned to legal professionals and (extra) judicial proceedings in the past year? Which were these? And for what reasons did they decide not to use service providers and procedures?
- How did the most important conflict of the past year end, and what were the results of the approach taken?
- How do businesses assess the services provided by legal professionals and ruling authorities that they have used?
- In general, how do businesses perceive their access to justice and what is their level of trust in the legal system?[32]

---

28 The Research and Data Centre (WODC) is an independent knowledge institute that falls under the Dutch Ministry of Justice and Security. It aims to contribute to upholding and improving the rule of law by, inter alia, carrying out scientific research (or commissioning others to do so, on its behalf). See also Nylund, Chapter 2.

29 T Geurts and MJ Ter Voert, 'Geschillen in het MKB. Over het verloop van conflicten bij bedrijven tot tien werkzame personen' (Disputes and the SME sector. On the course of conflicts at companies with up to ten employees) (*WODC Cahier 2019–11*). The two researchers who carried out this Report are social scientists. A summary in English is available at: https://repository.wodc.nl/bitstream/handle/20.500.12832/229/Cahier_2019-11_Summary_tcm28-410974.pdf?sequence=3&isAllowed=y (accessed 17 August 2026).

30 Due to the focus of this book, we will use the term 'small businesses'; note that the WODC-report is about small and medium businesses.

31 For the citizen's perspective on the landscape, we refer to M Ter Voert and M Hoekstra, 'Geschilbeslechtingsdelta 2019/Paths to justice in the Netherlands 2019' (*WODC- Cahier 2020–18*).

32 Geurts and Ter Voert (n 29) 88.

To answer our research questions, the researchers conducted a survey among businesses. The report focused on small businesses up to ten employees, considering that these businesses are presumably more vulnerable than larger businesses (up to 249 employees) when confronted with a conflict and that they have less economic and legal resources, as well as less experience with solving legal problems.

At the time of the research, there were just below 800,000 active small businesses in the Netherlands with up to ten employees. From that population of 778,000 active small businesses, a random sample of 4,130 businesses was drawn, and these selected businesses were invited to participate in the study by completing an online questionnaire. A total of 1,697 businesses participated in the survey. So, the researchers weighed the sample to estimate the actual numbers.[33]

Of the 778,000 businesses, an estimated 35% had one or more conflicts in the year preceding the survey.[34] The majority of those conflicts were trade conflicts. Around 17% had one or more conflicts concerning purchases, and about 13% had one or more conflicts about sales. These conflicts (purchase and sales) were usually about the product itself, the payment, or the invoice. Other, less prevalent types of conflicts include labour disputes.

The results of the study were described in two themes: 1) businesses' conflicts and getting justice and 2) businesses' approach to their most important conflict, including the results of this approach and satisfaction with any legal services used.

The first theme addressed general opinions about 'getting justice':

> Many businesses were unable to give their opinion about getting justice. On questions pertaining to various aspects of this topic, 21% to 41% of the businesses filled in 'I don't know'. Many of these businesses (26% to 51%) did not have a conflict in the past year, indicating that a lack of experience may be the reason why they have no opinion on this. Only few businesses (6%) believed that, in general, it is easy for a business to get their justice. Others were indifferent (22%) or reported that getting justice is hard for a business like their own (36%). Reasons behind a negative evaluation include the expectation that legal proceedings are difficult and time-consuming, as well as the high costs that are expected to come along with such procedures. Yet, about half of the entrepreneurs consider it worthwhile to take legal action in the event of a serious conflict. About a quarter of businesses find it difficult to find a qualified legal service provider (24%) and one fifth believe that there are insufficient facilities

33 Geurts and Ter Voert (n 29) para. 1.3.2.
34 Geurts and Ter Voert (n 29) 6 and para. 3.1.

> for advice or assistance (20%). Around 10% have no faith in a fair decision by the court or in the craftsmanship of a lawyer. Businesses that have had a conflict in the past year are more negative about access to or trust in the legal system than businesses without a conflict.[35]

The second theme focused on businesses' experience with what they consider their most important conflict. The summary of the 'valuation of access to justice and trust' reads as follows:

> All in all there were relatively many entrepreneurs with a conflict who have a negative opinion about access to justice and trust in the legal system in general. These entrepreneurs were the most negative about the costs of legal advice or court proceedings. About half consider control over the costs to be a problem. Moreover, more than half considered access to justice to be difficult (59%) and thought court proceedings to be difficult (55%) or time-consuming (73%). Entrepreneurs were a little less negative about finding a legal service provider: about a third thought there are insufficient facilities for advice or assistance or found it difficult to find a good legal service provider. About a quarter of the entrepreneurs who experienced a conflict, had no faith in a fair decision of a judge, 13% had no faith in the craftsmanship of a lawyer and 30% had little expectations from legal action.[36]

Both themes show that access to justice is difficult, costly and time-consuming.

The branch organisation of small and medium businesses in the Netherlands – *MKB Nederland* – embraced the report and advocated an experiment with a specific court for small businesses, which, together with the parties, would aim at resolving disputes as well and definitively as possible, combining elements of the summary proceedings and the proceedings on the merits. This should prevent lawsuits from dragging on and ultimately ending without a verdict. Small companies cannot keep that up and want to be able to move on.[37]

The report and the plea of small businesses make sense, taking into account that in court, some parties are in the habit of using every straw that the law offers, in the field of substantive civil law, as well as procedural law and private international law. This habit is often motivated not so much by the desire to

35 Geurts and Ter Voert (n 29) 89.

36 Geurts and Ter Voert (n 29) 94–95.

37 'Kleine bedrijven vinden de rechter te duur', *Het Financieele Dagblad* (Amsterdam 17 October 2019).

make a materially correct assessment possible but rather by the desire to postpone a conviction for as long as possible. Consider, for instance, a case involving the sale of fertiliser by a Belgian seller to a Dutch buyer. The fertiliser turned out to be contaminated, and the buyer went to the Dutch court. The lawyers of the Belgian seller used a fairly well-known form of strategic operationalisation of private international law: the opening of an incident on jurisdiction. Thus, the defendant can strengthen its negotiating position by calling into question the jurisdiction of the court seized by the claimant before putting forward defences of a substantive nature. The seller's lawyers expected that it would take some time to settle the jurisdictional incident, which would allow costly fact-finding into the cause and consequences of the contamination of the fertiliser to be postponed. It was also expected that after some time of litigation, the buyer would settle for a lower amount than it initially claimed. And so it happened: the case dragged from the District Court to the Court of Appeal, the Dutch Supreme Court, the European Court of Justice,[38] and back to the Dutch Supreme Court. By the time it was established that Dutch courts had jurisdiction to hear the case, the buyer was tired of litigating. The case was settled, more than 11 years after the delivery of fertiliser and nearly 9 years after the start of the proceedings. And in fact, the seller had to pay much less than the buyer had claimed in the proceedings.[39]

Taking this example into account, taken from the practice of an esteemed Dutch lawyer, it is for good reasons that *MKB Nederland* embraced the report. However, the comments of the Dutch government, sending the report to the Parliament, were – to put it mildly – less ambitious. The government announced that the report will be included in the ongoing project of simplifying the court procedure for the collection of claims. The Government also expressed its intention to promote easily accessible information and advice for all litigants.[40]

Thus, we cannot be sure that procedural law effectively supports the protection offered to small businesses by the CSDDD. Whereas the CSDDD aims at saving small businesses from bankruptcy, a claim for protection may contribute to the opposite, since we may expect that large companies are in the habit of using every straw that the law offers in court. Small businesses will face not only disputes on jurisdiction but also on their financial ability to live

38 Case C-189/08 *Zuid-Chemie v Philippo's* [2009] EU:C:2009:475.

39 MV Polak, *IPR-abracadabra: Internationaal privaatrecht voor tovenaars, hogepriesters en mandarijnen* (Leiden University Press 2013) 4–5.

40 Letter to the House of Representatives, 17 October 2019, *Parliamentary papers* 2019–2020 32 637, no. 383.

up to due diligence obligations laid down in the large company's code of conduct, without the support of the large company.

This prompts the question of whether it is imperative that procedural mechanisms give effect to the protective framework that the CSDDD establishes for small businesses.

5 Access to Justice as a Right under EU Law

The Dutch government, transposing the CSDDD into national law, assessed whether the new law, based on the CSDDD, would meet the standards of primary EU law. It argued that the due diligence obligations may constitute a restriction of the freedom to conduct a business, enshrined in Article 16 of the Charter of Fundamental Rights of the EU (EU Charter). The companies that fall within the scope of the CSDDD and the new national law must meet the additional obligations in the exercise of their economic activities. In addition, the freedom of contract of those companies may be restricted, as they may no longer be able to cooperate with business relations whose activities have adverse human rights or environmental impacts. According to the government, the restriction meets all the requirements, since it is provided for by law and the essence of the freedom of contract will remain unaffected. Without further ado, the government considered the restrictions necessary, while they meet the objectives of either the general interest recognised by the EU or the need to protect the rights and freedoms of others (Article 52(1) of the EU Charter).[41]

Apparently, the small businesses were not involved in this assessment. Obviously, their businesses will be affected by the new law. In order to meet the obligations of the large companies that are addressed by the new law explicitly, the small businesses will be induced to ensure that they will comply with the code of conduct of the large companies, cascade this assurance to their business partners and make the necessary investments accordingly. Whereas the CSDDD itself has explicitly addressed the potential existential burden on small businesses, national lawmakers and courts should be warned: the transposition of the CSDDD into national law and the application of national law should be in line with Article 16 of the EU Charter.

41 *Consultatie versie Memorie van Toelichting wetsvoorstel internationaal verantwoord ondernemen* (Consultation version of the explanatory memorandum of the law on international responsible business conduct) (18 November 2024) 20–21.

One may argue that the position is ascertained by the obligation of large companies to provide targeted and proportionate support to a small business which is a business partner of the company, as necessary in light of the resources, knowledge and constraints of the small business. But it will take some time before we know what 'as necessary' does entail, and how this will be proven.

It is not inconceivable that some large companies will hide behind this 'as necessary' clause because it is difficult to prove why it is actually necessary and to what extent. A cynical perspective will argue that this support is only legally necessary if it is simply impossible for a company to obtain the funds and knowledge. Moreover, when a small business is financially mean and lean, then it will be quite impossible to prove the causal link between compliance with the code of conduct of the large company and the upcoming bankruptcy. In the absence of means for compliance, it may be asked whether such a due diligence expectation is the drop in the ocean that drives a company to bankruptcy or one of the many drops in the ocean that together lead to bankruptcy. Even if this causal link can be substantiated and a large company still refuses to provide services and resources to achieve sufficient due diligence, the small business concerned will have limited means to initiate legal proceedings to claim these services and resources from the large company.

For these reasons, Article 47 of the EU Charter comes into play. Whereas the CSDDD explicitly aims to protect the interests of small businesses, the question arises whether national procedural provisions make the application of the CSDDD with regard to protecting small businesses impossible or excessively difficult. In the abstract, we cannot single out a specific provision. Several provisions are involved, from jurisdiction to timing, evidence and costs. The answer is complicated, since the matter must be analysed by reference to the role of those provisions in the procedure, their progress and their special features, viewed as a whole, and, where relevant, principles which lie at the basis of the national legal system, such as the protection of the rights of the defendant, the principle of legal certainty and the proper conduct of the proceedings.[42] Ensuring the effectiveness of the rights that individuals derive from EU law implies a requirement for effective judicial protection, reaffirmed in Article 47 of the Charter of Fundamental Rights of the European Union, which applies, inter alia, to the definition of detailed procedural rules relating to actions based on such rights.[43]

---

42 Case C-869/19 *Unicaja Banco SA* [2021] EU:C:2022:397 para 28.

43 Case C-869/19 *Unicaja Banco SA* [2022] EU:C:2022:397 para 29, referring particularly to the rights derived from Directive 93/13 as well as Joined Cases 776/19 to 782/19 *BNP Paribas Personal Finance* [2021] EU:C:2021:470 para 29.

Thus, the question of whether procedural provisions are adequately fit for assessing the small businesses' claim for support is not merely a matter of fact. It is a matter of law. If the procedural toolkit for small businesses under the CSDDD is indeed inadequate at present, what is the way forward?

6 A Complaint at the OECD National Contact Point

By 26 July 2027, Member States shall have adopted and published the laws, regulations and administrative provisions necessary to comply with the CSDDD.[44] On such short notice, two routes may enhance the position of small businesses to enable them to realise their claims against large companies.

The first is situated in the context of the OECD Guidelines for Multinational Enterprises on Responsible Business Conduct. Amongst other topics, they address the relationship between multinational companies and their business partners with a view to preventing and mitigating negative impacts on human rights, the environment and labour conditions. According to Guideline II.A.14, multinational enterprises should use their leverage and encourage, where practicable, entities with which an enterprise has a business relationship to apply principles of responsible business conduct compatible with the Guidelines. This is not only a matter of standard setting. Multinational enterprises may also engage with their business relationships to improve their performance, including through personnel training and other forms of capacity building, and support the integration of principles of responsible business conduct compatible with the Guidelines into their business practices. It is considered particularly important in this respect that multinational companies engage with and support small businesses with which they have business relationships.[45]

In this context, all Member States of the OECD and other adherents to the Guidelines have set up National Contact Points (NCPs) for Responsible Business Conduct, to contribute to the resolution of issues that arise in relation to the implementation of the Guidelines in specific instances.[46] The NCP serves

44 Directive (EU) 2025/794 of the European Parliament and of the Council of 14 April 2025 amending Directives (EU) 2022/2464 and (EU) 2024/1760 as regards the dates from which Member States are to apply certain corporate sustainability reporting and due diligence requirements [2025] OJ L 2025/794, Article 2.

45 OECD, *OECD Guidelines for Multinational Enterprises on Responsible Business Conduct* (OECD Publishing 2023) Commentary on Chapter II: General Policies 26.

46 OECD Council, *Decision of the Council on the Guidelines for Multinational Enterprises on Responsible Business Conduct*, (OECD Publishing 2023) 56.

as a non-judicial grievance mechanism. It offers a forum for discussion and its expertise on the Guidelines to assist the business community, worker organisations, other non-governmental organisations (NGOs) and other interested parties concerned to resolve the issues raised. Depending on the characteristics of each case, this assistance may include supporting constructive dialogue, facilitating agreements between the parties and/or issuing recommendations. The aims of such assistance may include furthering the implementation of the Guidelines in the future and addressing adverse impacts in a way consistent with the Guidelines.[47] NCPs will not charge a submission fee, and requirements to file a case will be clearly stated, readily available and not unnecessarily burdensome.[48]

Any person with a legitimate interest in the issue in question can file a case with an NCP. Usually, NGOs, individuals and trade unions submit cases. They have each been responsible for around one-third of the cases submitted to NCPs since 2000.[49] We did not come across any case submitted by a small business or its branch organisation, but we expect their case to be admissible, considering their legitimate interest in getting support from multinationals. The NCP should be able to offer guidance with regard to the application of Guideline II.A.14.

This first route cannot suffice. It may serve as an alternative but not as a substitute for access to justice. The NCPs will refrain from any legal interpretation of the applicable law such as the due diligence obligations of the CSDDD. Its findings will not be legally enforceable.

7 An Experimental Reforming of Civil Procedural Law

A second route should be aimed at reforming procedural law, making proceedings easier, faster and more affordable. This may take considerable time and effort, but in the Netherlands, the so-called Temporary Experiments on the Judicial System Act (the Experiments Act) could be invoked.[50] This Experiments Act, which has been in force since April 2023, aims to promote

---

47 OECD, *OECD Guidelines* (n 45).

48 OECD, *OECD Guidelines* (n 45) 65.

49 OECD, *Cases handled by the National Contact Points for Responsible Business Conduct*, https://www.oecd.org/content/dam/oecd/en/networks/national-contact-points/Flyer-OECD-National-Contact-Points.pdf (accessed 17 August 2026).

50 Temporary Experiments Act Judicial System Act (*Wet van 24 juni 2020 houdende regels inzake invoering van een tijdelijke mogelijkheid voor experimenten in de rechtspleging (Tijdelijke Experimentenwet rechtspleging)*) Stb. 2020, 223; Act of 24 June 2020, laying

simple, fast, efficient and de-escalating dispute resolution.[51] To achieve this, certain parts of various codes, such as the Code of Civil Procedure, the Code of Judicial Practice, some parts of the Civil Code and the Bankruptcy Act, may be deviated from for a maximum period of 3 years. The experiment must be based on a general administrative measure. This Experiments Act, therefore, does not contain the experiments themselves. It offers the framework for setting up experiments. The experiments must be evaluated and may also be terminated prematurely if necessary. Various restrictions apply.[52] For example, each experiment must guarantee at least the right of access to the courts, as well as, among other things, the right to a fair trial by an independent and impartial judge, the principle of hearing both sides of the argument and the principle of open court proceedings.[53] An important element of the Act is that parties can be compelled to participate in the experiment.[54]

The Experiments Act mentions one example of a possible experiment: lay judges, or, in the words of the Act itself, an additional expert member.[55] The parliamentary documents accompanying this Act also mention various other examples of possible experiments. One of these is a procedure for simple commercial disputes.[56] During the preparation of the Experiments Act, discussions were held with practitioners about what was needed in the field of procedural law. From the business side, it was emphasised that small businesses particularly need a procedure in which a final decision can be obtained more quickly in disputes between small businesses, so that they can get on with doing business.[57] Another example mentioned in the parliamentary documents is an alternative divorce procedure.[58]

Obligations relating to the CSDDD do not appear at all in the Explanatory Memorandum to the Temporary Experiments Act. This does not necessarily mean that the Experiments Act does not provide a basis for an experiment in which small businesses can ensure that the larger companies with which they collaborate enforce their CSDDD obligations towards them. These are not simple commercial disputes, but the matter is sufficiently serious and, at

---

down rules on the introduction of a temporary possibility for experiments in the administration of justice.

51 Temporary Experiments Act Judicial System Act Article 1.

52 Temporary Experiments Act Judicial System Act Articles 3 and 4.

53 Temporary Experiments Act Judicial System Act Article 1(5).

54 Cf CJM Klaassen, 'Rechtzoekenden als proefdieren (?)' (2020) Ars Aequi 995, 997.

55 Temporary Experiments Act Judicial System Act Article 5 (1).

56 Explanatory Memorandum, *Parliamentary Papers* 2018–2019, 35 263, no 3, 23 ff.

57 Explanatory Memorandum (n 56) 23.

58 Explanatory Memorandum (n 56) 27 ff.

least in some respects, is in line with the objectives of that Act: to promote simple, fast, efficient and de-escalating dispute resolution, preferably before 26 July 2027.

References

Baaij J and Castermans AG, 'The potential of contractual assurances to advance supply chain due diligence' in E de Jong (ed), *Corporate Accountability and Liability for Climate Change* (Edward Elgar 2024).

Dadush S, Schönfelder D and Strebelt M, 'What does the EU CSDDD say about contracts?' (2024) New York University Journal of Law & Business 245.

Geurts T and Ter Voert MJ, *Geschillen in het MKB: over het verloop van conflicten bij bedrijven tot tien werkzame personen* (WODC Cahier 2019–11, 2019).

'Kleine bedrijven vinden de rechter te duur', *Het Financieele Dagblad* (Amsterdam, 17 October 2019).

Klaassen CJM, 'Rechtzoekenden als proefdieren (?)' (2020) Ars Aequi 995.

OECD, *Cases handled by the National Contact Points for Responsible Business Conduct* https://www.oecd.org/content/dam/oecd/en/networks/national-contact-points/Flyer-OECD-National-Contact-Points.pdf (accessed 19 August 2026).

OECD, *OECD Guidelines for Multinational Enterprises on Responsible Business Conduct* (OECD Publishing 2023).

OECD Council, *Decision of the Council on the Guidelines for Multinational Enterprises on Responsible Business Conduct* (OECD Publishing 2023).

Polak MV, *IPR-abracadabra: Internationaal privaatrecht voor tovenaars, hogepriesters en mandarijnen* (Leiden University Press 2013).

Ter Voert M and Hoekstra M, *Geschilbeslechtingsdelta 2019/Paths to justice in the Netherlands 2019* (WODC Cahier 2020–18, 2020).

Unilever, *General Terms and Conditions for the Purchase of Products and Services* (December 2024).

Unilever, *Responsible Partner Policy* (2022).

CHAPTER 6

The Complex Nordic Dispute Resolution Landscape and Access to Justice for Small Businesses

Anna Nylund

1 Introduction

A civil justice system that includes a variety of dispute-resolution processes can be very advantageous, even for small businesses. Diversity might lead to quicker, cheaper, and more accessible justice. Some processes could offer alternatives to adversarial procedures intended to promote justice through the law by fostering collaboration and (at least partly) interest-based outcomes, thereby reducing the indirect and intangible costs of disputes.[1] Other procedures could provide a swifter and cheaper alternative to regular court proceedings, and some could be tailored for multi-party disputes.

For inexperienced disputants with limited resources, a complex justice system could be a maze of crossing pathways, making access to justice difficult and expensive.[2] When disputants must use multiple processes, pathways to justice could become longer, costlier, and riskier. Complexity increases the risk of selecting an inappropriate process with repercussions for efficiency and quality. In addition to the challenges associated with the initial selection of a dispute resolution process, disputants may have to decide whether to switch processes and, if so, how to select the next process or when to proceed to it. Different procedures not only produce different substantive outcomes but also tend to have different procedural effects, such as limited or no access to direct enforcement or limited estoppel effects.[3] Understanding the implica-

1 Eg, Klaus J Hopt and Felix Steffek, 'Mediation: Comparison of Laws, Regulatory Models, Fundamental Issues' in Klaus J Hopt and Felix Steffek, *Mediation. Principles and Regulation in Comparative Perspective* (Oxford University Press 2013) 97–99 and 103–104.

2 Hazel Genn, *Judging Civil Justice. The Hamlyn Lectures 2008* (Cambridge University Press 2010) 123.

3 Nadja Alexander and Shouyu Chong, *The Singapore Convention on Mediation. A Commentary* (Wolters Kluwer 2019) 69; Haris P Meidanis, 'Enforcement of Mediation Settlement Agreements in the EU and the Need for Reform' (2020) 16 Journal Private International Law 275, 281ff; Anna Nylund, 'Shaping Civil Litigation Using Procedural Agreements: Perspec-

 | HTTPS://DOI.ORG/10.1163/9789004779235-007

tions of such factors takes relatively advanced knowledge of procedural law. Making informed, rational decisions regarding the choice of procedure necessitates an adequate assessment of the direct and indirect, tangible and intangible costs and risks associated with each process.[4] The more complex the justice system, the more likely less informed disputants, such as many small businesses, are to face increased – not reduced – costs and risks. In multi-tier justice systems, small businesses risk depleting their resources before reaching a resolution or settling on unfavourable terms. Alternatively, ineffective navigation of the system could lead to apathy. In both cases, the result is inadequate access to justice.

This chapter investigates two alternatives to regular court litigation: simplified debt collection proceedings and mediation. Debt collection procedures are essential for maintaining the cash flow and ensuring that businesses and individuals fulfil their obligations promptly.[5] Mediation is potentially superior to litigation because it allows the parties to maintain their business relationship and to craft outcomes that meet their business interests.[6] They are examined from the perspective of small businesses in two dimensions: one in which the counterpart is another, often far larger, business (a business-to-business, B2B, dispute), and the other in which the counterpart is a consumer (a business-to-consumer, B2C, dispute). Finnish, Norwegian, and Swedish laws are used as examples to study these complexities.

Simplified debt collection procedures are often an efficient way to vindicate tenable claims. However, complexity becomes evident when the claim becomes contested, regardless of whether the contestation is tenable. In such cases, the choice between simplified and regular proceedings and the differences between them become apparent. In B2C cases, consumer dispute resolution (CDR) processes add another dimension to the selection of a strategy for pursuing the claim. The institutional and procedural design influences the challenges and risks involved in such processes.

---

tives and Prospectives' in Anna Nylund and Antonio Cabral (eds), *Shaping Civil Litigation Using Procedural Agreements* (Eleven 2024); Anna Nylund, 'Procedural Effects of Court Settlements' (2025) 2 Law & Criminology Journal 32.

4 Michaela Keet, Heather Heavin and John Lande, *Litigation Interest and Risk Assessment* (ABA Publishing 2020) 65 ff; Nylund and Bernt, Chapter 4, Section 2.

5 See also Ahmed, Chapter 9, Section 2.

6 Shirley Shipman, Ben Waters and William Wood, *Brown and Marriott's ADR Principles and Practice* (4th edn, Sweet & Maxwell 2019) 29–38 and 123 ff.

Mediation is interesting because out-of-court mediation is still limited in many European countries.[7] In many jurisdictions, disputants still tend to mediate only when mandated to do so;[8] this may be because mediation is not well known, and there is limited cultural support for choosing mediation. However, the institutional and regulatory design of out-of-court mediation could also prevent small businesses from participating. In contrast, some CDR processes include mediation or components similar to mediation as integral elements, making mediation the norm. Notwithstanding the mandatory mediation processes discussed by Masood Ahmed in his chapter,[9] in many European countries, including the Nordic countries, mediation is primarily available as an ad hoc process in B2B disputes. This type of mediation epitomises the alternative nature of mediation: it is privately organised and funded (although a mediation institution could assist with administrative issues similar to those of arbitration institutions), the mediator's role is to facilitate negotiations toward a consensual outcome, and the process is highly flexible. This flexibility could entail challenges for small businesses.

Access to court, particularly in cases where the amount in dispute is relatively low, is essential even when alternatives exist. If disputants lack real access to court because proceedings are too costly or lengthy, their access to justice will be curtailed. Therefore, this chapter first provides a brief overview of access to small-claims courts in Finland, Norway, and Sweden in Section 2. Thereafter, Section 3 discusses simplified procedures for pecuniary claims in B2B and B2C disputes. Then, Section 4 examines mediation as an alternative to adjudicative processes. Finally, in Section 5, some concluding observations are provided on when and how a more complex justice system could increase access to justice for small businesses.

7 Directorate-General for Internal Policies, *'Rebooting' the Mediation Directive: Assessing the limited impact of its implementation and proposing measure to increase the number of mediations in the EU.* Study. Policy Department C: Citizens' rights and constitutional affairs. Legal Affairs. European Parliament. PE 493.042, 6; and European Commission for the Efficiency of Justice. Working Group on Mediation (CEPEJ-GT-MED), *The Impact of CEPEJ Guidelines on Civil, Family, Penal and Administrative Mediation* (16 May 2018) CEPEJ-GT-MED(2017)8, 9–10.

8 Peter Grajzl, Agnė Tvaronavičienė and Bryan Clark, 'From Promise to Practice: Resolving the Mediation Paradox in Europe' JAMS ADR Blog (June 17, 2025) https://www.jdsupra.com/legalnews/from-promise-to-practice-resolving-the-1706683/ (accessed 10 November 2025).

9 Ahmed, Chapter 10; Vandenbussche and Onraedt, Chapter 8.

2 The Access to Court in Small Claims Cases in the Nordics

Given that Finland, Norway, and Sweden are neighbouring countries with, in many ways, similar legal systems and societies, and relatively similar procedural systems, the differences between them regarding access to court proceedings are surprising. This is reflected in the number of incoming cases. In 2023, Finland had only 180 and Norway only 206 general civil and commercial (non-family) cases per 100,000 inhabitants, while Sweden had 501, more than twice as many. In Sweden, the amount in dispute in about 40% of incoming general civil and commercial cases was below SEK 26,250 (approximately EUR 2,400), which is the threshold for small claims. Although the threshold for small claims was far higher in Norway, NOK 250,000 (approximately EUR 21,000), only 15% of the cases were small cases. Finland has no small claims proceedings. There is no data on the distribution of cases by the disputed value for Finnish cases. However, a survey conducted in Finland found that when the amount in dispute is EUR 10,000, only 31% of respondents would bring an action, considerably lower than in any other EU Member State.[10] The main reason was the high cost of litigation. The average case processing time is fairly low in Norway (176 days) and Sweden (152 days), but high in Finland (327 days).[11]

While Norway has a small claims procedure, in which costs for lawyers are capped at 20% of the amount in dispute, the number of small claims is low.[12] One reason is that small claims, unless the parties have used an alternative to the courts, such as CDR, must first be filed with the Conciliation Boards (*forliksråd*). Conciliation Boards, the members of which are lay persons, have limited power to issue a binding judgment. They may do so if the case is relatively simple. Their primary role is to bring about a settlement.[13] Because the members do not have legal training, they do not facilitate settlements or hand down rulings based on the law, but rather on what they find equitable or what

---

10 Oikeusministeriö, Pienriitamenettely. Arviomuistio (Oikeusministeriön julkaisuja, Mietintöjä ja lausuntoja 2023:1) 18–22.

11 European Commission for the Efficiency of Justice, *European Judicial Systems Evaluation Report. 2024 Cycle (2022 Data)* https://public.tableau.com/app/profile/cepej/viz/QuantitativeDataEN/Tables (accessed 17 August 2026).

12 Norwegian Dispute Act (*tvisteloven*) Section 10-5.

13 Anna Nylund, 'Alternative dispute resolution, justice and accountability in Norwegian civil justice' in Jos Hoevenaars, Betül Kas, Xandra Kramer and Erlis Themeli (eds), *Frontier in Civil Justice: Privatisation, Monetisation and Digitisation* (Edward Elgar 2022) 98–99; and Anna Nylund, 'Alternative dispute resolution and the judiciary' in Sophie Turenne and Mohamed Moussa (eds), *Research Handbook on Judging and the Judiciary.* (Edward Elgar 2025) 26–27.

they believe the law is (or should be). The findings of a recent study on the Boards are telling. According to it, only 9.4% of lawyers and 14.14% of judges agree that Conciliation Boards function adequately, while 77.67% of lawyers and 63.21% of judges surveyed disagree.[14] When asked to assess the legal certainty of Conciliation Boards, 68.01% of lawyers and 63.21% of judges consider it inadequate, while only 7.79% and 10.38%, respectively, consider it adequate. In contrast, representatives of debt collection companies held much more favourable views, with 63.64% considering legal certainty adequate and only 18.18% regarding it as inadequate.[15] Lawyers used characteristics such as 'headache', 'hindrance on the way to the courts', 'bingo', 'lottery', and 'Russian roulette' to describe Conciliation Boards.[16] While Conciliation Boards can sometimes facilitate a settlement that delivers justice, small businesses risk settling the case or receiving a ruling without realising it does not reflect the likely litigated outcome. Moreover, Conciliation Boards make the process to reach a final decision in a District Court longer and more expensive, which could result in disputants depleting their resources before reaching the courts. The high cost of litigation is considered a problem in Norway.[17]

The Swedish system is more balanced. Although most rules are the same for small claims as for regular claims, costs are capped for small claims.[18] Consequently, small claims proceedings are both relatively cheap and fast, and therefore, it is not surprising that the number of small claims is high.

3 Simplified Procedures for Pecuniary Claims

3.1 Introduction

Access to efficient procedures for pecuniary claims is essential to incentivise recalcitrant debtors to pay on time and to increase the likelihood of payment when debtors face economic difficulties. A core challenge in debt collection is when a claim that was presumed uncontested becomes contested. Understanding the consequences of a claim becoming contested, whether the small

14 Lisbeth Fullu Skyberg, Tale Røijen Størdal and Selma Øverland Lie, *Gjennomgang av forliksrådsordningen – en kunnskapsoppdatering* (Politihøyskolen 2025) 149–150.

15 Skyberg et al. (n 14) 152–153.

16 Skyberg et al. (n 14) 151.

17 Eg, Advokatforeningen, *Kostnader ved å gå til retten – tall og fakta* (https://www.advokatforeningen.no/om-advokatforeningen/rettspolitikk/sakskostnader/ (accessed 17 August 2026).

18 Swedish Code of Judicial Procedure (*Rättegångsbalk*) Chapter 18 Section 8a.

business is the claimant or the defendant, is key to estimating the risks and justice barriers that such processes entail.

CDR is sometimes perceived as a way for the consumer-debtor to avoid paying for a non-conforming product or service. However, CDR could also be the flip side of pecuniary claims: dissatisfied consumers withhold (part of) payment and initiate the CDR process, and some consumers could even deliberately attempt to avoid paying.[19] Depending on whether the consumer or the business initiates the process, and whether the business perceives it as an uncontested or contested claim, the case could start in one of three tracks: CDR, simplified proceedings, or regular court (small claims) proceedings.

Next, Section 3.2 discusses simplified court procedures, and Section 3.3 discusses CDR processes, their advantages, and disadvantages.

3.2 Simplified Court Procedure for Enforcing Pecuniary Claims

Many legal systems provide special proceedings for creditors seeking to enforce a pecuniary claim, such as order-for-payment procedures for uncontested claims. In Finland, there is a simplified (summary) process for uncontested claims (*summaarinen riita-asia*); in Norway, pecuniary claims can be directly enforced if the debtor has been given advance notice; and in Sweden, the payment order (*betalningsföreläggande*) process is available.[20] The Norwegian process stands out because it is not a payment order but an enforcement process administered by the enforcement agency (*namsmannen*), and it involves more steps than regular enforcement of court judgments and arbitral awards. In Sweden, the payment order procedure is also placed at the enforcement agency (*Kronofogdemyndigheten*).

The advantage of these proceedings is that the creditor can quickly move to enforcement. The costs of evidence are also almost non-existent, and no lawyer is needed. The challenge across all three is minimal control over the claim.[21] In Finland and Sweden, the claimant does not have to file evidence

19 Antonina Bakardjieva Engelbrekt, 'Effectiveness and Enforcement of Consumer Law in Sweden' in Hans-W Micklitz and Genevieve Saumier (eds), *Enforcement and Effectiveness of Consumer Law* (Springer 2018) 631–634; Nylund, 'ADR, justice and accountability' (n 13) 98–99.

20 Finnish Code of judicial procedure (*oikeudenkäymiskaari*) Chapter 5 Section 3; Norwegian Act relating to compulsory enforcement (*tvangsfullbyrdelsesloven*) Chapter 7 Section 4 litra f; Swedish Act relating to order for payment and judicial assistance (*lagen om betalningsföreläggande och handräckning*).

21 Although this is not so formally, this is the case in practice, Ari Luukinen, Juha Jokinen, Jari Suurla, Jarkko Vuorinen, Antti Sieppi, Matti Sipiläinen, Julia Sjöström, Lauri Wilenius and Netta Heiskanen, *Summaarisen menettelyn epäkohdat ja mahdollinen väärinkäyttö*

to support the claim, making it challenging to determine whether the claim is well-founded. Given that the Norwegian and Swedish procedures take place at the enforcement authorities, which are part of the executive, not the adjudicative branch, the threshold for intervention is high.

If the creditor does not need to provide evidence and the requirements for initiating the process under the statement of claim or petition are low, the basis for the claim could be unclear. This could make contesting the claim risky, as the debtor could challenge well-founded claims. Consequently, it could be better to pay the claimed amount rather than challenge it, even if there is reason to suspect that the claim is unfounded or even fictitious. Although the process is simple and inexpensive for the parties, a dishonest trader could exploit small businesses by filing unfounded claims or pursuing claims after the statutory time limit has expired. A recent report from the Finnish Competition and Consumer Authority found that debt collection companies exploit the Finnish system to pursue unfounded pecuniary claims.[22] Because the claimant only needs to provide minimal information about the claim, it is sometimes unclear which debt is being collected.[23] This happens even if Finnish courts are aware of their obligations to apply EU consumer law on their own motion. Because the prevailing party is entitled to recover all necessary and proportionate costs under Finnish law, the risks of contesting the claim are very high.

Another challenge concerns the consequences of the contestation. In Finland, contested claims are automatically transferred to the regular track for proceedings. In contrast, in Norway, an application for direct enforcement of an uncontested pecuniary claim must include information on whether the case shall be transferred to a Conciliation Board or dismissed if the claim, or

kuluttajien velkomusasioissa. Kilpailu- ja kuluttajaviraston Tutkimusraportteja 4/2025. Kilpailu- ja kuluttajavirasto 2025; Anna Nylund, 'Hverdagsjuss, rettssikkerhet og retten til en rettferdig rettergang' in Trude Haugli, Siri Gerrard, Anne Hellum and Eva-Maria Svensson (eds), *Dette brenner jeg for! Festskrift til Hege Brækhhus 70 år* (Fagbokforlaget 2020) 310–313; Torbjörn Andersson, '*Ex Officio* Application of the Unfair Terms Directive Cases against Consumers. A Swedish Perspective' in Anna Nylund and Magne Strandberg (eds), *Civil Procedure and Harmonisation of Law* (Intersentia 2019) 162–167.

22 Luukinen et al. (n 21).

23 This practice is against the case law of the European Court of Justice on the obligations of the courts of the Member States to act on their own motion in certain consumer cases, see eg, Bart Krans, 'EU law and national civil procedure law: an invisible pillar' (2015) 23 European Review of Private Law 567; and Mateusz Grochowski and Maciej Taborowski, 'Effectiveness and EU consumer law: the blurriness in judicial dialogue' in Federica Casarosa and Madalina Moraru (eds), *The Practice of Judicial Interaction in the Field of Fundamental Rights* (Edward Elgar 2022).

any part of it, becomes contested.[24] In Sweden, when a claim or part of a claim becomes contested, the claimant is informed that the case may be transferred to a court or dismissed. A transfer request shall be submitted in writing within four weeks.[25]

The Finnish approach is problematic because contestation results in costly, time-consuming court proceedings, which are particularly concerning given the long disposition times and high costs. The Swedish approach poses the least risk because the claimant decides whether to pursue a contested claim only after the claim has been contested. It allows the claimant to assess the grounds for contesting the claim and to conduct a new risk assessment before deciding whether to pursue it in court. It probably also lowers the threshold for contesting unclear claims, and claimants are probably less likely to pursue untenable claims in court than Finnish claimants are. Thus, the likely cost of a well-founded contestation is low. In Norway, the creditor-claimant must decide in advance of filing whether to pursue the claim in uncontested proceedings. However, claimants may change their minds before the Conciliation Board sets the hearing date or before the enforcement agency dismisses the case.[26] This gives the claimant maximum freedom to select and adjust the approach. The initial information, of course, also provides some predictability for the defendant, even if claimants can change their minds. However, the process at the Conciliation Board entails considerable risks, given the Board's limited knowledge of the law and the fact that the procedure essentially delays access to real courts.

In all three countries, powerful debtors could exploit financially weaker claimants' fear of the costs of pursuing a claim in regular proceedings by contesting the claim. The contestation, even if without any real prospect of success, could prompt the claimant to withdraw the case. In fact, small businesses that are creditors may refrain from pursuing their claim if they consider there is a risk that the debtor will contest it, even if the contestation would be unfounded.

To conclude: the design of the juncture between simplified and regular proceedings appears consequential. The Swedish design is likely to reduce risks for claimants and defendants acting in good faith; it is likely to provide better access to justice than systems that transfer contested cases to regular proceedings. To improve access to justice, the challenges posed by potentially unfounded claims or contestations can be addressed by requiring claimants to

24 Norwegian Enforcement Act Section 7–5.
25 Swedish Payment Order Act Sections 33–37.
26 Norwegian Enforcement Act Section 7–7.

provide sufficient details about the claim and, when available, supporting documentation. Given that claims are often filed electronically, these requirements are not onerous. Courts could develop an AI tool to perform an initial scan of the file before serving it on the defendant, and if the AI tool flags a case, a staff member could check it and, when necessary, require the claimant to specify the claim.[27] Furthermore, the organisational structure and educational backgrounds of those who decide the cases seem vital to whether the process delivers justice. Above all, this also illustrates how effective access to justice in simplified proceedings for pecuniary claims depends on the cost, duration, and quality of regular proceedings.

3.3 Consumer Dispute Resolution Processes as Simplified Adjudication

Consumer dispute resolution processes are, to some extent, an alternative to both regular and simplified court proceedings. In Norway, the public CDR process consists of two parts: a first stage with mediation or evaluation (sometimes both) and, unless the parties settle, a second, quasi-adjudicative stage.[28] In fact, the outcomes of the quasi-adjudicative stage in Norwegian public CDR have the same effect as court judgments: they become res judicata and enforceable unless a party initiates court proceedings.[29] In Sweden, decisions from the Swedish National Board for Consumer Disputes are only recommendations, yet the majority of businesses abide by them.[30] The Finnish structure is similar to the Swedish one and will not be discussed for the sake of simplicity. In Norway, there is a tendency for courts to follow the rulings of private CDR bodies, because CDR bodies are specialised and therefore better positioned than courts to assess the validity of claims.[31]

Although a binding decision could at first sight appear contrary to the interests of traders, this might not be so. If the business prevails, the outcome becomes enforceable and res judicata unless the consumer initiates court proceedings. The outcome is a sword that allows the business to proceed directly

27 Eg, Amy J Schmitz, 'Expanding Access to Remedies through E-Court Initiatives' (2019) 67 Buffalo Law Review 89; Amy J Schmitz and John Zeleznikow, 'Intelligent Legal Tech to Empower Self-Represented Litigants' (2022) 23 Columbia Science and Technology Law Review 142.

28 Consumer Complaints Act (*Lov om behandling av forbrukerklager i Forbrukertilsynet og Forbrukerklageutvalget*) Sections 15 and 16.

29 Consumer Complaints Act Section 17 Subsection 4.

30 Allmänna reklamationsnämnden, *Allmänna reklamationsnämndens årsredovisning 2025* https://arn.se/globalassets/extern/arsredovisningar/allmanna-reklamationsnamndens-arsredovisning-2025.pdf (accessed 18 August 2026) 24.

31 NOU 2010:11 Nemndsbehandling av forbrukertvister, Chapters 3 and 6.

to enforcement from low-cost CDR, and a shield against the consumer making further attempts to avoid paying. If the consumer prevails, the business must yield. However, the same would apply to its competitors if they had been parties to the case. Consumers have access to an effective remedy, and a process that delivers quality justice helps combat rogue traders, thereby benefiting traders seeking to comply with the law. In fact, the Norwegian financial services sector, which operates its own CDR body with non-binding outcomes, mandates its members to bear all costs, both their own and those of consumers, if they challenge the outcome.[32] This illustrates the value of a strong CDR mechanism for businesses, not just for consumers.

While Scandinavian CDR mechanisms are widely used and generally considered to deliver high-quality outcomes, they also have several problematic aspects. The challenges are likely to be more troublesome for small businesses and consumers with limited resources than for large businesses. These differences relate to limitations on evidence, limited cost-shifting, and the duration of proceedings.

Typically, CDR processes are exclusively written.[33] Although written proceedings may be cheaper than oral proceedings, they prevent the parties from relying on oral evidence. Therefore, when key information is exchanged orally, proving conformity could be an insurmountable task for a business. In these cases, court proceedings could be preferable for the small business.

In the Norwegian CDR, cost-shifting is limited to expert opinions and only applies to manifestly unfounded claims.[34] In Sweden, the parties bear their own costs, including expert opinions, although the CDR body recommends that the trader bear the costs if the consumer prevails.[35] Thus, even if the small business prevails, the costs could be nearly equal to, or exceed, the amount gained. This is particularly problematic in complex cases.

CDR procedures in Norway and Sweden are also relatively slow compared to courts. The average case processing time was 5.3 months in Norway and 5.5

32 Agreement on the Norwegian Financial Services Complaints Board, between the Norwegian Consumer Council, Finance Norway, the Association of Norwegian Finance Houses, the Norwegian Fund and Asset Management Association, FoodDrinkNorway and the Federation of Norwegian Enterprise (Virke) In force from 28 March 2023. Available at https://www.finkn.no/om-oss/regelverk (accessed 17 August 2026).

33 Eg, Norwegian Consumer Complaints Act Section 16; and Decree on Swedish National Board for Consumer Disputes (SNBCD) (Decree on SNBCD, *Förordning med instruktion för Allmänna reklamationsnämnden*) Section 19.

34 For the public body, see Norwegian Consumer Complaints Act Section 19.

35 Allmänna reklamationsnämnden https://arn.se/foretag/ (accessed 17 August 2026).

months in Sweden.[36] In contrast, the average processing time in CDR was 311 days (about 10 months) at the Norwegian Consumer Dispute Resolution Board[37] and 174 days (more than 6 months) in the Swedish Consumer Dispute Board.[38] In Sweden, the result is not even enforceable. Thus, if the business prevails but the consumer refuses to pay, the business must bring an action to obtain an enforceable judgment. Consequently, although the average disposal time in CDR has been reduced in both countries, the process to an enforceable decision takes considerably longer in CDR than in both regular court proceedings and simplified proceedings, such as payment order proceedings. Since the 90-day maximum processing time under the EU Consumer ADR Directive[39] Article 8, only commences when the case is ripe for decision-making, these systems comply with it despite the long overall disposition time.

The combination of limited outcome accuracy, the absence of cost-shifting, lengthy disposition times, and a non-enforceable outcome makes CDR processes less favourable than court proceedings in some instances.[40] This could be remedied by also imposing time limits on the preliminary stages and by considering rules on cost-shifting, particularly in cases where evidence is needed. Moreover, because oral evidence can be given online, thus removing the requirement of synchronisation and physical presence, the exclusively written nature of the proceedings should be questioned, and oral elements should be implemented whenever they increase access to justice. Increasing the speed and quality of CDR proceedings improves access to justice for both consumers and businesses, as court proceedings currently provide better access to justice.

---

36 Domstoladministrasjonen, *Tingrettene 2020–2024* https://www.domstol.no/contentassets/b6c751a96c724cfdad1d2b6c671eff7f/tingrettene-2020-2024.pdf (accessed 17 August 2026); and Domstolsverket, *Verksamhetsmål – tingsrätterna* https://pxweb.etjanst.domstol.se/PxWeb/pxweb/sv/DOMstat/DOMstat__Verksamhetsmal/01_Verksamhetsmal_TR.px/table/tableViewLayout2/ (accessed 17 August 2026).

37 Forbrukertilsynet, *Årsrapport 2025*, https://www.forbrukertilsynet.no/wp-content/uploads/2026/06/forbrukertilsynet-arsrapport2025.pdf (accessed 17 August 2026) 25–30.

38 Allmänna reklamationsnämnden (n 30) 20; Forbrukertilsynet (n 37).

39 European Parliament and Council Directive 2013/11/EU on alternative dispute resolution for consumer disputes and amending Regulation (EC) No 2006/2004 and Directive 2009/22/EC [2013] OJ L165/63.

40 See also Anna Wallerman Ghavanini, 'Access to justice för små anspråk i den svenska civilprocessen' in Anna Wallerman Ghavanini and Sebastian Wejedal (eds), *Access to justice i Skandinavien* (Santérus Academic Press Sweden 2022).

4 Mediation as an Alternative to Adjudicative Processes

4.1 Out-of-Court Mediation as a Private, Flexible Procedure

Mediation, as a process aimed at reaching a settlement agreement and encouraging voluntary compliance, could be advantageous for small businesses in several ways.[41] First, it may reduce indirect costs and generate future benefits by helping the parties preserve a business relationship and achieve outcomes that are more commercially favourable than those in court proceedings. Second, the parties may mitigate risks by retaining control over the outcome. Third, the process could be quicker and more cost-effective. Fourth, because the outcome is negotiated rather than imposed on the parties, they are more likely to comply voluntarily, and thus incur no enforcement costs.[42]

Under the EU Mediation Directive,[43] the parties to a mediated settlement agreement can jointly request that the agreement be made enforceable. Although the Directive has given the parties to a mediated settlement agreement the option to make the settlement enforceable, it does not address other challenges that mediation entails for small businesses.

Private mediation is costly because the parties to mediation must pay for the process. The Stockholm Chamber of Commerce (SCC), the leading provider of commercial dispute resolution services in Scandinavia, charges a standard mediation fee of EUR 16,000 and an administration fee of EUR 4,000.[44] The costs are, hence, likely to be similar to or exceed those of litigation. Consequently, for mediation to become a feasible option for small businesses, many European countries need more institutionalised mediation, and above all, more affordable mediation. In Finland, disputants may request that a court mediate their case even if they do not have a pending court case.[45] The mediation service is provided at regular court fees, and a judge acts as the mediator, making the process accessible. Nevertheless, this kind of independent court mediation is relatively little used.[46]

41 Shipman et al. (n 6) 29–38 and 123 ff.

42 Jennie J Long, 'Compliance in small claims court: Exploring the factors associated with defendants' level of compliance with mediated and adjudicated outcomes' (2003) 21 Conflict Resolution Quarterly 139.

43 European Parliament and Council Directive 2008/52/EC on certain aspects of mediation in civil and commercial matters [2008] OJ L136/3.

44 SCC Arbitration Institute, *SCC Mediation Rules 2025* Rule 12.

45 Act on mediation in civil matters and confirmation of settlements in general courts (*Laki riita-asioiden sovittelusta ja sovinnon vahvistamisesta yleisissä tuomioistuimissa*).

46 The Finnish Courts Administration does not publish data regarding requests for mediation, only the number of cases resolved in mediation. Most mediation requests are

Even if small businesses could afford mediation, they still face challenges related to the agreement to mediate. Negotiating an individual agreement to mediate requires extra resources.[47] Of course, the parties could include a standard mediation clause, but this might not suit their needs. When negotiating the clause ex ante, before the dispute has arisen, one must foresee whether mediation will be appropriate for the dispute that will actually arise. If the dispute requires clarification for future cases, litigation could be more suitable, but the mediation clause could force a party to mediate before litigating. Similarly, a party's economic situation could have deteriorated unexpectedly, and there may be a dire need to proceed with enforcement quickly, without first mediating. However, if the agreement to mediate is postponed until a dispute arises, the other party may no longer be willing to mediate.

The mediation clause itself could become a point of contention.[48] For example, it might be unclear what constitutes fulfilment of the obligation to mediate, or whether a party can initiate legal action under certain conditions despite the mediation clause. As mediation is a vague concept, it could also be unclear what it refers to, and mediators practise it in surprisingly different ways.[49] For instance, the SCC Mediation Rules do not define mediation at all, and regulate the mediation process only minimally.[50] Similarly, Section 6 of the Finnish Mediation Act only gives a minimal definition of mediation. Thus, foreseeing what mediation entails and how the selection and appointment of the mediator influences the process, and consequently, probably also the outcome, could be an insurmountable task for a small business. Shaping the mediation process could also be challenging because it requires knowledge of mediation and its possibilities. One-shot players, such as small busi-

---

made when the case is pending. The number of mediated settlement agreements is about 300 annually in non-family civil cases, https://tuomioistuimet.fi/fi/index/tuomioistuinlaitos/tilastoja.html (accessed 18 August 2026).

47 Gerhard Wagner, 'Dispute Resolution as a Product: Competition between Civil Justice Systems' in Horst Eidenmüller (ed), *Regulatory Competition in Contract Law and Dispute Resolution* (CH Beck 2013) 376–385.

48 Ronán Feehily, *International Commercial Mediation. Law and Regulation in Comparative Context* (Cambridge University Press 2022) 57–68.

49 John Lande, 'Moving Negotiation Theory from the Tower of Babel toward a World of Mutual Understanding' (2017) Journal of Dispute Resolution 1, 7; Rachel Field and Jonathan Crowe, *Mediation Ethics* (Edward Elgar 2020) 150–151; Feehily (n 48) 57–68; and Anna Nylund, 'Agreements Related to Alternative Dispute Resolution' in Anna Nylund and Antonio Cabral (eds), *Shaping Civil Litigation Using Procedural Agreements* (Eleven 2024).

50 SCC Arbitration Institute, SCC Mediation Rules 2025 https://sccarbitrationinstitute.se/wp-content/uploads/2025/01/3-scc_mediation_rules_2025_eng.pdf (accessed 17 August 2026).

nesses, are unlikely to exploit these opportunities fully and may be at a disadvantage compared to more experienced counterparts.

Mediation could also put small businesses at risk of being pressured into settling the dispute. If mediation does not result in a settlement, the small business may need to choose between bringing an action, which is costly and time-consuming, or relinquishing the claim. As a result, the small business could be pressured to settle on unfavourable terms.

Given the inherent risks and potential costs, it is not evident that mediation is appropriate for all small businesses. Instead, there is reason to believe that mediation could be made more accessible and less risky if it is provided by an institution, such as an industry organisation, a chamber of commerce, or a similar body that administers the process, helps appoint suitable mediators, and maintains a certain level of standardisation – and thus predictability and quality control.

4.2 Institutionalised Mediation in CDR Processes

Institutional mediation could alleviate some of the challenges posed by the unpredictability and vagueness of mediation. However, institutionalised mediation is not always unproblematic, as institutionalisation could lead to problematic practices. Additionally, institutionalisation is often associated with mediation becoming one step in a multi-tiered process, which can be bundled or unbundled. Sometimes, different dispute resolution processes are combined into a single stage, which could affect access to justice.

The Norwegian and Swedish public CDRs serve as examples of institutionalised mediation within a multi-tiered process. Both include a mediation component before the decision-making stage. In Norway, the process comprises two distinct stages: the mediation stage occurs first, and only if the parties do not settle may they proceed to the quasi-adjudicative process.[51] In Sweden, mediation and quasi-adjudication are components of the same process.[52] The Norwegian system provides a clear mandate for the public CDR body to explore the potential of a consensual outcome and explain its benefits.[53] The principles for the process are also outlined in greater detail than for private and court mediation. Thus, disputants are more likely to have a clear idea of the mediation process and are offered mediation as a default. In contrast,

51 Nylund, 'ADR, justice and accountability' (n 13) 82–85; and Nylund, 'ADR and the judiciary' (n 13) 27–29.

52 Decree on SNBCD Section 22.

53 Decree on SNBCD Section 11.

when mediation is not a distinct stage, as is the case in Sweden, the body might not facilitate such negotiations, or do so only to a limited extent.

The Norwegian public CDR system attempts to address some of the quandaries related to informed decision-making, specifically, the lack thereof, for less informed parties. It does so by requiring mediators to inform the parties regarding consumer law.[54] This could be regarded as 'informative' or 'educative'[55] interventions in which the mediator informs the disputants of the applicable rules, typical outcomes, and the procedural implications of settling and not settling the case.[56]

However, mediation as a separate step also poses problems because it makes the body more prone to pressure from disputants to settle.[57] One reason is that the mediator or body providing mediation is frequently rewarded, directly or indirectly, for settling cases. For instance, the higher a CDR body's caseload is relative to available resources, the more tempting it will be to minimise the resources spent on each case through early settlement, thereby also improving its average processing time and the number of cases processed. Scoring well on disposition time and the settlement ratio could enhance the body's funding. Performance is often measured by easily quantifiable metrics rather than by the quality of the outcomes.[58] The Norwegian public CDR body is measured primarily by its case-disposal rate and by the resolution of cases within the time limit set by EU rules.[59] The quality of proceedings and outcomes is measured only indirectly through customer surveys conducted at irregular intervals. As a result, the third party may be incentivised to push for a settlement even when proceeding to the quasi-adjudicative stage would be better.

Institutionalised mediation is often bundled: to reach a quasi-adjudicative process, the parties must first participate in mediation. As a result, disputants have few opportunities to bypass mediation, even when there is a good reason to do so. In a worst-case scenario, the necessary steps to secure the claim could be unduly delayed and, even if the claim is enforceable, enforcement could be

54 Nylund, 'ADR, justice and accountability' (n 13).

55 Ellen A Waldman, 'Identifying the role of social norms in mediation: A multiple model approach' (1996) Hastings Law Journal 703.

56 Decree on SNBCD Section 11; and Nylund, 'ADR, justice and accountability (n 13).

57 Nylund, 'ADR and the Judiciary' (n 13) 19–23.

58 Nylund, 'ADR and the Judiciary' (n 13) 19–23.

59 Forbrukertilsynet (n 37), 2025, https://www.forbrukertilsynet.no/wp-content/uploads/2026/06/forbrukertilsynet-arsrapport2025.pdf 26–35 (accessed 17 August 2026).

impossible due to insolvency or otherwise impractical.[60] Given the excessive length of Norwegian public CDR proceedings, small businesses may find that settling on unfavourable terms is preferable to pursuing the claim through the adjudicative stage of CDR. The low quality of justice at the Conciliation Boards is likely to exacerbate this problem because the alternative to CDR is poor. In Sweden, this dilemma is equally present; despite shorter processing times in CDR than in Norway, the CDR outcome is not enforceable. In this regard, institutionalised CDR processes have the same drawback as mediation clauses: they subject small businesses to settlement pressure. The risks of spending time on mediation when it is not appropriate and of being pressured to settle could deter small businesses from participating in dispute resolution schemes that involve mediation.[61]

The Norwegian and Swedish public CDR processes illustrate how mediation could be made accessible to small businesses by embedding it in institutionalised (multi-stage) processes. The Norwegian system also shows how 'educative' mediation can increase access to justice by reducing the need to engage a lawyer, helping level the playing field, and enabling disputants with limited legal capacity to make informed decisions. This model could serve as a model for mediation in B2B cases involving small businesses. However, the process as a whole and its alternatives must be efficient.

5 Complexity: From Hindering to Bolstering Access to Justice

While Nordic justice systems with diverse processes increase the likelihood that disputants will find a suitable process for their dispute, they also carry a significant risk that uninformed disputants will choose an unsuitable process. These risks are probably greater for small businesses, which have less information about the processes and less experience in selecting and using them. Therefore, providing information about each process – including its advantages and disadvantages, legal effects, costs, duration, and so on – is paramount to ensuring access to justice for small businesses. Many small busi-

60 Nylund, 'ADR and the Judiciary' (n 13) 32–33.

61 See also Andrea Fejos and Chris Willet, 'Consumer Access to Justice: The Role of the ADR Directive and the Member States' (2016) 1 European Review of Private Law 33; Marte Knigge and Charlotte Pavillon, 'The Legality Requirement of the ADR Directive: Just Another Paper Tiger?' (2016) 5 Journal of European Consumer and Market Law 155; Alexandre Biard, 'Impact of Directive 2013/11/EU on Consumer ADR Quality: Evidence from France and the UK' (2019) 42 Journal of Consumer Policy 109, 113.

nesses would probably benefit from a tool to triage their disputes, select a suitable process, and help them navigate the justice system.

At least three additional conclusions can be drawn from comparing selected processes in Finland, Norway, and Sweden. First, not all alternatives to regular court proceedings offer efficient, high-quality procedures. On the contrary, several of them are inefficient, may not deliver sufficient quality, or both. Second, the linkages between processes are essential. It matters whether the case is automatically transferred to another process, and the combined length and cost of the processes are paramount. Thirdly, and perhaps most importantly, real, not just formal, access to regular court proceedings is vital; it is the centrepiece of the justice system, the sine qua non of its functioning.

CDR illustrates how institutionalised, sectoral alternatives to courts could be valuable, particularly when the process is appropriate. Business and professional organisations could facilitate access to justice for small businesses by developing dispute resolution processes tailored to their respective domains.[62]

References

Advokatforeningen, *Kostnader ved å gå til retten – tall og fakta* (https://www.advokatforeningen.no/om-advokatforeningen/rettspolitikk/sakskostnader/ (accessed 17 August 2026).

Alexander N and Chong S, *The Singapore Convention on Mediation. A Commentary* (Wolters Kluwer 2019).

Allmänna reklamationsnämnden, *Allmänna reklamationsnämndens årsredovisning 2024*, ARN 2025.

Andersson T, '*Ex Officio* Application of the Unfair Terms Directive Cases Against Consumers. A Swedish Perspective' in A Nylund and M Strandberg (eds), *Civil Procedure and Harmonisation of Law* (Intersentia 2019).

Bakardjieva Engelbrekt A, 'Effectiveness and Enforcement of Consumer Law in Sweden' in H-W Micklitz and G Saumier (eds), *Enforcement and Effectiveness of Consumer Law* (Springer 2018).

Biard A 'Impact of Directive 2013/11/EU on Consumer ADR Quality: Evidence from France and the UK' (2019) 42 Journal of Consumer Policy 109.

Brazil WD, *Early Neutral Evaluation* (ABA Publishing 2012).

62 Amy J Schmitz and Janet Martinez, *Digital Dispute System Design. Using Technology in Preventing and Resolving Conflicts* (Aspen Publishing 2025).

Directorate-General for Internal Policies, *'Rebooting' the Mediation Directive: Assessing the limited impact of its implementation and proposing measure to increase the number of mediations in the EU.* Policy Department C: Citizens' rights and constitutional affairs. Legal Affairs. European Parliament. PE 493.042.

Domstoladministrasjonen, *Tingrettene 2020–2024* https://www.domstol.no/contentassets/b6c751a96c724cfdad1d2b6c671eff7f/tingrettene-2020-2024.pdf (accessed 17 August 2026).

Domstolsverket, *Verksamhetsmål – tingsrätterna* https://pxweb.etjanst.domstol.se/PxWeb/pxweb/sv/DOMstat/DOMstat__Verksamhetsmal/01_Verksamhetsmal_TR.px/table/tableViewLayout2/ (accessed 17 October 2025).

European Commission for the Efficiency of Justice. Working Group on Mediation (CEPEJ-GT-MED), *The Impact of CEPEJ Guidelines on Civil, Family, Penal and Administrative Mediation* (16 May 2018) CEPEJ-GT-MED (2017)8.

European Commission for the Efficiency of Justice, *European Judicial Systems Evaluation Report 2024 Cycle* (2022 Data) https://public.tableau.com/app/profile/cepej/viz/QuantitativeDataEN/Tables (accessed 17 August 2026).

Feehily R, *International Commercial Mediation. Law and Regulation in Comparative Context* (Cambridge University Press 2022).

Fejos A and Willet C, 'Consumer Access to Justice: The Role of the ADR Directive and the Member States' (2016) 1 European Review of Private Law 33.

Field R and Crowe J, *Mediation Ethics* (Edward Elgar 2020).

Forbrukertilsynet, *Årsrapport 2025*, https://www.forbrukertilsynet.no/wp-content/uploads/2026/06/forbrukertilsynet-arsrapport2025.pdf (accessed 17 August 2026).

Genn H, *Judging Civil Justice. The Hamlyn Lectures 2008* (Cambridge University Press 2010).

Grajzl P, Tvaronavičienė A and Clar B, 'From Promise to Practice: Resolving the Mediation Paradox in Europe' JAMS ADR Blog (June 17 2025) https://www.jdsupra.com/legalnews/from-promise-to-practice-resolving-the-1706683/ (accessed 17 August 2026).

Grochowski M, and Taborowski M, 'Effectiveness and EU consumer law: the blurriness in judicial dialogue' in F Carosa and M Moraru (eds), *The Practice of Judicial Interaction in the Field of Fundamental Rights* (Edward Elgar 2022).

Hopt KJ and Steffek F, 'Mediation: Comparison of Laws, Regulatory Models, Fundamental Issues' in K J Hopt and F Steffek (eds), *Mediation: Principles and Regulation in Comparative Perspective* (Oxford University Press 2013).

Keet M, Heavin H and Lande J, *Litigation Interest and Risk Assessment* (ABA Publishing 2020).

Knigge M and Pavillon C, 'The Legality Requirement of the ADR Directive: Just Another Paper Tiger?' (2016) 5 Journal of European Consumer and Market Law 155.

Krans B, 'EU law and national civil procedure law: an invisible pillar' (2015) 23 European Review of Private Law 567.

Lande J, 'Moving Negotiation Theory from the Tower of Babel toward a World of Mutual Understanding' (2017) Journal of Dispute Resolution 1.

Long JJ, 'Compliance in small claims court: Exploring the factors associated with defendants' level of compliance with mediated and adjudicated outcomes' (2003) 21 Conflict Resolution Quarterly 139.

Luukinen A, Jokinen J, Suurla J, Vuorinen J, Sieppi A, Sipiläinen M, Sjöström J, Wilenius L and Heiskanen N, *Summaarisen menettelyn epäkohdat ja mahdollinen väärinkäyttö kuluttajien velkomusasioissa.* Kilpailu- ja kuluttajaviraston tutkimusraportteja 4/2025. Kilpailu- ja kuluttajavirasto 2025.

Meidanis HP, 'Enforcement of Mediation Settlement Agreements in the EU and the Need for Reform' (2020) 16 Journal of Private International Law 275.

NOU 2010:11 Nemndsbehandling av forbrukertvister.

Nylund A, 'Agreements Related to Alternative Dispute Resolution', in A Nylund and A Cabral (eds), *Shaping Civil Litigation Using Procedural Agreements* (Eleven 2024).

Nylund A, 'Alternative Dispute Resolution' in JM Smits, J Husa, C Valcke and M Narciso (eds), *Elgar Encyclopedia of Comparative Law* (Edward Elgar 2023).

Nylund A, 'Alternative dispute resolution and the judiciary', in S Turenne and M Moussa (eds), *Research Handbook on Judging and the Judiciary* (Edward Elgar 2025).

Nylund A, 'Alternative dispute resolution, justice and accountability in Norwegian civil justice', in J Hoevenaars, B Kas, X Kramer and E Themeli (eds), *Frontier in Civil Justice: Privatisation, Monetisation and Digitisation* (Edward Elgar 2022).

Nylund A, 'Hverdagsjuss, rettssikkerhet og retten til en rettferdig rettergang' in T Haugli, S Gerrard, A Hellum and E-M Svensson (eds), *Dette brenner jeg for! Festskrift til Hege Brækhhus 70 år* (Fagbokforlaget 2020).

Nylund A, 'Procedural Effects of Court Settlements' (2025) 2 Law & Criminology Journal 32.

Nylund A, 'Shaping Civil Litigation Using Procedural Agreements: Perspectives and Prospectives', in A Nylund and A Cabral (eds), *Shaping Civil Litigation Using Procedural Agreements* (Eleven 2024).

Oikeusministeriö, *Pienriitamenettely. Arviomuistio* (Oikeusministeriön julkaisuja, Mietintöjä ja lausuntoja 2023:1).

Schmitz AJ, 'Expanding Access to Remedies through E-Court Initiatives' (2019) 67 *Buffalo Law Review* 89.

Schmitz AJ and Martinez J, *Digital Dispute System Design. Using Technology in Preventing and Resolving Conflicts* (Aspen Publishing 2025).

Schmitz AJ and Zeleznikow J, 'Intelligent Legal Tech to Empower Self-Represented Litigants' (2022) 23 Columbia Science and Technology Law Review 142.

Shipman S, Waters B and Wood W, *Brown and Marriott's ADR Principles and Practice* (4th edn, Sweet & Maxwell 2019).

Skyberg LF, Størdal TR and Lie SØ, *Gjennomgang av forliksrådsordningen – en kunnskapsoppdatering* (Politihøyskolen 2025).

SCC Arbitration Institute, SCC Mediation Rules 2025 https://sccarbitrationinstitute.se/wp-content/uploads/2025/01/3-scc_mediation_rules_2025_eng.pdf (accessed 17 August 2026).

Wagner G, 'Dispute Resolution as a Product: Competition between Civil Justice Systems' in Horst Eidenmüller (ed), *Regulatory Competition in Contract Law and Dispute Resolution* (CH Beck 2013).

Wallerman Ghavanini A, 'Access to justice för små anspråk i den svenska civilprocessen' in A Wallerman Ghavanini and S Wejedal (eds), *Access to justice i Skandinavien* (Santérus Academic Press Sweden 2022).

Waldman EA, 'Identifying the role of social norms in mediation: A multiple model approach' (1996) Hastings Law Journal 703.

PART 3

Pathways for Improving Access to Justice for Small Businesses

CHAPTER 7

Contract-Based Mechanisms as a Pathway to Access to Justice for Small Businesses: Examples from Norway

Magne Strandberg

1 Introduction

The civil justice systems of most Western jurisdictions are characterised by a massive difference between the legal regulation of the phase after commencement of a lawsuit and the legal regulation of the phase before commencement. The codes of civil procedure apply after commencement,[1] and contain rather detailed regulations of most aspects of the proceedings till a final judgment has been produced and enforced. Another characteristic feature of these codes is that they consist of general rules applicable to all types of cases within the broad category of civil procedure.[2] These rules are non-sectoral in the sense that one set of rules applies to all cases within the civil procedure code's field of application, and the parties' opportunity to agree on rules deviating from the common model is rather limited.[3] These rules are also general in that a uniform set of rules applies to whichever parties are involved. Regular civil procedure law does not contain special rules for small businesses, which, combined with the non-sectoral style of the regulation, means that small businesses face some common challenges and shortcomings related to civil lawsuits. The shortcomings are first and foremost that the proceedings are

1 There are some exceptions to this, see for instance the ELI-UNIDROIT Model European Rules of Civil Procedure Rule 9 on the parties' obligation to seek a consensual resolution to the dispute before and after commencement. Such exceptions are also found in national rules, eg, the Norwegian Dispute Act (civil procedure act) (*tvisteloven*) Chapter 5 containing general rules on the parties' obligations before commencement, Chapter 28 regulates securing of evidence before commencement, and Chapters 32–34 contain rules on provisional measures.

2 The precise scope of application for these codes varies somewhat between the jurisdictions. The Dispute Act applies to all cases except for criminal cases, see the Norwegian Criminal Procedure Act (*straffeprosessloven*) Sections 1-3 *e contrario.*

3 See, eg, Anna Nylund and Antonio Cabral (eds), *Contractualisation of Civil Litigation* (Intersentia 2023) for a comprehensive overview of several jurisdictions.

 | HTTPS://DOI.ORG/10.1163/9789004779235-008

extremely expensive, and that judges typically lack the specialised expertise that may be asked for in lawsuits between businesses.

In order to avoid the shortcomings of civil proceedings, small businesses and other professional parties may seek contract-based out-of-court alternatives. In the pre-commencement phase, more precisely when a case is not pending before a court, the general freedom of contract applies to the choice of methods for dispute resolution. As a result of that freedom, a number of alternatives for dispute resolution have been established. In contrast to the non-sectoral rules applying to in-court proceedings, these out-of-court alternatives are highly sectoral in the sense that different schemes have developed for different areas of law, markets, professions, or businesses. In contrast to regular civil proceedings, no principle of public hearing applies. The proceedings are not open to the public, and the decisions are not made available on a regular basis for anyone other than the parties. As a result of that lack of openness, updated statistical and other information on these out-of-court alternatives is hard to find. Even though statistics are not available, contract-based out-of-court mechanisms are obviously of high practical importance for small businesses within certain branches of business.

In this chapter, I will describe and analyse two such contract-based schemes for out-of-court dispute resolution in Norway. I will first describe insurance claim valuation (*forsikringsskadeskjønn*),[4] which has been developed within certain branches of insurance law (Section 2 below). Thereafter, I will describe the decision by assessor (*oppmannsavgjørelse*), which typically applies to construction contracts and craftsman contracts within larger construction projects. Although both schemes are known in other European jurisdictions as well, I will concentrate on their role, content and development in Norwegian law.

At least under Norwegian law, and probably also in most other jurisdictions, these schemes are not considered as arbitration. The purpose of developing these schemes is to provide alternatives to arbitration, and they are typically constructed in order to be affordable, faster and more suitable for the substantive claims in question. Since these schemes are not arbitration, the Arbitration Act[5] does not apply,[6] which, for instance, means that the decisions have no res judicata effect, and that the time limits for bringing a lawsuit

4 The translation 'insurance claim valuation' is the author's.

5 The Norwegian Act on Arbitration (*voldgiftsloven*).

6 The Supreme Court's judgments Rt. 1958 p. 471 A at 473; Rt. 1981 p. 651 A; Rt. 2007 p. 69 A para 60; Henry John Mæland, *Voldgift* (Universitetsforlaget 1988) 32–34; Andreas Arntzen, *Forsikringsrett. Tingskadeoppgjør – brann og kombinertforsikring* (Brevik 1993) 283.

on the invalidity of arbitral awards do not apply.[7] However, there are also important similarities between arbitration and these schemes, which may prepare the ground for using arbitration law as a source of inspiration or as a basis for analogical application.

2 Insurance Claim Valuation

2.1 General Aspects

Insurance claim valuation has a relatively long history, at least compared to other out-of-court mechanisms for handling disputes or disagreements. Although I am not sure when the mechanism was first in use, it was well-defined and established when the Supreme Court heard the first case on such valuations in 1958.[8] Although it is hard to find up-to-date information about the scheme, a working group appointed by the Ministry of Finance in 2010 underlined the practical importance of such valuations for some branches of insurance law.[9] According to the working group, approximately 300 insurance valuations are conducted annually based on approximately identical insurance terms and conditions set by various insurance companies.[10] This is a small fraction of the total number of insurance claims in Norway each year, but it is a relatively large fraction of the insurance claims concerning high-value property, and it is high compared to the low number of proceedings before the regular courts.

Insurance claim valuation is most commonly used to estimate the value of damaged buildings and certain types of valuable movable property, and the scheme is particularly common for fire insurance. It is applied both in the private insurance market and in the insurance market for businesses. However, insurance claims between a small business and an insurance company are among the typical claims solved under this scheme. The last case on insurance claims valuation handled by the Supreme Court is illustrative.[11] In that case, the business premises of a small, local company in the eastern part of

7 The time limits are found in the Arbitration Act Section 44.
8 The Supreme Court's judgment Rt. 1958 p. 471 A.
9 The report is, unfortunately, only in Norwegian language, see *Forsikringsskjønn i skadeoppgjør – rapport fra arbeidsgruppe*, levert 30 Nov 2012, available at: https://www.regjeringen.no/contentassets/9cb7e3b09c084f69857b3c01a04358/forsikringsskjonn_skadeoppgjor.pdf (accessed 17 August 2026).
10 *Forsikringsskjønn i skadeoppgjør* (n 9) 10.
11 The Supreme Court's judgment Rt. 2007 p. 69 A.

Norway had been severely damaged in a fire, and an insurance claim valuation was conducted to assess the value of the damaged buildings.

Insurance claim valuation may have been inspired by judicial valuation (*skjønn*), which was established by the Judicial Valuation Act (*skjønnsloven*). Some elements of insurance claim valuation clearly resemble judicial valuation; both are specialised mechanisms particularly well-suited to the assessment of damages, and both are faster and more affordable than ordinary civil proceedings. Parties may also agree to apply judicial valuation because the Judicial Valuation Act is applicable whenever prescribed by law or contract.[12] However, insurance claim valuation differs significantly from judicial valuation. Firstly, judicial valuation is managed by the district courts and ends with a settlement or a formal judgment. Judicial valuation is thereby a separate and somewhat simplified form of court proceeding, and a judgment will have res judicata effect and be enforceable. Insurance claim valuation is not managed by a court, and the process does not lead to a judgment. Secondly, the object for judicial valuation is a full-blown legal claim, which in insurance cases will be a case concerning the insurance company's obligation to compensate for a given damage, or the company's obligation to pay a sum of money in compensation.[13] The object for insurance claim valuation is whatever the contract leaves to it. Most often, it does not leave an entire legal claim to valuation; most insurance claim valuations deal with more narrowly defined elements of a legal claim, for instance, the value of specified moveable or non-moveable property. The main function of insurance claim valuation is not to solve entire disputes, but to make binding assessments of damaged moveable or immovable property within an insurance claim dispute.

The contract between the parties is the most important legal source or instrument for insurance valuation, and the insurance valuation board derives its entire competence from that contract. It may be an ad hoc contract entered into after the emergence of the damage, but it is most often a clause or set of clauses contained in the general insurance contract. When such a contract or clause is established between the parties, insurance claim valuation may be initiated by any party who may base a claim on the insurance contract and any party who may be liable based on that contract. However, other sources of law may also be of importance. Firstly, customs within the insurance industry may be relevant because insurance claim valuation has developed through practice within the insurance businesses. The mechanism has had the same characteristics for a long time and may be described as a more or less standardised

12 Judicial Valuation Act Section 4.

13 This is because Dispute Act Section 1-3 also applies to judicial valuation.

scheme for out-of-court dispute resolution.[14] Secondly, rules for arbitration and judicial valuation have been applied for filling in the scheme for insurance claim valuation, and for establishing mandatory minimum standards for such valuations.[15] Thirdly, general procedural principles may also be applied.[16] Since these principles are fundamental to the proper handling of disputes, one may reasonably expect them to be fulfilled even by a contract-based mechanism such as insurance claims valuation, especially when parties to such contracts have agreed to regard the valuation as binding.

2.2 Composition, Competence, and Proceedings

In most cases, the valuation board consists of two members. Each party appoints one member of the board. If the two members cannot agree on the valuation, they will appoint a senior board member who will make the decision. Both the board members and the senior board members are experts, most often appraisers or engineers, without a law degree. The members are expected to have expertise in the valuation of the buildings or objects in question, but there are no formal registers of experts; it may become difficult to find proper experts, and quite a few experts may have been involved in many valuations initiated by a particular insurance company.

The competence of the board is defined in the contract or other agreements between the parties. The board is only competent to deal with the elements of the claims that are left to the board by the parties. The board's competence is further limited or specified by a set of assumptions agreed upon by the parties. Such assumptions may, for instance, determine whether the damages shall compensate for the costs of reconstruction of a damaged building or for the construction of a new building. The board members shall assess the damaged building on the basis of those assumptions.

The proceedings, which are simplified compared to regular court proceedings, follow a more or less standardised pattern in all cases unless the parties have agreed otherwise. The proceedings contain at least one short meeting between the parties and the board members, where the assumptions and other issues are clarified. Parties are allowed to argue their case; they are normally (not always) represented by a lawyer. Parties are allowed to present evidence, such as documents and evidence by visual inspection, and the deci-

---

14 Arntzen (n 6) 276–358.

15 The Supreme Court's judgment Rt. 2007 p. 69 A paras 64–69.

16 The Supreme Court's judgment Rt. 2007 p. 69 A para 87 concerning minimum requirements on impartiality.

sion is in writing and must contain proper reasons. Compared to regular court proceedings, these proceedings are more cooperative in the sense that the parties have a shared responsibility for pleading facts and presenting evidence.[17]

2.3 The Court's Review of the Decision's Validity

A party may bring a dispute to court even if there has been a prior insurance claim valuation of parts of the dispute. The court will conduct a valuation of the damaged goods. The valuation is left to the parties in accordance with their agreement, and the court will merely review the valuation and decide whether it is valid or not. If the court declares the valuation invalid, the court will still not do the valuation. The insurance claim valuation contract is valid even though the decision taken by the board members is found invalid. Therefore, the parties still have a valid contract saying that the valuation shall be taken by a board, and that agreement is also binding on the court.

There are substantive and procedural grounds for invalidity. The substantive grounds typically arise if the valuation is based on a misinterpretation of the law, a wrongful application of the law, a misunderstanding of the facts, or a misunderstanding of the assumptions agreed upon by the parties.

The most important procedural grounds for invalidity are: Firstly, a decision may be deemed invalid if one or several of the board members did not meet the criteria of impartiality. As has been underlined by the Supreme Court, the board members must meet the rather strict criteria of impartiality that apply to judges.[18] These strict criteria are applied due to the binding effect of such valuations and in order to secure the trustworthiness of such valuations. Secondly, the decision may be deemed invalid if it does not contain proper reasons.[19] In the process before the Supreme Court's judgment on insurance claim valuation in 2007, both the district court and the court of appeal had applied the rule of required reasons for judicial valuation analogically to insurance claim valuation.[20] The Judicial Valuation Act, Section 28, contains the required reasons for judgments following from judicial valuation:

17 The Supreme Court's judgment Rt. 1981 p. 651 A at pp. 657–658. Please note that regular court proceedings may also take a cooperative form, see eg, ERCP Rule 2.

18 The Supreme Court's judgment Rt. 2007 p. 69 A para 87. The requirements for judges' impartiality are found in Chapter 6 of the Act relating to the Courts of Justice (*domstolloven*).

19 The Supreme Court's judgment Rt. 2007 p. 69 A paras 64–69.

20 The Supreme Court's judgment Rt. 2007 p. 69 A para 63.

> The grounds for the valuation shall explain the legal basis on which the valuation is made and the factual circumstances and other factors of significant importance to the decision.

These requirements are rather limited compared to the requirements for judgments in ordinary civil proceedings,[21] cf the Norwegian Dispute Act (DA) Section 19-6(4). However, the Supreme Court would not even apply these rather soft requirements analogically for insurance claim valuations. The required reasons for judicial valuation were still applied similarly to insurance claim valuation, and the Supreme Court underlined that the main ingredients of these requirements must be fulfilled. On the other hand, the Supreme Court emphasised that the application of these requirements must be softer for the simpler and more informal insurance claim valuations than for judicial evaluations.[22]

In addition to these two procedural reasons for invalidity, arguably, insurance claim valuation is also invalid if basic procedural rights or safeguards have been violated. That will, for instance, cover situations where a party's right to be heard has been violated,[23] or if one of the parties has been allowed to bring forward procedural steps that the opposing party has been disallowed.

2.4 The Decision's Substantively Binding Effect

As long as the decision is not found invalid, it is regarded as binding, and a key feature of the insurance claim valuation scheme is that parties, when entering into the agreement, accept that the board's decision will become binding. But what does that mean? Clearly, the decision does not have a res judicata effect and is not enforceable. Under Norwegian law, the parties cannot agree that a decision by a tribunal shall have a res judicata effect. Such an effect is exclusive to judgments taken by the court and for other decisions when prescribed by law.[24] The law does prescribe such an effect for arbitral awards,[25] but as we

21 Eg, the Supreme Court's decisions Rt. 1983 p. 1507 A; Rt. 1988 p. 595 A; Rt. 1989 p. 532 A.
22 The Supreme Court's judgment Rt. 2007 p. 69 A paras 64–69.
23 The Supreme Court's judgment Rt. 1981 p. 651 A at 655–656; Arntzen (n 6) 313–314.
24 The Supreme Court's judgment HR-2016-867-A. An example is the Patient Injury Act (*pasientskadeloven*) Section 18 Subsection 2 which prescribes that decisions by the patient injury compensation board has a res judicata effect when the time limit for bringing a lawsuit concerning the decision has passed.
25 The Arbitration Act Section 46.

have underlined, insurance claim valuation is not arbitration, and the law does not prescribe a res judicata effect on such valuations.

What is the binding effect, then? Arguably, it is binding in a substantive sense similar to the effect of entering into contracts by agents.[26] Just as two persons who are about to enter a contract may leave the finalising of the contract to a joint agent representing both, two parties to an insurance contract may agree that a joint expert or two experts may set up a solution that is binding for both parties. A bit simplified, we may say that the decision taken by the board members, or the senior board member, becomes a part of the substantive contract unless the decision is found invalid. Similar to a situation where two parties entered an out-of-court settlement, the parties may still take the claim to court since the decision has no res judicata effect, but as long as the decision is valid, the rights and obligations of the parties are now due to the board decision.

However, there are similarities between the substantive effects of decisions taken by insurance claim valuation and the positive res judicata effect of judgments. Since the court shall not conduct the valuation, a valid decision after an insurance claim valuation limits the court's competence in a manner similar to a res judicata effect. Just as the court must respect a final judgment on claim A when dealing with claim B (assuming that A is relevant for B),[27] the court must respect the valuation of element A when dealing with element B (assuming that A is relevant for B). However, the difference is fundamental because a res judicata effect is always related to a claim, while the effect of an insurance claim valuation is only related to a part of a claim. Furthermore, the binding effect of the valuation is still based on contract, which means that rules for the interpretation of contracts apply when a valuation is unclear – the rules for the interpretation of judgments do not apply.

3 Decision by Assessor

3.1 Introduction

Decision by assessor is a scheme developed for disputes connected to certain types of construction contracts. Although there may be some minor differ-

26 Jens Edvin A Skoghøy, 'Rettskraftens objektive grenser i sivile saker' (1995) Jussens Venner 1, 17; Borgar Høgetveit Bergh (ed), *Voldgiftsloven med kommentarer* (Gyldendal 2006) 73.

27 Dispute Act Section 19–15(2).

ences between the regulations on decision by assessor in different standard contracts, it is a more or less standardised scheme across all types of contracts where it is applied. The assessor's competence is typically based on standard contracts, see, for instance, Norsk Standard (NS) 8407:2011 *Standard Contractual Clauses for Turnkey Projects,* Section 50.3.1.

> Unless otherwise agreed, each of the parties may, until takeover, demand that a dispute concerning the contractual relationship be settled by an assessor, unless the dispute has already been brought before the court or arbitration.

Traditionally, disputes within Norwegian construction projects were handled by arbitration for established and continuous sets of arbitrators. From the 1990s onwards, a scheme for the use of assessors or experts was introduced as an agreed alternative to arbitration (or ordinary court proceedings). Initially, there was a two-track scheme where disputes under a defined and rather high value should be arbitrated,[28] other disputes should go to assessors. In the current scheme, the value thresholds are replaced by full freedom of choice for both parties when a dispute arises. Any party may choose decision by assessor or arbitration (or regular court proceedings if there is no arbitration clause). The contracts also include a scheme of project-integrated mediation, which is available to both parties before or after entering into arbitration or engaging an assessor.[29]

The scheme of decisions by assessors may concern smaller or larger contracts, but the contract is typically part of a larger construction project. One of the main reasons for establishing this scheme is the need to save money (compared to full proceedings), but even more important is the need for a swift and speedy process that does not hinder the progress of the project. As these construction contracts are regularly rather large, they may also involve some rather massive companies. However, the scheme is normally also applicable to subcontractors. There may be a high number of subcontractors involved in the development of larger buildings, bridges, or highways, and these subcontractors may very well be medium or small-scale entrepreneurs.

---

28 Karl Marthinussen, Heikki Giverholt and Hans-Jørgen Arvesen, *NS 8405 med kommentarer*, (4th ed, Oslo 2016) 732. The value was set to 100 G. G is short for *Grunnbeløp*, which is primarily used for the calculation of compensations based on the public welfare system. Because the G is regulated annually and more or less keeps track with inflation, it may be used for setting value thresholds in various legal settings. From 1 May 2025 is 1 G equivalent to NOK 130,160.

29 NS 8407 Section 50.2.

3.2 Composition and Proceedings

In general, decision by assessor involves a single decision-maker. The assessor is normally a legal expert, very often a law professor specialised in contract law, but it may also be an expert on factual matters that are decisive for the dispute – for instance, an engineer or appraiser.[30] If the parties cannot agree on the appointment of a decision-maker, he or she will be appointed by Standard Norge, a business organisation that develops the standard contracts for these disputes.[31]

The proceedings are regulated by the standard contracts, but not in much detail. Pursuant to NS 8407 sec 50.3.1(3), proceedings start with introductory statements by all parties involved. The requirements are modified versions of the requirements for statements of claim (DA Section 9–2) and written replies (DA Section 9–3). The complaining party shall, in writing, define a prayer for relief, shall, to the extent necessary, provide factual and legal reasons, and shall produce documentation. The opposing party shall, within a short time limit set by the assessor, have the opportunity to reply in writing. Both parties have a right to produce one further document to the assessor and the opposing party, and the assessor may call for a hearing whenever necessary in order to clarify each party's opinion.

The assessor's decision shall contain reasons and shall be taken within 14 days after the closing of the preparatory stage, cf NS 8407 sec 50.3.1(4). There is a specialised rule concerning cost-shifting: Each party covers their own costs, but the losing party is responsible for the costs of the assessor, cf NS 8407 sec 50.3.1(5).

3.3 The Decision's Substantively Binding Effect

Since a decision by assessor obviously is not an arbitral decision, it is not a hindrance to a later lawsuit. A party that has a legal interest in bringing a lawsuit may very well do so even though a decision has been taken by an assessor, but the standard contracts stipulate that a party must notify the opposing party if they do not regard the decision as binding, cf NS 8407, Section 50.3.2.

> The parties shall notify each other in writing within one month of receipt of the assessor's decision whether they will accept the decision as binding.

---

30 Marthinussen et al (n 28) 736.

31 NS 8407 Section 50.3.1(3).

If a party initiates litigation or arbitration, the court or the tribunal examines the entire claim and does not review the validity of the assessor's decision. In this situation, the assessor's decision does not have any binding effect at all, and the court's competence is, in essence, as if there was no initial decision.

However, a decision by assessor is temporarily binding whenever it concerns some legal claims or legal situations defined in NS 8407 Section 50.3.2 (2). I cannot dwell on the details of this, which would lead us far away into the peculiarities of these rather complex contracts, but the claims and situations described cover a considerable portion of the most practically important claims that could go to decision by assessor. Therefore, such a temporarily binding effect is in fact the main rule. Furthermore, pursuant to NS 8407 Section 50.3.2(3), a decision by assessor becomes permanently binding

> [i]f the parties have not brought the decision before court or arbitration within six months after the date of the decision.

However, none of these clauses defines 'binding'. As we have seen for insurance claim valuations, defining 'binding' is challenging and may depend on the context.

What does 'binding' mean in the context of a decision by assessor? Obviously, a decision taken by assessor does not have a res judicata effect since it does not preclude the commencement of a lawsuit or an arbitration proceeding. As was emphasised in Section 2.5, such an effect would require a legal basis in a statutory provision. One may argue that such an effect emerges when the decision has become permanently binding.[32] Of course, there is a difference between the temporary binding effect and the permanent binding effect. But it is not a distinction between a procedural res judicata effect and a substantive effect; it is a distinction between two forms of substantive effects. Whenever an assessor's decision is merely temporarily binding, any party may initiate court proceedings or arbitration proceedings, and the competence of the courts or tribunals will be as if the decision was not taken – the competence covers the entire claim and not just the validity of the assessor's decision. Whenever a lawsuit or arbitration proceeding commences after the permanent binding effect has emerged, the action shall not be rejected. The assessor's decision has become binding, but in a substantive sense, which

32 Marthinussen et al (n 28) 415 and 738.

means that a lawsuit is still possible, but the decision shall be regarded as a part of the contract.[33] The effect is very similar to the effect of out-of-court settlements.

4 Some Concluding Remarks

Insurance claim valuation and decision by assessor are important schemes for procedural handling of legal claims involving small businesses. These schemes are examples of specialised patterns of decision-making and conflict-solving which, over the years, have developed for the special needs of the businesses to which they apply. In general, the schemes seem to work relatively well in practice. However, the extreme sectoral approach is also problematic. Very little cooperation is found between the highly specialised sectors or businesses in which the respective schemes have been developed, and one wonders whether a cross-sectoral approach to this could have produced fruitful findings that could enhance the schemes. At least partly due to the sectoral approach, some quite fundamental procedural sides of these schemes have never been thoroughly analysed. A part of the problem is also the lack of attention that has been brought to these issues from academia. Most of the schemes are both developed and applied by practitioners, in some fields orchestrated by law professors specialising in the relevant substantive contracts.

Some problematic issues concerning these schemes, especially for insurance claim valuation, are the unbalanced access to resources between the parties. One side of these disputes, insurance companies, are repeat players who have access to plenty of experience, expertise and resources. The opposing party, typically a small business, is a one-shot player with very limited access to experience, expertise and economic resources. On the other hand, these schemes are still a better solution for small businesses than regular court proceedings, especially because these solutions are quicker and cheaper.

33 Knut Kaasen, *Tilvirkningskontrakter. Med kommentarer til NTK 15 og NF 15* (Universitetsforlaget 2018) 499–500.

References

Arntzen A, *Forsikringsrett. Tingskadeoppgjør – brann og kombinertforsikring* (Brevik 1993).

Bergh BH (ed), *Voldgiftsloven med kommentarer* (Gyldendal 2006).

Forsikringsskjønn i skadeoppgjør – rapport fra arbeidsgruppe (30 November 2012) https://www.regjeringen.no/contentassets/9cb7e3b09c084f6985857b3c01a04358/forsikringsskjonn_skadeoppgjor.pdf (accessed 17 August 2026).

Kaasen K, *Tilvirkningskontrakter. Med kommentarer til NTK 15 og NF 15* (Universitetsforlaget 2018).

Mæland HJ, *Voldgift* (Universitetsforlaget 1988).

Marthinussen K, Giverholt H and Arvesen H-J, *NS 8405 med kommentarer* (4th ed, Oslo 2016).

Nylund A and Cabral A (eds), *Contractualisation of Civil Litigation* (Intersentia 2023).

Skoghøy JEA, 'Rettskraftens objektive grenser i sivile saker' (1995) Jussens Venner 1.

CHAPTER 8

Small Businesses and Consumer Dispute Resolution

Wannes Vandenbussche and Silke Onraedt

1 Introduction

The term alternative dispute resolution (ADR) is generally used to describe the wide range of dispute resolution methods that operate outside of the traditional court system, with the 'A' variously understood to stand for 'appropriate', 'amicable', or 'alternative'.[1] In the EU, the use of ADR in consumer disputes has been a topic of increasing interest over the past thirty years, driven by both legislative initiatives[2] and an expanding academic literature,[3] to the point that consumer ADR, referred to as consumer dispute resolution (CDR), could even be considered a sub-field in its own right. At its core, consumer dispute reso-

1 Arnold Ingen-Housz, 'Editor's Preface' in Arnold Ingen-Housz (ed), *ADR in Business: Practice and Issues across Countries and Cultures II* (Kluwer Law International 2010).

2 See amongst others, European Commission, *Green Paper on the access of consumers to justice and the settlement of consumer disputes in the single market* COM (1993) 576 final; European Parliament and Council Directive (EU) 2013/11/EU on alternative dispute resolution for consumer disputes and amending Regulation (EC) No 2006/2004 and Directive 2009/22/EC (Consumer ADR Directive) [2013] OJ L165/63; European Parliament and Council Directive (EU) 2015/2302 on package travel and linked travel arrangements, amending Regulation (EC) No 2006/2004 and Directive 2011/83/EU of the European Parliament and of the Council and repealing Council Directive 90/314/EEC [2015] OJ L 326/1; European Parliament and Council Directive (EU) 2019/2161 amending Council Directive 93/13/EEC and Directives 98/6/EC, 2005/29/EC and 2011/83/EU of the European Parliament and of the Council as regards the better enforcement and modernisation of Union consumer protection rules (Consumer Omnibus Directive) [2019] OJ L328/7; European Parliament and Council Directive (EU) 2020/1828 on representative actions for the protection of the collective interests of consumers and repealing Directive 2009/22/EC (Representative Actions Directive) [2020] OJ L409/1; European Parliament and Council Directive (EU) 2025/2647 amending Directive 2013/11/EU on alternative dispute resolution for consumer disputes and amending Directives (EU) 2015/2302, (EU) 2019/2161 and (EU) 2020/1828 following the discontinuation of the European Online Dispute Resolution Platform [2025] OJ L2025/2647.

3 See, eg, Christopher Hodges, Iris Benöhr and Naomi Creutzfeldt-Banda, *Consumer ADR in Europe* (Hart 2012); Hans-W Micklitz and Geneviève Saumier, *Enforcement and Effectiveness of Consumer Law* (Springer 2018); Stephanie Law and Vincent Richard, *Public and Private Enforcement of Consumer Law – Insights for Luxembourg* (Nomos 2021).

lution is intended to enable consumers to settle complaints against traders through the intervention of an entity (eg, arbitrator, conciliator, mediator, ombudsman, and complaints board), outside of court.[4] Practice-based figures confirm that these processes have gained considerable traction. By 2025, it was reported that ADR bodies had examined around 300,000 eligible consumer-trader disputes in the EU, with resolution rates ranging from 17% to 100% across the Member States.[5] Nevertheless, considerable efforts are still needed to raise public awareness of ADR as a widespread means of resolving consumer disputes.[6]

This chapter examines the potential of consumer dispute resolution to address the access-to-justice needs of small businesses. This is particularly relevant given that small businesses face risks similar to those encountered by consumers in their relationships and disputes with larger businesses. Like consumers, small businesses are often economically less powerful than multinational businesses.[7] On the other hand, small businesses may also be in a weaker position than some well-informed consumers who find it easier to navigate the dispute resolution landscape or, more generally, to enforce their rights.[8] Despite consumer dispute resolution's potential to play a meaningful role in practice, this topic has thus far attracted little scholarly attention.[9] For this reason, the analysis is primarily exploratory in nature. More specifically,

4 David Ashton, *Alternative Dispute Resolution* (European Parliamentary Research Service 2025) PE 757.639, 1. https://www.europarl.europa.eu/RegData/etudes/BRIE/2024/757639/EPRS_BRI(2024)757639_EN.pdf (accessed 18 August 2026); Jules Stuyck *1993 – Twenty Years Later: The Evolution of Consumer Law in the European Union* (Intersentia 2013).

5 Ashton (n 4) 1. For the Nordic context, see Nylund, Chapter 6, Section 3.3.

6 After all, the same report indicates that only 5% of EU consumers (approximately 2.25 million persons) who experienced a problem when purchasing a product or service proceeded to submit their complaint to an ADR body. Moreover, the 2019 Consumer Conditions Scoreboard found that 43% of surveyed retailers were unaware of the existence of ADR (ibid, 2 and 4).

7 Pieter-Jan De Koning, 'CDR' in Belgium: The Special Place of the Belgian Residual ADR Body' in Xandra Kramer, Alexandre Biard, Jos Hoevenaars and Erlis Themeli (eds), *New Pathways to Civil Justice in Europe: Challenges of Access to Justice* (Springer 2021) 146. See also Castermans and Krans, Chapter 5; Ghavanini, Chapter 3, Section 3; Stadler, Chapter 10.

8 Ibid, 146. Illustrative in this respect is a decision of the Amsterdam District Court allowing the buyer of a €5,400,000 yacht to rely on a favourable consumer regime (Amsterdam District Court, 4 August 2021 RBAMS:2021:4531, S&S 2021/103).

9 For one of the few exceptions, see Anirudh Gundumi, 'The Impact of ADR on SME Development: A Comparative Study between England and India' (2025) 6 York Law Review 34–63. The following article also devotes some attention to the relationship between small businesses and ADR; Stefanie Hartog and Michael Hammes, 'Dispute Resolution and Conflict Management in Germany' (2017) Nederlands-Vlaams tijdschrift voor Mediation en conflictmanagement 21, 25.

this chapter examines whether, and under what circumstances, this mechanism is accessible to small businesses, at the level of EU law and in a selected Member State. Where such access exists, the chapter explores whether it could provide insight into the extent to which the mechanism could be a viable option for small businesses when it comes to resolving disputes with larger retailers or other business counterparts.

This chapter proceeds as follows. The first and most substantial part traces the four main stages in the development of consumer dispute resolution within the EU. Our focus here is, of course, on the role of small businesses as complainants in this dispute resolution mechanism. As the title of this section indicates, small businesses have generally been approached as incidental beneficiaries, but seldom as actors warranting any substantive consideration beyond that (see Section 2). The following part of this chapter will focus on Belgium as a case study. There are two main reasons for this choice. Firstly, it is the legal system with which both authors are most familiar. Secondly, small and medium-sized enterprises (SMEs), defined as businesses with fewer than 250 employees, play a crucial role in the Belgian economy, representing the large majority of all businesses in the country. More specifically, this section sets out the state of play regarding the past and present accessibility of consumer dispute resolution for small businesses and draws a number of lessons from this analysis (see Section 3). The chapter concludes with a brief final section offering a number of overarching reflections on the topic.

2 The Common Thread in the EU Development of Consumer Dispute Resolution: The Marginal Position of Small Businesses

2.1 The Period Prior to the ADR Directive

It is well established that, as in the United States, ADR in many European jurisdictions first emerged in an ad hoc manner, developed by private actors operating largely outside the regulatory framework.[10] Since the 1990s, however, the EU has been a driving force behind initiatives to promote and institutionalise ADR.

The EU's work on consumer protection provided the initial context for its engagement with ADR. An important milestone was the 1993 Green Paper on

10 Wannes Vandenbussche and Piet Taelman, 'Consumer Protection Proceedings' in Burkhard Hess, Margareth Woo, Loïc Cadiet, Sevérine Menétrey and Enrique Vallines García

the access of consumers to justice and the settlement of consumer disputes in the single market,[11] followed in 1996 by the Action Plan on Consumer Access to Justice and the Settlement of Consumer Disputes in the Internal Market.[12] The Action Plan referred to a study on the 'Cost of legal barriers to consumers in the single market' conducted in 1995, which contained at least one finding directly relevant to small businesses. Specifically, the study observed that transborder legal uncertainty, understood as the risk of incurring higher transaction costs in order to obtain payment for goods delivered, had a relatively greater impact on small businesses than on larger ones, 'small businesses tend to be outcompeted'.[13]

By the late 1990s, and following the well-known Presidency Conclusions of the 1999 Tampere Summit, the EU broadened its agenda towards improving access to justice for all.[14] A notable illustration of this, in the context of promoting ADR, is Article 17 of the Electronic Commerce Directive,[15] which introduced a specific provision on out-of-court dispute settlement. The ambition remained modest. Member States were only required to ensure that their legislation did not hinder the use of existing out-of-court schemes in disputes between information society service providers and recipients.[16] A 2002 Green Paper on alternative dispute resolution in civil and commercial law nonetheless referred to this provision as evidence of the EU's efforts to foster ADR and to bolster the confidence of both consumers *and* small (and medium-sized) businesses in electronic commerce.[17] In summary, throughout this period, the consideration given to small businesses in the ADR context at EU level amounted to little more than sporadic mentions.

(eds), *Comparative Procedural Law and Justice* (Part XII Chapter 6) https://www.cplj.org/publications/12-6-consumer-protection-proceedings (accessed 18 August 2026) para 123.

11 COM (1993) 576 final (n 2).

12 European Commission *Action Plan on consumer access to justice and the settlement of consumer disputes in the internal market*, COM (96) 13 final.

13 European Commission (n 12) 11.

14 Burkhard Hess, 'Nouvelles Techniques de La Coopération Judiciaire Transfrontière En Europe' (2003) Revue critique de droit international privé 215, 217.

15 European Parliament and Council Directive 2000/31/EC on certain legal aspects of information society services, in particular electronic commerce, in the Internal Market (Electronic Commerce Directive) [2000] OJ L178/1.

16 Electronic Commerce Directive Article 17 para 1.

17 COM (1993) 576 final (n 2) 6.

2.2 The Adoption of the Consumer ADR Directive

The 2013 Consumer ADR Directive represents, as is widely recognised, the cornerstone of EU regulatory intervention in this domain. It required Member States to establish a comprehensive institutional framework for consumer dispute resolution intended to complement and, where appropriate, substitute court proceedings. Therefore, the framework incorporated the existing private and public ADR schemes of the Member States, such as ombudsmen, complaint boards and consumer mediation services. In addition, it obliged the Member States to set up new ADR entities in areas of EU consumer law that were not yet covered by existing bodies.[18] The Directive also established a set of principles designed to ensure the quality of ADR services. These principles include guaranteeing the independence and impartiality of ADR bodies, ensuring the transparency and effectiveness of the system as a whole, and promoting fair procedures.[19]

What is most significant for this chapter is recital 16 of the preamble, which limits the Directive's scope to consumer complaints against traders relating to contractual obligations stemming from sales or service contracts. It explicitly excludes complaints submitted by traders against consumers, as well as disputes between traders. This means that small businesses, in the same way as all other undertakings, are in principle excluded from being able to submit complaints. However, according to the same recital, Member States should not be prevented from adopting or maintaining in force provisions on procedures for the out-of-court resolution of such disputes.

Interestingly, the EU Commission initially adopted a broader approach in its proposal for the Directive. In the original text of this recital, the envisaged scope likewise covered disputes between consumers and traders arising from the sale of goods or the provision of services, but it explicitly added that this should also include 'complaints submitted by traders against consumers', while excluding only trader against trader disputes.[20] Under the Commission's approach, all traders, not just small businesses, would have been able to rely

18 Burkhard Hess, 'The State of the Civil Justice Union' in Burkhard Hess, Maria Bergström and Eva Storskrubb (eds), *EU Civil Justice: Current Issues and Future Outlook* (Hart 2016) 6–7.

19 Consumer ADR Directive Articles 6–9.

20 Proposal for a Directive on alternative dispute resolution for consumer disputes and amending Regulation (EC) 2006/2004 and Directive 2009/22/EC, COM (2011) 793 final, 2011/0373 (COD) recital 7. The proposal also refers to a business consultation conducted between March and May 2011 through the SME survey platform, in which 927 small and medium-sized businesses responded to questions on ADR (Proposal, para. 2.1).

on ADR entities in disputes with consumers. This extension beyond the consumer sphere aligned with the broader policy climate at the time, which aimed to provide small businesses with the same level of protection as consumers, particularly against unfair commercial practices and unfair contract terms. This approach was also reflected in the proposal for a Common European Sales Law (CESL), which ultimately failed.[21]

As noted, the Commission's proposal was ultimately reversed, and the final text of the Directive expressly excluded complaints submitted by traders against consumers. The reasons for this shift remain unclear. The European Economic and Social Committee (EESC) was reluctant to the idea of such an extension, warning that it would contradict prevailing national traditions and transform ADR bodies into de facto debt-collection mechanisms. This would bypass the EU small-claims framework and overload structures that are not equipped for such caseloads. The EESC nonetheless acknowledged, with reference to the Small Business Act,[22] that micro and small businesses could, under clearly defined conditions, have access to ADR for disputes concerning uncollected orders, repairs or reservations.[23]

2.3 Developments Since the Implementation of the Consumer ADR Directive

A significant development after the implementation of the ADR Directive was the adoption of the European Electronic Communications Code in late 2018. For the first time, the EU legislature explicitly allowed Member States to extend access to ADR procedures 'to *end-users other than consumers*, in particular micro businesses and small businesses'.[24] This marked a departure from the earlier 2002 regulatory framework for electronic communications networks and services, which had focused exclusively on ensuring a high

21 Stuyck (n 4) 27.

22 Communication from the Commission to the Council, the European Parliament, the European Economic and Social Committee and the Committee of the Regions: 'Think Small First – A "Small Business Act" for Europe' COM (2008) 394 final, 25 June 2008.

23 European Economic and Social Committee, 'Opinion of the Proposal for a Directive of the European Parliament and of the Council on alternative dispute resolution for consumer disputes and amending Regulation (EC) 2006/2004 and Directive 2009/22/EC' COM (2011) 793 final, 2011/0373 (COD).

24 European Parliament and Council Directive (EU) 2018/1972 establishing the European Electronic Communications Code (Recast) (Electronic Communications Code Directive) [2018] OJ L321/36 Article 25(1).

level of protection for *consumers* through simple and inexpensive dispute-resolution mechanisms.[25]

The preamble to the 2018 European Electronic Communications Code emphasises the speed and cost-effectiveness of out-of-court procedures for enforcing the rights of end-users, particularly consumers and micro and small businesses. It also calls on Member States to designate a national regulatory authority or another independent body with recognised expertise in end-user rights to act as the relevant ADR entity, operating independently. Importantly, the preamble clarifies the relationship with the Consumer ADR Directive, reiterating that the latter does not apply to end-users other than consumers. However, since many Member States have nonetheless established dispute resolution procedures also for non-consumer end-users, the EU legislature considers it reasonable to retain the sector-specific dispute resolution mechanism for consumers and, where Member States so provide, also for other end-users, in particular micro and small businesses.[26]

The EU legislator's explicit permission for Member States to extend consumer protection to non-consumers, such as start-ups and small businesses, also appears in other non-enforcement-oriented directives from the same period. These include those on the sale of goods,[27] and the supply of digital content and services.[28] However, this approach has not been universally welcomed, as it has been criticised for introducing additional scope for fragmentation.[29]

Finally, the Electricity Market Directive is also noteworthy in this regard. It expressly requires Member States to ensure that final customers have access to simple, fair, transparent, independent, effective and efficient out-of-court dispute resolution mechanisms, provided by an independent body (such as an

---

25 European Parliament and Council Directive 2002/21/EC on a common regulatory framework for electronic communications networks and services [2002] OJ L108/33 Article 8(4)(b).

26 Electronic Communications Code Directive recital (68).

27 European Parliament and Council Directive (EU) 2019/771 on certain aspects concerning contracts for the sale of goods, amending Regulation (EU) 2017/2394 and Directive 2009/22/EC, and repealing Directive 1999/44/EC [2019] OJ L136/28, recital (21).

28 European Parliament and Council Directive (EU) 2019/770 on certain aspects concerning contracts for the supply of digital content and digital services (Digital Services Directive) [2019] OJ L136/1, recital (16).

29 Laura Seritti, 'Online Shopping and Quality Problems: What Safeguards for Platform Users Under the EU Consumer Protection Regime?' (2021) 10 Journal of European Consumer and Market Law 180, 185.

energy ombudsman, a consumer body or a regulatory authority).[30] Small businesses seem to fall under the definition of final customer, which refers to a customer who purchases electricity for their own use. This directive even goes a step further than the framework of the Consumer ADR Directive[31] by making the participation of electricity undertakings in out-of-court dispute resolution mechanisms mandatory,[32] albeit only with respect to household customers. As household customers are defined as those who purchase electricity for household consumption only, excluding commercial or professional activities, small businesses cannot benefit from this mandatory participation regime for traders. The same principles can likewise be found in the Gas and Hydrogen Directive.[33]

2.4 The Reform of the Consumer ADR Directive

On 17 October 2023, the European Commission presented a proposal for a directive amending the Consumer ADR Directive. The proposal was deemed necessary in light of three main objectives: (1) adapting the ADR framework to digital markets, (2) facilitating the use of ADR in cross-border disputes, and (3) simplifying ADR procedures. Following the ordinary legislative procedure, the Council approved the reform of the ADR Directive on 17 November 2025, after which it was endorsed by the European Parliament in plenary session on 16 December 2025. The revised Consumer ADR Directive was published in the Official Journal on 30 December 2025 and entered into force on 19 January 2026, giving the Member States until 20 March 2028 to transpose it into their national legal systems.

In terms of scope, the revised Consumer ADR Directive is intended to continue to apply exclusively to disputes between consumers and traders. Disputes between traders remain outside its scope. Nevertheless, the principle

30 European Parliament and Council Directive (EU) 2019/944 on common rules for the internal market for electricity and amending Directive 2012/27/EU (recast) (Electricity Market Directive) [2019] OJ L158/125 Article 26(1).

31 For instance, only six Member States transposed the ADR Directive 2013/11/EU by creating an obligation for traders to participate in ADR across economic sectors, seven other Member States created such an obligation only for specific economic sectors, while eleven other Member States made participation entirely voluntary (Ashton (n 4) 4).

32 This applies unless the Member State demonstrates to the Commission that other mechanisms are equally effective; see Electricity Market Directive Article 26(3).

33 European Parliament and Council Directive (EU) 2024/1788 on common rules for the internal markets for renewable gas, natural gas and hydrogen, amending Directive (EU) 2023/1791 and repealing Directive 2009/73/EC [2024] (Gas and Hydrogen Directive) OJ L2024/1788 Article 25(3).

of minimum harmonisation is preserved,[34] enabling Member States to maintain existing practices or exceed them by granting small businesses access to ADR entities as complainants. Of particular significance is the addition to the preamble introduced by the European Parliament in its resolution of 13 March 2024[35]: 'Member States can, in accordance with Union law, facilitate access to ADR procedures for the self-employed or microenterprises so that such businesses have the possibility to benefit from independent, impartial, transparent, effective, fast and fair ADR systems'.[36]

Shortly before, the EESC had also devoted some attention to small businesses, or more generally to SMEs, in its opinion. Rather than expressly addressing an extension of consumer dispute resolution to small businesses as complainants, the EESC focused on the opportunities offered by fair, neutral and efficient ADR procedures for SMEs in their capacity as traders,[37] and on the idea that traders, including SMEs, should likewise be encouraged to participate on a voluntary basis.[38] This last issue is closely linked to the broader debate on whether trader participation in consumer dispute resolution should be made mandatory or whether policy efforts should instead focus on incentives to encourage participation and compliance. This question has been extensively discussed in the literature.[39] The preamble of the final

34 European Commission, 'New Measures to Simplify the Resolution of Disputes out of Court and Boost Consumer Rights' (17 October 2023) <https://ec.europa.eu/commission/presscorner/detail/nl/ip_23_5049> (accessed 18 August 2026).

35 European Parliament, Legislative Resolution of 13 March 2024 on the proposal for a Directive of the European Parliament and of the Council amending Directive 2013/11/EU on alternative dispute resolution for consumer disputes COM (2023), P9_TA (2024) 0139.

36 Council compromise text on the Directive amending Directive 2013/11/EU on alternative dispute resolution for consumer disputes and amending Directives (EU) 2015/2302, (EU) 2019/2161, (EU) 2020/1828 following the discontinuation of the European Online Dispute Resolution Platform, Recital (39).

37 European Economic and Social Committee, opinion of 14 February 2024 on Alternative Dispute Resolution, INT/1047 para 2.2.

38 Ibid para 1.3.

39 See, amongst others Chris Willett and Andrea Fejos, 'Consumer Access to Justice: The Role of the ADR Directive and the Member States' (2016) 24 European Review of Private Law 33, 42; Giacomo Pailli and Cristina Poncibò, 'The Transformation of Consumer Law Enforcement: An Italian Perspective' (2017) Comparative Law Review 1, 37; Caroline Daniels, 'Alternative Dispute Resolution for European Consumers: A Question of Access to and Standards of Justice' in Loïc Cadiet, Burkhard Hess and Marta Requejo Isidro (eds), *Privatizing Dispute Resolution* (Nomos Verlagsgesellschaft 2019); Stefaan Voet, 'ADR, Mandatory Consumer Mediation and the Impact on Civil Litigation' in Xandra Kramer Ahmed Masood, Adriani Dori and Maria Carlota Ucin (eds), *Sustaining Access to Justice* (Hart 2025) 217.

text of the Directive ultimately provides that Member States may introduce mandatory trader participation in consumer dispute resolution in sectors with persistently low participation rates and recurrent consumer complaints, notably in transport and tourism, including air passengers' rights.[40] This issue, however, falls outside the scope of the present chapter and will therefore not be examined further.[41]

3 Belgium as a Case Study

The following section takes a closer look at the Belgian legal system with the purpose of providing an overview of the accessibility of consumer dispute resolution for small businesses, both in the past and in the present. At the outset, it is important to note that Belgium hosts approximately 1.186 million small and medium businesses, understood as businesses employing fewer than 250 employees, which correspond to 98.8 such businesses per thousand inhabitants.[42]

3.1 The Belgian Consumer Dispute Resolution Landscape at a Glance

The Belgian Act of 14 April 2014[43] transposed the ADR Directive. This resulted in Book XVI, entitled 'Out-of-Court Settlement of Consumer Disputes', being introduced into the Belgian Code of Economic Law. As with the Directive

40 Council, compromise text for Directive amending Directive 2013/11/EU on alternative dispute resolution for consumer disputes and amending Directives (EU) 2015/2302, (EU) 2019/2161 and (EU) 2020/1828 following the discontinuation of the European Online Dispute Resolution Platform, recital (16).

41 Nevertheless, in this context, it is worth noting that SMEunited, a European interest group representing national cross-sectoral craft and SME federations and claiming to speak on behalf of 25.8 million SMEs in Europe, advocated maintaining a voluntary ADR system for European businesses at EU level. In its view, participation in ADR procedures is more effectively fostered by easing obligations and providing incentives than by imposing mandatory participation Sophia Zakari, 'Alternative Dispute Resolution (ADR)' (SME United, 7 October 2024) https://www.smeunited.eu/admin/storage/smeunited/20241007-smeunited-key-articles-onepager-adr.pdf (accessed 18 August 2026).

42 FOD Economie, 'Statistieken over kmo's in België. FOD Economie' <https://economie.fgov.be/nl/themas/ondernemingen/kmos-en-zelfstandigen-cijfers/statistieken-over-kmos-belgie> (accessed 18 August 2026).

43 *Act on the insertion of Book XVI "Extrajudicial settlement of consumer disputes" in the Code of Economic Law* (Wet van 4 april 2014 houdende de invoeging van Boek XVI "Buitengerechtelijke regeling van consumentengeschillen" in het Wetboek van economisch recht) *Belgisch Staatsblad* 12 mei 2014, 38262.

itself, the Belgian implementation is characterised by a scope that is limited to consumer disputes. By refraining from explicitly extending this scope to business-to-business disputes, the Belgian legislator sought to avoid creating an overly broad framework that might prove unmanageable for ADR entities.[44] However, parliamentary documents suggest that the legislation does not prevent qualified ADR entities from settling other types of disputes, such as business-to-business disputes.[45] As will be discussed below, six of the thirteen qualified ADR entities in Belgium are indeed doing so.

In essence, the transposition of the Consumer ADR Directive brought about two significant changes. First, the legislation resulted in the designation of thirteen qualified ADR entities, whether of a private nature or established by a public authority. These entities include both pre-existing bodies that were integrated into the new framework and newly established entities, all of which are required to comply with the quality requirements already set out in the Directive (such as independence and impartiality)[46] and to be included on the list drawn up by the Federal Public Service for Economic Affairs.[47] Currently, the thirteen qualified ADR entities, listed in chronological order of recognition as of 2015, and their respective mandates are as follows:

- The Ombudsman for Telecommunication Services, responsible for resolving disputes between users and providers of electronic communications services.[48]
- The Ombudsman for Financial Services (Ombudsfin), which handles complaints from consumers of financial services.[49]

---

44 Draft Law of 28 February 2014 on the insertion of Book XVI "Extrajudicial settlement of consumer disputes" in the Code of Economic Law, report on behalf of the Committee on Business, Scientific Policy, Education, National Scientific and Cultural Institutions, the Self-Employed and Agriculture (*Wetsontwerp van 28 februari 2014 houdende de invoeging van Boek XVI "Buitengerechtelijke regeling van consumentengeschillen" in het Wetboek van economisch recht, verslag namens de commissie voor het bedrijfsleven, het wetenschapsbeleid, het onderwijs, de nationale wetenschappelijke en culturele instellingen, de middenstand en de landbouw*) [53 3360/004] 22.

45 Ibid 20.

46 Code of Economic Law (*Wetboek van economisch recht*) Article XVI.25.

47 Code of Economic Law Article XVI.24.

48 Ombudsdienst Telecommunicatie 'Een klacht indienen bij de ombudsdienst' <https://www.ombudsmantelecom.be/nl/een-klacht-indienen/> (accessed 18 August 2026).

49 Ombudsfin – Bemiddelingsdienst voor banken, kredieten en beleggingen <https://www.vlaanderen.be/organisaties/ombudsfin-bemiddelingsdienst-voor-banken-kredieten-en-beleggingen> (accessed 18 August 2026).

- The Ombudsman for Notaries, established to address complaints from third parties concerning the professional conduct of notaries.[50]
- The Ombudsman for Insurance, competent to deal with disputes between an applicant and an insurer or intermediary.[51]
- The Reconciliation Commission for Construction, which intervenes in all technical disputes that arise between a consumer and an architect and/or a contractor involved in the private construction or renovation works.[52]
- The Consumer Mediation Service, responsible for providing information, referrals, and mediation to consumers and businesses involved in disputes (see below).
- The Ombudsman for Energy, which manages complaints from any end-user purchasing electricity or natural gas for personal use.[53]
- The Travel Disputes Committee, which is responsible for handling complaints filed by travellers and tour operators against each other regarding the course of the trip.[54]
- The Ombudsman for the Postal Sector, which handles disputes between senders or recipients and postal service providers operating on the Belgian market, including both national and international shipments.[55]
- The Ombudsman Service for Consumer Disputes relating to the Legal Profession authorised to address questions and/or complaints relating to the relationship between a lawyer and a client.[56]
- The Ombudsman of the lawyers of the French and German-speaking Bar Association, responsible for resolving disputes arising from the relationship between a lawyer and a client.[57]

50 Ombudsnotaris 'Opdracht' <https://www.ombudsnotaris.be/ombudsdienst/> (accessed 18 August 2026).

51 Ombudsman Insurance 'Bevoegdheid' <https://www.ombudsman-insurance.be/nl/over-ons/#bevoegdheid> (accessed 18 August 2026).

52 Bouwverzoening 'Voor wie' <https://bouwverzoening.be/voor-wie> (accessed 18 August 2026).

53 Ombudsdienst voor Energie 'Wie kan een beroep doen op de Ombudsdienst voor Energie?' <https://www.ombudsmanenergie.be/nl/faq/wie-kan-een-beroep-doen-op-de-ombudsdienst-voor-energie> (accessed 18 August 2026).

54 CLV-GR <https://clv-gr.be/> (accessed 18 August 2026).

55 Ombudsman Post 'Vaak gestelde vragen' <https://www.ombudsmanposte.be/nl/info/faq/> (accessed 18 August 2026).

56 OCA 'FAQ' <https://oca.ligeca.be/en/facq/> (accessed 18 August 2026).

57 OBFG 'A propos du service' https://obfg.ligeca.be/ (accessed 18 August 2026).

- The Arbitration Committee for Consumers and Textile Carers, created to handle disputes regarding textile items that were damaged during a professional treatment.[58]
- The Ombudsman for bailiffs, responsible for resolving problems that individuals, companies, debtors, creditors, etc., have with a candidate bailiff or a bailiff.[59]

Second, the implementation of the Consumer ADR Directive led to the establishment in 2015 of a new autonomous public body: the Consumer Mediation Service (CMS). The CMS's primary task is to guide consumers and businesses through the rather heterogeneous and complex Belgian ADR landscape, both by providing information and by referring disputes to the appropriate ADR entity. Where a dispute cannot be referred to a sector-specific entity,[60] the CMS may itself attempt to mediate a solution.[61]

Even before the ADR Directive was enacted, Belgian law provided for a digital ADR portal, BELMED, which still exists alongside the CMS to this day. BELMED provides information on the Belgian ADR landscape and allows users to submit complaints,[62] which are then forwarded to one of its forty partners, including qualified ADR entities[63] and individual mediators.[64] Based on the sector, language and region, BELMED proposes various neutral third parties to handle the dispute.[65] However, if a particular partner is competent in the relevant sector, the application is automatically forwarded to them.[66]

Finally, consumers and, by extension, small businesses may also resolve their disputes amicably through alternative means. As already mentioned, there are independent mediators who are recognised by the Federal Public

58 CACET vzw 'Welkom bij CACET vzw' <https://www.cacet.be/> (accessed 18 August 2026).

59 Ombudsdienst voor de Gerechtsdeurwaarders 'Tot uw dienst' <https://www.ombudsgdw.be/tot-uw-dienst-0> (accessed 18 August 2026).

60 CMS is one of Belgium's thirteen qualified ADR entities and can forward disputes to any of the other twelve qualified ADR entities.

61 Pieter-Jan De Koning, 'CDR in Belgium: The Special Place of the Belgian Residual ADR Body' in Xandra Kramer, Alexandre Biard, Jos Hoevenaars and Erlis Themeli (eds), *New Pathways to Civil Justice in Europe: Challenges of Access to Justice* (Springer 2021) 131.

62 FOD Economie, 'Gebruiksvoorwaarden Belmed' <https://economie.fgov.be/nl/themas/online/belmed-onlinebemiddeling/alternatieve/bemiddelingsaanvraag/gebruiksvoorwaarden-belmed> (accessed 18 August 2026).

63 BELMED can forward a dispute to twelve of Belgium's thirteen qualified ADR entities.

64 Unlike BELMED, CMS cannot refer disputes to individual recognised mediators.

65 IBR-IRE, 'Belmed – Platform voor de online buitengerechtelijke beslechting van geschillen' <https://www.ibr-ire.be/nl/actueel/news-detail/belmed-platform-voor-de-online-buitengerechtelijke-beslechting-van-geschillen> (accessed 18 August 2026).

66 FOD Economie (n 53).

Service for Justice and who meet specific training requirements.[67] In addition, consumers as well as small businesses can bring a dispute before a judge at the Chamber for Amicable Settlements before any judicial proceedings have been initiated, completely free of charge.[68] As of 1 September 2025, a Chamber for Amicable Settlement exists within all Belgian civil and commercial courts, at both first-instance and appellate levels. The judge sitting in such a chamber has received specialised training and endeavours to facilitate an amicable settlement in a completely voluntary[69] and confidential[70] setting. However, no data are available if consumers actually rely on this form of dispute resolution to settle their conflicts with businesses.

3.2 Key Findings on Access of Small Businesses to Consumer Dispute Resolution in Belgium

Although the Code of Economic Law only covers disputes between consumers and traders, six of the thirteen qualified ADR entities seem to accept complaints from small businesses, meaning they also deal with disputes between traders.[71] More specifically, this concerns the following entities.

- The Ombudsman for Telecommunication Services
- The Ombudsman for Financial Services
- The Ombudsman for Notaries
- The Ombudsman for Insurance
- The Ombudsman for Energy
- The Ombudsman for the Postal Sector

Accordingly, small businesses in these sectors have access to ADR entities for resolving disputes with other businesses. This offers an alternative to court proceedings, which may entail the drawbacks frequently identified in the literature, such as being time-consuming, costly, and potentially affecting ongoing commercial relationships.[72]

---

67 Belgian Judicial Code Book VI 'Mediation' Articles 1724–1737.

68 Wannes Vandenbussche, 'De impact van de Wet van 19 december 2023 op de KMS-praktijk in familiezaken' (2025) Tijdschrift voor familierecht 59, 63.

69 Ibid 74.

70 Ibid 67.

71 The authors derived this figure from an analysis of the relevant ADR entities' legislative frameworks, annual reports and websites. While some qualified entities, such as the Ombudsman Service for Consumer Disputes in the Legal Profession, explicitly limit their activities to consumer disputes, the position of several other entities is less clear in this regard.

72 Gundumi (n 9) 34.

Based on our analysis of these six qualified ADR entities, three broader conclusions can be drawn regarding the relationship between consumer dispute resolution and small businesses from the perspective of Belgian law.

First, there is no consistent approach to extending the material scope of ADR beyond consumer disputes. Such extensions are articulated through different concepts and labels, including 'users', 'professionals', 'self-employed', and 'businesses'. For instance, the Ombudsman for Telecommunication Services has competence over complaints brought by 'users', which refers not only to natural persons but also to (micro) businesses and organisations.[73] Similarly, the Energy Ombudsman handles complaints from any end-user, interpreted in line with the Electricity Market Directive (see above), allowing residential customers, craftsmen, micro and small businesses and associations to submit disputes.[74] The Ombudsman for the Postal Sector appears to accept complaints from anyone, irrespective of whether the complainant is a private individual, a company or another organisation.[75] The Ombudsman for Insurance handles complaints from applicants, which include consumers, policyholders, associations and (micro) businesses.[76] The Ombudsman for Notaries states that it deals with complaints from private individuals or professionals,[77] whereas Ombudsfin processes complaints from both consumers and (micro) businesses.[78]

Secondly, chronologically speaking, no parallel can be drawn with what was outlined above regarding the relationship between small businesses and the development of consumer dispute resolution within the EU. Notably, none of the Belgian ADR entities has opened its doors to small businesses in direct response to EU developments in this area. Rather, several entities had already done so long before. For example, the Ombudsman for Telecommunication

73 Act on the reform of certain public economic undertakings (*Wet van 21 maart 1991 betreffende de hervorming van sommige economische overheidsbedrijven*) Article 43 §1.

74 Ombudsdienst voor energie, 'Missie' <https://www.ombudsmanenergie.be/nl/missie> (accessed 18 August 2026).

75 Ombudsdienst voor de postsector, 'Wie kan een klacht indienen?' <https://www.ombudsmanposte.be/nl/over-ons/onze-werking/wie-kan-klacht-indienen/> (accessed 18 August 2026).

76 Ombudsman van de verzekeringen 'De Ombudsman: jaarverslag 1999' 17 https://ombudsman-insurance.be/wp-content/uploads/2024/11/ra-nl-1999.pdf (accessed 18 August 2026).

77 Ombudsnotaris, 'Klachten, Ombudsnotaire – Ombudsnotaris' <https://www.ombudsnotaris.be/klachten/> (accessed 18 August 2026).

78 Ombudsfin 'Jaarverslag 2016' 28 <https://www.ombudsfin.be/storage/app/uploads/public/640/098/899/640098899570943829233.pdf> (accessed 18 August 2026).

Services,[79] the Ombudsman for the Postal Sector,[80] and the Ombudsman for Insurance[81] have accepted complaints from (small) businesses since the 1990s. Others, including the Ombudsman for Energy and Ombudsfin, began handling complaints from businesses after their establishment in the mid-2010s, following the implementation of the Consumer ADR Directive. This may, of course, change in the future. It remains to be seen how the Belgian legislator will respond following the implementation of the recast Consumer ADR Directive, which indicates that Member States may facilitate access to ADR procedures for micro businesses.

The third and final observation concerns the scarcity of empirical data on the relation between small businesses and alternative dispute resolution. This may be explained, on the one hand, by the limited attention paid to small businesses' access to consumer dispute resolution in the Belgian legal doctrine. On the other hand, research on the interaction between small businesses' and dispute resolution mechanisms often remains unpublished or inaccessible. The available material is limited to annual reports produced by one of the six qualified ADR entities. These reports occasionally include data on businesses' use of their services.[82] Further insight is provided by a survey conducted in 2022 by the Union of Self-Employed Entrepreneurs (UNIZO), in which entrepreneurs were questioned about business disputes, the justice system, and ADR methods.[83] The survey indicates that 38% of respondents seek to avoid legal proceedings, primarily due to the associated costs and law-

79 For example, the first annual report emphasises conflict prevention and resolution, in particular by bridging the positions of the public sector and 'users', see Ombudsdienst Belgacom, 'Het jaarverslag 1993 van de Ombudsdienst Belgacom' 6 <https://www.ombudsmantelecom.be/wp-content/uploads/1993_NL.pdf> (accessed 18 August 2026).

80 This is more difficult to ascertain as the earliest available annual report dates back only to 2012. However, legislation from 1991 already refers to 'all users of companies within the postal sector', which suggests that companies have been entitled to complain for a long time.

81 See, eg, the annual report of 1999, referring to complaints lodged by lawyers, companies, individuals, governments, etc. 'De Ombudsman: jaarverslag 1999' (n 74) 17.

82 For instance, the report of the Ombudsman for energy states that 7% of the complaints submitted in 2010 and 6% of the complaints submitted in 2011 were from professional end-users: Ombudsdienst voor energie 'Activiteitenverslag 2011' (Ombudsdienst voor energie 2011) 19 <https://www.ombudsmanenergie.be/sites/default/files/content/download/files/ombudsdienst_voor_energie_activiteitenverslag_2011_nl.pdf>) (accessed 18 August 2026).

83 UNIZO Studiedienst 'Enquête: Zakelijke geschillen en justitie', (2023), <www.unizo.be/onderzoek-en-statistiek> (accessed 18 August 2026). It should be noted, however, that no information was provided about the methodology used or the number of respondents.

yers' fees,[84] while 71% report a willingness to negotiate in order to prevent litigation.[85] Most notably, 85% of respondents who had never made use of ADR attributed this to insufficient awareness of the available ADR mechanisms.[86] These findings suggest that a lack of knowledge may (still) be a factor in the limited use of consumer dispute resolution by small businesses.

4 Conclusions

This chapter has sought, in a holistic and exploratory manner, to assess the relationship between consumer dispute resolution and small businesses in the EU.

The first section examined the development of consumer dispute resolution at the EU level, as well as its accessibility for small businesses. The main finding was that small businesses were generally considered incidental beneficiaries of consumer dispute resolution rather than actors warranting substantive consideration in their own right. During the period when the EU began to show interest in ADR, references to the position of small businesses were sporadic at best. Furthermore, the 2013 Consumer ADR Directive, the cornerstone of this framework, explicitly excluded complaints submitted by traders against consumers, as well as disputes between traders, from its scope. However, it should be noted that Member States were not precluded from adopting or maintaining in force provisions on procedures for the out-of-court resolution of such disputes. The recently revised Consumer ADR Directive maintains the principle of minimum harmonisation and goes a step further by expressly indicating that Member States may facilitate access to ADR procedures for micro businesses. In doing so, the EU legislator continues the trajectory already visible in sector-specific instruments, such as the European Electronic Communications Code.

The second section analysed the complex consumer dispute resolution landscape in Belgium, with a specific focus on small businesses. Currently, Belgium has thirteen qualified ADR entities, six of which are authorised to handle complaints submitted by businesses. Three key insights emerged from this analysis. Firstly, there is no consistent approach to extending the scope of ADR beyond consumer disputes. Where such extensions exist, they are framed through a variety of concepts and labels, such as 'users', 'professionals', 'self-

84 UNIZO Studiedienst (n 83) 4.
85 Ibid 3.
86 Ibid 5.

employed persons' and 'businesses', resulting in a fragmented and opaque framework. Secondly, the Belgian landscape does not mirror the EU-level evolution concerning the position of small businesses in consumer dispute resolution. Notably, none of the Belgian ADR entities extended their scope to small businesses in direct response to EU-level developments. Rather, the entities that accept business complaints had already done so well before these initiatives emerged at the EU level. Thirdly, it is not possible to draw any firm conclusions regarding the actual use of consumer dispute resolution by small businesses in Belgium, as the available empirical data remains too limited and fragmented.

Even in the Belgian context, it remains unclear how often small businesses use consumer dispute resolution, and why they choose to use or avoid it. One explanation frequently given in legal literature on ADR is a lack of awareness among small businesses of the existence of ADR mechanisms and their applicability to disputes with other traders.[87] Other factors that have been identified include limited logistical and financial resources, a comparatively higher degree of risk aversion, continued reliance on traditional dispute resolution practices and a lack of accessible precedents and institutional experience with ADR mechanisms.[88]

As noted above, the scope of this chapter does not permit definitive conclusions on these explanations. However, what can be stated with greater certainty for Belgium is that consumer dispute resolution is not the only way in which small businesses can seek an out-of-court settlement. Other options include attempting an amicable settlement before initiating judicial proceedings with the Chambers for Amicable Settlement, which operate free of charge within all Belgian civil and commercial courts, and seeking the help of independent mediators.

In sum, while this chapter does not permit firm conclusions regarding effectiveness or uptake, it suggests that greater conceptual coherence and empirical transparency are required for consumer dispute resolution to play a more meaningful role for small businesses.

---

87 Christopher Hodges, 'Delivering Justice' in Xandra Kramer Stefaan Voet, Lorenz Ködderitzsch, Magdalena Tulibacka and Burkhard Hess (eds), *New Pathways to Civil Justice in Europe: Challenges of Access to Justice* (Springer 2021) 84; Stuyck (n 4) 24.

88 Hartog and Hammes (n 9) 25.

References

Ashton D, *Alternative Dispute Resolution* (European Parliamentary Research Service 2025) https://www.europarl.europa.eu/RegData/etudes/BRIE/2024/757639/EPRS_BRI(2024)757639_EN.pdf (accessed 18 August 2026)

Benöhr I, Creutzfeldt-Banda N and Hodges C, *Consumer ADR in Europe* (Hart 2012)

Bouwverzoening, 'Voor wie' https://bouwverzoening.be/voor-wie (accessed 18 August 2026)

CLV-GR, 'Welkom' https://clv-gr.be/ (accessed 18 August 2026)

CMS, 'Tot uw dienst' (Ombudsdienst voor de Gerechtsdeurwaarders) https://www.ombudsgdw.be/tot-uw-dienst-oc (accessed 18 August 2026)

Daniels C, 'Alternative Dispute Resolution for European Consumers: A Question of Access to and Standards of Justice' in L Cadiet, B Hess and M Requejo Isidro (eds), *Privatizing Dispute Resolution* (Nomos Verlagsgesellschaft 2019)

De Koning PJ, 'CDR in Belgium: The Special Place of the Belgian Residual ADR Body' in X Kramer, A Biard, J Hoevenaars and E Themeli (eds), *New Pathways to Civil Justice in Europe: Challenges of Access to Justice* (Springer 2021)

FOD Economie, 'Gebruiksvoorwaarden Belmed' https://economie.fgov.be/nl/themas/online/belmed-onlinebemiddeling/alternatieve/bemiddelingsaanvraag/gebruiksvoorwaarden-belmed (accessed 18 August 2026)

FOD Economie, 'Statistieken over kmo's in België. FOD Economie' <https://economie.fgov.be/nl/themas/ondernemingen/kmos-en-zelfstandigen-cijfers/statistieken-over-kmos-belgie> (accessed 18 August 2026)

Gundumi A, 'The Impact of ADR on SME Development: A Comparative Study Between England and India' (2025) 6 York Law Review 34

Hartog S and Hammes M, 'Dispute Resolution and Conflict Management in Germany' (2017) Nederlands-Vlaams Tijdschrift voor Mediation en Conflictmanagement 21

Hess B, 'Nouvelles Techniques de la Coopération Judiciaire Transfrontière en Europe' (2003) Revue critique de droit international privé 215

Hess B, 'The State of the Civil Justice Union' in B Hess, M Bergström and E Storskrubb (eds), EU Civil Justice: Current Issues and Future Outlook (Hart 2016)

Hodges C, 'Delivering Justice' in X Kramer, S Voet, L Ködderitzsch, M Tulibacka and B Hess (eds), *New Pathways to Civil Justice in Europe: Challenges of Access to Justice* (Springer 2021)

IBR-IRE, 'Belmed – Platform voor de online buitengerechtelijke beslechting van geschillen' https://www.ibr-ire.be/nl/actueel/news-detail/belmed-platform-voor-de-online-buitengerechtelijke-beslechting-van-geschillen (accessed 18 August 2026)

Ingen-Housz A (ed), *ADR in Business: Practice and Issues across Countries and Cultures II* (Kluwer Law International 2010)

OCA, 'FAQ' https://oca.ligeca.be/en/facq/ (accessed 18 August 2026)

OBFG, 'A propos du service' https://obfg.ligeca.be/fr (accessed 18 August 2026)

Ombudsman Insurance, 'Bevoegdheid' https://www.ombudsman-insurance.be/nl/over-ons/#bevoegdheid (accessed 18 August 2026)

Ombudsman Post, 'Vaak gestelde vragen' https://www.ombudsmanposte.be/nl/info/faq/ (accessed 18 August 2026)

Ombudsman van de verzekeringen, *De Ombudsman: jaarverslag* 1999 17 https://www.ombudsmaninsurance.be/images/uploads/dossier_general/Procedurereglement_definitief_juni_2024.pdf (accessed 18 August 2026)

Ombudsfin – Bemiddelingsdienst voor banken, kredieten en beleggingen, 'Organisaties' https://www.vlaanderen.be/organisaties/ombudsfin-bemiddelingsdienst-voor-banken-kredieten-en-beleggingen (accessed 18 August 2026)

Ombudsfin, *Jaarverslag* 2016 28 https://www.ombudsfin.be/storage/app/uploads/public/640/098/899/640098899570943829233.pdf (accessed 18 August 2026)

Ombudsnotaris, 'Klachten' https://www.ombudsnotaris.be/klachten/ (accessed 18 August 2026)

Ombudsdienst Belgacom, Het jaarverslag 1993 van de Ombudsdienst Belgacom (1993) 6 https://www.ombudsmantelecom.be/wp-content/uploads/1993_NL.pdf (accessed 18 August 2026)

Ombudsdienst Telecommunicatie, 'Een klacht indienen bij de ombudsdienst' https://www.ombudsmantelecom.be/nl/een-klacht-indienen/ (accessed 18 August 2026)

Ombudsdienst voor de Postsector, 'Wie kan een klacht indienen?' https://www.ombudsmanposte.be/nl/over-ons/onze-werking/wie-kan-klacht-indienen (accessed 18 August 2026)

Ombudsdienst voor Energie, 'Missie' https://www.ombudsmanenergie.be/nl/missie (accessed 18 August 2026)

Pailli G and Poncibò C, 'The Transformation of Consumer Law Enforcement: An Italian Perspective' (2017) Comparative Law Review 1

Seritti L, 'Online Shopping and Quality Problems: What Safeguards for Platform Users Under the EU Consumer Protection Regime?' (2021) 10 Journal of European Consumer and Market Law 180

Stuyck J, 1993 – Twenty Years Later: The Evolution of Consumer Law in the European Union (Intersentia 2013)

UNIZO Studiedienst, Enquête: Zakelijke geschillen en justitie (2023) www.unizo.be/onderzoek-en-statistiek (accessed 18 August 2026)

UNIZO Studiedienst, KMO cijfers (2023) 4

Vandenbussche W and Taelman P, 'Consumer Protection Proceedings' in B Hess, M Woo, L Cadiet, S Menétrey and E Vallines García (eds), *Comparative Procedural Law and Justice* (Part XII Chapter 6) https://www.cplj.org/publications/12-6-consumer-protection-proceedings (accessed 18 August 2026)

Voet S, 'ADR, Mandatory Consumer Mediation and the Impact on Civil Litigation' in X Kramer, A Masood, A Dori and MC Ucin (eds), *Sustaining Access to Justice* (Hart 2025)

Willett C and Fejos A, 'Consumer Access to Justice: The Role of the ADR Directive and the Member States' (2016) European Review of Private Law 33

Zakari S, 'Alternative Dispute Resolution (ADR)' (SME United, 7 October 2024) https://www.smeunited.eu/admin/storage/smeunited/20241007-smeunited-key-articles-onepager-adr.pdf (accessed 18 August 2026)

CHAPTER 9

Pre-action Protocols: Increasing Access to Justice for Small Businesses in England and Wales

Masood Ahmed

1 Introduction

Small businesses have been described as 'the engine of the UK economy and at the heart of their local communities'.[1] Of the 5.5 million private sector businesses in the UK, approximately 5.45 million are small businesses.[2] They employ nearly half of the private workforce and generate a significant share of national output.[3] Yet, despite their economic significance, small businesses have long faced acute challenges in accessing legal services and support to understand and manage their disputes before they become complex and costly.[4] Research by the Legal Services Board[5] has shown that the inability of small businesses to resolve their legal disputes costs the UK economy approximately £40 billion per year.[6] Where proceedings are issued, small businesses

1 Goldman Sachs, *10,000 Small Businesses UK Programme* (2025) https://www.goldmansachs.com/community-impact/10000-small-businesses/uk?utm_source=chatgpt.com (accessed 27 August 2026); and Enterprise Research Centre, *The State of Small Business Britain 2024: Rising to the Challenge* (Economic and Social Research Council 2024) https://www.enterpriseresearch.ac.uk/wp-content/uploads/2025/03/The-State-of-Small-Business-Britain-2024-Final-1.pdf (accessed 27 August 2026).

2 Department of Trade and Industry, *Business Population Estimates 2024* https://www.gov.uk/government/statistics/business-population-estimates-2024 (accessed 27 August 2026).

3 Annalise Murray, *Business Statistics: Research Briefing* (House of Commons Library, 3 December 2025).

4 Legal Services Board, *Small Business Legal Needs: Wave Four Survey 2021* (April 2022).

5 The Legal Services Board (LSB) is the independent oversight regulator for the legal profession in England and Wales.

6 Legal Services Board, 'New research reveals the legal struggles facing small businesses: LSB calls on the government for a legal support strategy' (23 May 2022) https://legalservicesboard.org.uk/news/new-research-reveals-the-legal-struggles-facing-small-businesses-lsb-calls-on-the-government-for-a-legal-support-strategy (accessed 27 August 2026). The Federation of Small Businesses has also estimated that the inability to resolve disputes costs the economy approximately £11.6 billion per year, see Federation of Small Businesses, *Tied-up* https://www.fsb.org.uk/resources/policy-reports/tied-up-MCYQSHZP7PDRESNN573SGHQLINQU (accessed 27 August 2026).

 | HTTPS://DOI.ORG/10.1163/9789004779235-010

struggle to bring and defend claims as a consequence of high and unpredictable litigation costs, the exorbitant delays within the civil courts and the complexities of court procedures. This has created a significant 'access to justice gap'[7] and a growing lack of confidence among small businesses in the civil justice system.[8]

In response to these persistent access to justice challenges, the current reforms in England and Wales[9] are primarily[10] focused on the creation of a digital justice system[11] and the integration and expansion of alternative dispute resolution (ADR) and online dispute resolution (ODR) processes within the courts and tribunals.[12] More interestingly, policy makers and the senior judiciary are seeking to reform the pre-action stage[13] – the stage at which disputes arise but before the parties initiate court proceedings – to promote the early resolution of disputes. To this end, the Online Procedure Rule Committee (OPRC)[14] was established with the stated aim to improve access to justice for all by harnessing the potential of digital technology. The OPRC has the power to make procedural rules for specific types of online court and tribunal proceedings. It also has the power to make rules affecting the pre-action stage,[15] including allowing for the digital transfer of information held

---

7 Legal Services Board, *Small business legal needs* (n 4).

8 Written evidence from the Federation of Small Businesses research shows that the average value of dispute being £18,000 and attempts to resolve a dispute to almost £17,000 with legal representation and time spent dealing with the dispute and other resources are taken into account. See https://committees.parliament.uk/writtenevidence/127780/pdf/ (accessed 27 August 2026).

9 In this chapter, 'English' and 'England' include Wales.

10 Other reforms include, eg, the fixed recoverable costs regime for claims up to £100,000.

11 Eg, HM Courts & Tribunals Service *Modernising courts and tribunals: benefits of digital services* 24 March 2025; Ministry of Justice *Ministry of Justice Digital Strategy 2025* 8 April 2022. See also the speeches of Sir Geoffery Vos MR, eg, Sir Geoffrey Vos, Master of the Rolls and Head of Civil Justice, 'The Digital Justice System – an engine for resolving disputes' International Forum on Online Dispute Resolution (ODR) Greenwich University Wednesday 30 April 2025; Master of the Rolls The Right Honourable Sir Geoffrey Vos 'The Future of Courts: Expert Panel and Discussion' University College London, Bentham House Tuesday 14 May 2024.

12 Eg, the recent implantation of mandatory mediation in the Small Claims Track.

13 Also referred to as the 'pre-action space'.

14 Chapter 2 of the Judicial Review and Courts Act 2022 provides for the creation of the OPRC. The OPRC consists of three senior judges and three expert representatives. The Online Procedure Rules (specified Proceedings Regulations) 2025 provide the OPRC with the power to make rules for (a) civil and tribunal proceedings in relation to property, and (b) family proceedings for financial remedies.

15 The Judicial Review and Courts Act 2022 Section 24.

by public and private pre-action ODR providers to a court or tribunal.[16] In July 2025, the OPRC issued a public engagement document[17] which explains its proposed inclusion framework and pre-action model. The inclusion framework seeks to ensure that the civil justice system supports the participation of all court users, particularly those with vulnerabilities. The pre-action model sets out guidance for providers of online legal information, advice, and dispute resolution services to assist users in navigating the various pre-action service providers and to set data standards that should apply to facilitate the smooth transfer of data between providers and, eventually, from providers to the online court and tribunal process. Furthermore, the recently enacted Online Procedure Rules 2026 promote party cooperation, ADR and emphasis the importance of early dispute resolution in the courts and tribunals.[18]

The pre-action protocols (the protocols) fall within the OPRC's remit. The protocols have long formed[19] a significant part of the English civil justice landscape.[20] They provide a procedural framework that aims to encourage early party co-operation and settlement before disputes reach the courts and, where disputes cannot be settled and proceedings are issued, they help to facilitate efficient judicial case management. There are currently seventeen sector-specific protocols[21] and one general protocol.[22] Between 2021 and 2024, the Civil Justice Council (CJC)[23] conducted an extensive review of the protocols, which culminated in the publication of two final reports.[24] The CJC Final Report

16 The Judicial Review and Courts Act 2022 Section 24(2).

17 The Online Procedure Rule Committee, *Inclusion Framework and Pre-action Model for the Digital Justice System* (July 2025).

18 Online Procedure (Rules and Practice Directions) Rules 2026 SI 2026/696.

19 The protocols were first introduced by the Woolf reforms of the 1990s'. See Lord Woolf *Access to Justice – Final Report* (1996) Chapter 10.

20 See the comments of the Court of Appeal in *Jet2 Holidays Ltd v Hughes* [2019] EWCA Civ 1858. See also *Shah v Barnet LBC* [2021] EWHC 2631 (QB).

21 Eg, the protocol for Media and Communications Claims, Clinical Disputes, Professional Negligence and Pre-action Protocol for Judicial Review.

22 Practice Direction – Pre-action Conduct and Protocols.

23 The Civil Justice Council is an advisory public body which was established under the Civil Procedure Act 1997. The Council's statutory duty is to review the civil justice system and make recommendations to the Lord Chancellor, the judiciary and the Civil Procedure Rule Committee on the development of the civil justice system to make it more accessible, fair and efficient.

24 Civil Justice Council, *CJC Review of Pre-action Protocols Final Report Part I (August 2023);* Civil Justice Council *CJC Review of Pre-action Protocols Final Report Phase 2 (August 2024)*. In addition to the Final Report, the Civil Justice Council published its *Review of the Pre-action Protocols Interim Report* (November 2021).

(Part 1) (CJC Final Report) made recommendations for reforming the protocols to promote greater access to justice and more proportionate dispute resolution. As part of those proposals, the CJC recommended the introduction of a new General Pre-action Protocol (GPaP) to replace the current general protocol.[25] Should the recommendations be implemented, the proposed GPaP will have a significant impact on the ability of small businesses to access justice, especially given the types of disputes they frequently encounter.[26]

This chapter focuses on the pre-action stage of disputes and critically considers the CJC Final Report recommendations and, in particular, the GPaP's potential to enhance access to justice for small businesses. Given that small businesses are increasingly demanding access to ADR processes,[27] the chapter also provides a detailed analysis of the landmark decision of *Churchill v Merthyr Tydfil Borough Council*[28] in which the Court of Appeal confirmed that the courts could compel disputing parties to engage with ADR processes, provided any order or stay in favour of ADR did not undermine their right to proceed to a judicial hearing. Although *Churchill* and the subsequent ADR amendments to the Civil Procedure Rules (CPR) apply to court proceedings, they will also have an impact on the duty of small businesses to engage with ADR processes at the pre-action stage. It is argued that the combined effect of these recommendations and developments, together with the need to digitise the GPaP and link it to the civil court process, provides the greatest potential to effectively enhance access to justice for small businesses.

Including the introduction, this chapter is organised into five parts. Section 2 provides a brief overview of the various attempts to increase access to justice for small businesses. Section 3 explains the key recommendations of the CJC Final Report and evaluates the salient features of the GPaP. Section 4 critically analyses *Churchill* and its potential impact on the pre-action protocols. Finally, Section 5 considers the OPRC's proposed inclusion framework and pre-action model and concludes with reflections on the way forward for increasing access to justice for small businesses at the pre-action stage.

25 Civil Justice Council, *Final Report Part I* (n 24) Chapters 3 and 4 and Annex 2.
26 Research by the Legal Services Board found that trading issues were the most experienced legal issues by small businesses, which included 'goods or services purchased – late delivery', 'goods or services purchased – not as described' and 'goods/services late payments'. Legal Services Board *Small business legal needs* (n 4).
27 Legal Services Board, *Small business needs* (n 4) and Federation of Small Businesses (n 6).
28 *Churchill v Merthyr Tydfil County Borough Council* [2023] EWCA Civ 1416.

2 Attempts to Increase Access to Justice for Small Businesses

The access to justice challenges faced by small businesses have been recognised in successive civil justice reviews. In its *Improving access to justice for consumers and small businesses in collective claims*[29] report, the CJC recommended increasing the types of representative bodies that can bring claims on behalf of small businesses. Those recommendations, however, were not implemented. Sir Rupert Jackson's *Review of Civil Litigation Costs* discussed at length the need to improve access to justice for small businesses[30] and encouraged the government and insurers to make serious efforts to make small businesses aware of the benefits and availability of before-the-event insurance (BTE) as a way to promote greater access to justice.[31] Unfortunately, like the CJC recommendations before them, the Jackson recommendations were not implemented and were repeated by the CJC's most recent report, *Review of Litigation Funding Final Report 2025*, in which the CJC explained the benefits of BTE insurance for small businesses and called for the implementation of Sir Rupert's proposals.[32]

The help that is currently available for small businesses at the pre-action stage is limited. The Small Business Commissioner,[33] for example, was established to support small businesses to get paid quickly and on time. However, the Small Business Commissioner's remit is limited to resolving late payments and debt issues and does not extend to the wider range of disputes which small businesses encounter.[34] Furthermore, the Small Business Commissioner simply provides advice on how small businesses may negotiate their terms and conditions with their customers; it does not provide a formal dispute resolution service, such as mediation or early neutral evaluation, which can help small businesses to resolve legal disputes without having to issue or defend court proceedings. The UK government also introduced the Prompt Payments Code to address the problems with late payments to small businesses. The Code requires companies that have signed up to it to pay 95% of

29 Civil Justice Council *Improving access to justice for consumers and small businesses in collective claims* (7 May 2010).

30 Lord Justice Jackson, *Review of Civil Litigation Costs: Final Report* (Judiciary 14 January 2010).

31 Ibid Chapter 8 para. 7.5.

32 Civil Justice Council, *Review of Litigation Funding: Final Report* (June 2025) paras 13.9–13.10.

33 The Office of the Small Business Commissioner (OSBC) is an independent public body established by Government under the Enterprise Act 2016.

34 Eg, breach of commercial contract, supply of goods and services disputes.

invoices from small businesses within 30 days. However, becoming a signatory remains voluntary, and just over 3,500 companies have signed the Code out of an estimated 5.6 million businesses.

Stakeholders such as legal charities, regulatory bodies and legal professional organisations have also stressed the need for more to be done to improve the availability of information, advice and dispute resolution processes for small businesses to access at an early stage of disputes arising. In its *21st Century Justice Project Final Report*,[35] the Law Society of England and Wales has called on the government to build a publicly funded triage tool – a 'solutions explorer' – which would provide a trusted entry point to the civil justice system. It has also called for the creation of an online dispute resolution ombudsman using an application programming interface to create a 'single front door' to the civil justice system. Similarly, the Legal Services Board has called for the availability of early information and access to better ADR processes for small businesses.[36]

The various calls for reform of the pre-action stage for small businesses are notably convergent. Each approach focuses on the need for early intervention in the life of a dispute and emphasises the importance of accessible information, guidance, and access to ADR processes, as well as the use of technology to enhance access to justice. Yet, such proposals presuppose significant government investment – an assumption that appears unrealistic given that the Ministry of Justice is not a protected department and remains vulnerable to further government budgetary constraints.[37] A more pragmatic approach may lie in the implementation of the recommendations set out in the CJC Final Report. These recommendations build upon the established procedural framework of the protocols, which have long constituted a coherent and, in general, effective mechanism for facilitating early and proportionate dispute resolution. As will be discussed in the next part, the procedural structure of the GPaP has an inherent flexibility that allows it to be amended, refined, and adapted so as to effectively comply with the requirements of the OPRC's inclusion framework and the guidance under the pre-action model.

---

35 Law Society of England and Wales, *21st Century Justice: Final Report* (Law Society June 2025).

36 Legal Services Board, *Legal Support Strategy for small businesses – Key Asks* https://legalservicesboard.org.uk/wp-content/uploads/2022/05/Small-Business-Legal-Support-Strategy-key-asks-1.pdf (accessed 27 August 2026).

37 The Ministry of Justice is not a 'protected' government department, meaning its budget is not ring-fenced from cuts during public spending reviews and therefore remains susceptible to further reductions in funding.

3 The CJC Final Report and the GPaP

The CJC's Final Report proposes a number of key reforms, including making engagement with the protocols mandatory and sanctioning parties for failure to comply, and making explicit that starting court proceedings should be a last resort. It also makes a significant and far-reaching proposal: amending the overriding objective of the CPR to make explicit reference to the need for parties to comply with the protocols and for the courts to enforce compliance. This is significant because pre-action protocols traditionally sit outside of the court process, and the courts have limited jurisdiction over them. By incorporating the protocols within the most important rule within the CPR, the recommendation proposes to formally bridge the procedural gap between the protocols and the court process. Clearly, primary legislation will be required to implement such a change; however, the proposal reflects a major shift away from the outdated procedural structure to one in which the protocols are formally interconnected with the court process, which also lays the foundations for the protocols to form an essential part of the digital justice system.

A major proposal is the introduction of the GPaP, which will govern the types of disputes that small businesses regularly encounter. As well as reflecting the key recommendations of the CJC Final Report, the GPaP also explains the principle of proportionality by making clear that only proportionate costs must be incurred when complying with the GPaP and that disproportionate costs may not be recoverable. At its heart, the GPaP requires the parties to complete the following three sequential procedural steps before issuing proceedings:

- Step one: The early exchange of relevant information – the claimant must draft a letter of claim explaining the basis of its claim, including the facts, issues and any remedy that it is seeking from the defendant. The letter of claim must be sent to the defendant, who must acknowledge it within 21 days of receipt. The defendant must then provide a full reply. Both parties must disclose and attach key documents with their respective letters.
- Step two: Engagement with an ADR process – upon completion of step one, the parties must then engage with a dispute resolution process. The GPaP provides a non-exhaustive list of ADR processes, including mediation, early neutral evaluation and ombudsman schemes. If the parties cannot agree on an ADR process, they must hold a without prejudice pre-action meeting to discuss the issues and the ways the dispute may be resolved or narrowed. It should be noted that paragraph 4.14 of the GPaP exempts parties from any future requirement to engage with ADR if they have previously attempted ADR at the pre-action stage. This exemption

would apply to low-value disputes that have already been through a pre-action ADR process.[38] However, the decision in *Churchill* and the amended ADR rules alter the position for higher-value disputes. For those disputes, the courts may order the parties to engage with a second round of ADR after proceedings have been issued. This issue is discussed further in Part 4.

- Step three: Completion of a joint stocktake report – if the parties have complied with steps one and two but are unable to resolve the dispute, they must review their positions, continue to co-operate and prepare and file at court a joint pre-action stocktake report. The stocktake report must set out the issues the parties agree on, the issues they disagree on and the reasons for that disagreement, and the status of the parties' disclosure.

It should be noted that step two – the parties' ADR obligation under the GPaP – is solely a process-based obligation, and there is no requirement that the parties must settle their dispute; to say otherwise would be to undermine the right to a fair trial.[39] This is consistent with the CJC's previous report, *Compulsory ADR,*[40] which concluded that compulsory engagement with an ADR process would not, in principle, undermine the parties' right to a fair trial under Article 6 of the European Convention on Human Rights (ECHR), provided the parties are able to revert to the court process if the matter does not settle. More significantly, it is consistent with the Court of Appeal's decision in *Churchill,* which was decided three months after the publication of the CJC Final Report. It should also be noted that mediation has been given priority in the list of ADR processes, given its popularity among the judiciary and policy makers, and the recent expansion of mandatory mediation in the small claims track.[41]

The strongest criticism of the GPaP is that there is a risk of front-loading costs at the pre-action stage, which may erode any intended cost-efficiency benefits. This may be challenging for small businesses that have limited resources, and that may be forced to invest heavily in compliance with pre-action obligations, only to find that the dispute cannot be resolved or must proceed to court regardless. The CJC itself acknowledged this tension, noting that extensive information exchange and mandatory ADR engagement could 'impose a disproportionate burden in lower-value or straightforward dis-

38 Civil Justice Council, *Final Report Part I* (n 24) 68.

39 ECHR Article 6.

40 Civil Justice Council *Compulsory ADR Report* (June 2021); see also Civil Justice Council *ADR and Civil Justice, CJC ADR Working Group Final Report* (November 2018).

41 Practice Direction 51ZE – Small Claims Track Automatic Referral to Mediation Pilot Scheme.

putes'.[42] Moreover, the GPaP's emphasis on prescriptive compliance, coupled with the threat of cost sanctions for non-compliance, could encourage tactical behaviour. Stronger and better-resourced parties may attempt to exploit procedural technicalities to try to delay or pressure small businesses to settle their claims on unfair terms or cause them to abandon their claims. It is therefore unsurprising that critics have argued that the GPaP may 'formalise inefficiency', embedding a culture of procedural defensiveness rather than promoting substantive co-operation.

While concerns about the front-loading of costs and procedural rigidity are legitimate, they arguably underestimate the efficiencies and structural benefits that the GPaP is designed to achieve for the parties and the wider civil justice system. The GPaP provides clear and easy-to-understand guidance on the steps to take before issuing or defending a claim, for example, what a letter of claim must contain, how and when to respond, what is meant by 'key documents', and the nature and types of ADR processes. This has the potential to reduce the need for specialist advice at the earliest stage, cutting initial costs and helping small businesses to act confidently and without the need to incur the cost of lawyers. The three sequential procedural steps also increase the opportunities for early, proportionate settlement of disputes, thereby reducing the need to issue formal proceedings, saving the parties time and cost, and thereby preserving the courts' finite resources. For small businesses, early settlement means fewer legal costs, less cash-flow pressures, and more predictable procedural timelines. The obligation to engage in ADR after the exchange of information and key documents increases the likelihood of settlement and, in the absence of a settlement, engagement with ADR allows the parties to better understand the dispute, helps to narrow the issues, and can set the foundations for a future settlement. Furthermore, by expressly including a range of ADR processes, including mediation, early neutral evaluation, and ombudsman schemes, small businesses are presented with a range of processes and the autonomy to choose the most appropriate process for their dispute. By embedding the principle of proportionality, the GPaP sends out a clear message that the parties must only take steps and incur costs that are proportionate to the complexity and value of the dispute. By making compliance with the GPaP mandatory and having enforcement mechanisms (eg, cost sanctions), small businesses can expect genuine engagement from their opponent and can rely on judicial support if the other side refuses to co-operate. As will be discussed in Section 4, the simple procedural structure of

42 Civil Justice Council, *Final Report Part I* (n 24) paras 5.32–5.35. See also Nylund, Chapter 6.

the GPaP also means that it can easily be incorporated within the digital justice system and be connected to the court process.

4 ADR, Churchill, and the Impact on the Pre-action Stage

For small businesses, ADR processes offer many benefits, including greater control, autonomy and empowerment during the ADR process, the ability to protect their reputation in the market and to preserve trading relationships, and the ability to save time, cost, and reputational damage of litigating disputes in open court. It is unsurprising, therefore, that small businesses are increasingly calling for access to ADR processes at an early stage of when disputes arise. This part critically considers the landmark decision of *Churchill*. Although *Churchill* and the amendments that were subsequently made to the CPR to reflect the decision are concerned with court proceedings, these developments also have the effect of enhancing and reinforcing the parties' obligations at the pre-action stage and, in particular, under the proposed GPaP.

The Court of Appeal in *Churchill* declared that the courts could lawfully compel disputing parties to engage with ADR processes. The courts could do so provided that the order or stay allowing the parties to engage with ADR did not undermine their right to proceed to a judicial hearing, and was proportionate to achieving the legitimate aim of settling the dispute fairly, quickly and at reasonable cost. In reaching its decision, the Court of Appeal finally departed from its controversial comments in *Halsey v Milton Keynes General NHS Trust*[43] in which Dyson LJ, giving the judgment of the Court, observed that to compel parties to engage with ADR would be contrary to their right to a fair trial under Article 6 of the ECHR.[44] Those comments were, as the Court of Appeal made clear in *Churchill*, obiter dicta and did not, therefore, bind the courts on the issue of compulsory ADR.

The Court of Appeal identified three issues of principle: (i) Was the judge right to think that *Halsey* bound him? (ii) If not, can the court lawfully stay proceedings for, or order, the parties to engage in an ADR procedure? If so, (iii) How should the court decide whether to stay the proceedings for, or order, the parties to engage in an ADR process?

On issue (i), the Court held that the judge at first instance was not bound by *Halsey* because the passage on which the judge relied 'was not a necessary part of the reasoning that led to the decision in that case (so was not part of the

43 *Halsey v Milton Keynes General NHS Trust* [2004] EWCA Civ 576.
44 Ibid at [9].

ratio decidendi and was an *obiter dictum*)'.[45] This was because the Court of Appeal in *Halsey* was not concerned with whether or not the courts had the power to compel ADR, rather it was concerned with whether a costs sanction should be imposed against the successful parties on the basis that they had refused to engage with mediation. It was in that context that Dyson LJ had made his comments on compulsory ADR which were not a necessary step in reaching the court's conclusions on the costs questions decided in the appeals. On issue (ii), the Court held that the courts possessed the power to order disputing parties to ADR. In reaching that conclusion, the Court considered a number of European Court of Human Rights (ECtHR) cases, including *Deweer v Belgium*,[46] which Dyson LJ relied upon in *Halsey* in support of his Article 6 ECHR comments.

Deweer concerned a Belgian butcher who had allegedly committed an offence of selling meat at an illegal profit. The public prosecutor ordered the butcher to close his shop until either his prosecution was completed, or he paid a fine of 10,000 Belgian francs. Although he paid the fine under protest, he brought successful proceedings for breach of Article 6(1) ECHR. The ECtHR held that the pressure brought to bear on the butcher by the threat to close his shop if he did not pay the fine was an unlawful constraint that was incompatible with Article 6. In contrast, the ECtHR has found that compulsory ADR does not undermine Article 6 where it pursues a legitimate aim and is proportionate with the aims to be achieved.[47]

The Court in *Churchill* also referred to the decisions of *Alassini v Telecom Italia SpA*[48] and *Menini v Banco Popolare Societa Cooperativa*,[49] in which the Court of Justice of the European Union recognised the compatibility of compulsory ADR with Article 6 rights. The Court in *Churchill* then turned its attention to *R (UNISON) v Lord Chancellor*.[50] In that case, the UK Supreme Court held that the right of access to the courts could only be curtailed by express primary legislation and, therefore, the statutory instrument increasing fees to bring claims in the Employment Tribunal was unlawful because it prevented access to justice. The Court explained that *UNISON* was not authority for the proposition that a statutory basis was required for the court to mandate ADR

45 *Churchill* (n 28) at [20]; see also *Darren White v Michael and Sheila Alder* [2025] EWCA Civ 392 [19]–[20].

46 *Deweer v Belgium* [1980] E.C.C. 169.

47 *Momcilovic v Croatia* (2019) 69 EHRR 14.

48 Joined Cases C-317/08, C-301/08, C-319/08 *Alassini v Telecom Italia SpA* [2010] EU:C:2010:146.

49 Case C-75/16 *Menini v Banco Popolare Societa Cooperativa* [2017] EU:C:2017:457.

50 *R (UNISON) v Lord Chancellor* [2017] UKSC 51.

because (i) it was not concerned with either staying existing proceedings or with mandating the parties to participate in another dispute resolution process; (ii) it did not contradict the long-established right of the court to control its own process; (iii) none of the authorities referred to in *UNISON* suggested that the court cannot make orders that delay or prevent the resolution of existing proceedings in aid of making the court system accessible, fair and efficient; (iv) whilst the CPR itself is not primary legislation, nothing in *UNISON* suggested that one of the fundamental premises of the overriding objective in the CPR and even the CPR itself could be unlawful without primary legislation authorising it expressly. The Court concluded that the courts do have the power to lawfully stay proceedings for, or order the parties to engage with, ADR. The Court held: 'the court can lawfully stay proceedings for, or order, the parties to engage in a non-court-based dispute resolution process provided that the order made: (a) does not impair the very essence of the claimant's right to a fair trial; (b) is made in pursuit of a legitimate aim, and (c) is proportionate to achieving that legitimate aim.'[51]

On issue (iii), the Court refused to provide a list of factors which would assist the courts in determining when to exercise its powers to compel parties to engage with ADR; it would be a matter for the courts to determine in the circumstances of each case. Nevertheless, the Court explained that the overriding objective, the factors identified by the claimant, the Bar Council, and the *Halsey* factors were all likely to be relevant.

Following the decision in *Churchill*, amendments were made to the CPR to make explicit the court's powers to compel parties to ADR. The overriding objective was amended to make clear that dealing with cases justly and at proportionate cost includes 'promoting or using alternative dispute resolution'.[52] The court's duty to further the overriding objective through active case management[53] was also amended to refer to the court's powers in '*ordering* or encouraging the parties to use, and facilitating the use of, alternative dispute resolution'.[54] The court's general case management powers under CPR 3 were amended to refer to the court's powers to '*order* the parties to engage in alternative dispute resolution'.[55] and, when it is considering making procedural directions for cases allocated to the fast track and the multi-track, the court may make an '*order* or encourage the parties to engage

51 Ibid [54].
52 CPR 1.1(2)(f).
53 CPR 1.4 Emphasis added.
54 CPR 1.4(2)(e). Emphasis added.
55 CPR 3.1(2)(o). Emphasis added.

in alternative dispute resolution'.[56] Finally, when considering the conduct of the parties for the purposes of costs, the court may take account of 'whether a party failed to comply with *an order* for alternative dispute resolution, or unreasonably failed to engage in alternative dispute resolution'.[57] The procedural changes to the CPR make explicit what was previously implied within the overriding objective and what was subsequently confirmed by the Court of Appeal in *Churchill*: the courts do have the power to compel parties to ADR. In doing so, the revised rules provide much-needed clarity to the courts, the parties and their lawyers on the legality of compulsory ADR orders. The courts are, following *Churchill* and the amended CPR, willing to exercise their powers in making ADR orders[58] and they are also willing to penalise the parties in costs for unreasonably refusing to engage with ADR.[59]

The strengthened judicial ADR powers under the amended CPR have the potential to reduce litigation costs and to promote proportionate dispute resolution for small businesses. There are, however, risks for small businesses that may feel pressured into settlement, even where judicial determination would be more suitable, especially in disputes involving power imbalances. Nonetheless, the amended CPR are, on balance, beneficial for small businesses and consistent with calls from small business for early ADR processes within the civil justice system. By underpinning the amended CPR with the principle of proportionality, they have the potential to enhance access to justice and offer more efficient and economically sustainable pathways for resolving disputes for small businesses.

It is also worth examining the online rules[60] which place significantly greater emphasis on ADR and settlement than the amended CPR. The online rules introduce a new overriding objective, which is firmly focused on 'resolving disputes'[61] as compared with the overriding objective under the CPR,

56 CPR 28.7(1)(d) and CPR 28.14(f). Emphasis added.

57 CPR 44.2(5)(e). Emphasis added.

58 *DKH Retail v City Football Group Ltd* [2024] EWHC 3231 (Ch); *Elphick v Times Media* [2024] EWHC 2595 (KB).

59 *Conway v Conway and another* [2024] EW Misc. 19 (CC); *Northamber Plc v Genee World Limited and others* [2024] EWCA Civ 428; *Smith v Campbell* [2026] EWHC 144. A refusal to engage with ADR will not automatically result in a costs penalty; the courts will carefully scrutinise the circumstances of each case – see, eg, *Assensus Limited v Wirsol Energy Limited* [2025] EWHC 503 (KB); *Belson & Ors v Belson & Ors* [2025] EWHC 2989 (Ch); *Chassy v Left Shift IT Ltd* [2025] EWHC 1701 (KB); *Ellis v Ellis* [2025] EWHC 2609 (Ch).

60 Online rules (n 18).

61 Online rule 5.

which is concerned with 'dealing with cases'.[62] The online rules represent a major procedural shift away from the judicial determination of disputes as a central dispute resolution mechanism within the civil justice system, and a move towards settlement and ADR processes. This procedural shift also introduces a cultural shift by placing an obligation on the parties to 'do all they can'[63] to help achieve the overriding objective and to 'take all reasonable and appropriate steps to settle their disputes'.[64] Although ADR is not expressly mentioned, the online rules envisage an active judicial role in promoting 'mediated solutions'[65] and in managing cases so as to enable disputes to be resolved 'without the parties coming to court'.[66] The court is further empowered to direct parties towards 'the least burdensome or least costly means'[67] of dispute resolution, with early resolution routes expressly including 'online information, online advice, consensual online dispute resolution and adjudication'.[68]

For small businesses, the emphasis on early dispute resolution in the online rules, low-cost online processes, and judicial case management designed to avoid unnecessary hearings has the potential to reduce legal costs, minimise disruption to business operations, and improve access to justice. The availability of online information, advice, and consensual dispute resolution can empower small businesses to resolve disputes swiftly, proportionately, and without the need to instruct lawyers. However, the strong emphasis on resolving disputes through the 'least burdensome' may, in some cases, pressure some small businesses to settle prematurely or disadvantageously. It may also risk prioritising efficiency over substantive justice, especially in cases where judicial determination would be more appropriate. However, despite these concerns, the online rules are, on balance, well suited to the needs of small businesses: by prioritising proportionality, cost-effectiveness, and procedural flexibility, they are likely to deliver faster, more accessible, and cost-efficient routes to the resolution of disputes rather than through the traditional court processes.

Although *Churchill* and the CPR amendments formally apply only once court proceedings have been issued, they nevertheless have important implications for parties' ADR obligations at the pre-action stage and for the scope

62 CPR 1.1(1).
63 Online rule 6 and 8.
64 Online rule 8(b).
65 Online rule 7(d).
66 Online rule 9(f).
67 Online rule 18.
68 Online rule 18.

and exercise of the court's ADR powers thereafter. There are already early indications that the courts are willing to exercise their ADR powers to order parties to engage in a second round of ADR, even where they have previously complied with a relevant pre-action protocol. This judicial approach is consistent with, and reinforced by, paragraph 4.14 of the GPaP. It will be recalled that paragraph 4.14 of the GPaP exempts parties from any future requirement to engage with ADR if they have previously attempted ADR at the pre-action stage. This exemption would apply to low-value disputes that have already been through pre-action ADR, where a further round of ADR would be disproportionate.[69] However, the decision in *Churchill* and the amended ADR rules alter the position for higher-value disputes, which means that the courts may order the parties to engage with a second round of ADR after proceedings have been issued. Two recent post-*Churchill* High Court decisions support these observations. In *Heyes v Holt*,[70] the parties had attempted mediation before issuing proceedings but were unable to reach a settlement. HHJ Matthews, sitting as a judge of the High Court, ordered the parties to engage in a further mediation when he said:

> This is a case which cries out for mediation by the parties. I am aware that mediation has already been attempted between the parties … and on that occasion it failed. I commend them nevertheless for trying. But that was before the claim had even been issued. Now that the parties have full pleadings and disclosure, as well as (for what it may be worth) this judgment, the parties should try again. I will order a stay for that purpose.

Similarly, in *Francis v Pearson*,[71] HHJ Lewis, sitting as a judge of the High Court, recommended that the parties engage with a second mediation. As the judge explained:

> 88. Experience shows that it is often in entrenched cases such as this that ADR can make a real difference, often requiring honest conversations with parties as to the merits of their respective cases, and the potential downsides, as well as looking at pragmatic ways forward.....
>
> 91. The parties need to reflect on the reasons why the cases did not settle at mediation, and the costs of continuing this litigation – not just in terms of money, but the personal costs to each party for example from the time and

69 CJC Final Report, Part I, 68.

70 *Heyes v Holt* [2024] EWHC 779.

71 *Francis v Pearson* [2024] EWHC 605 (KB).

> energy spent fighting, the stress and worry the proceedings might cause, particularly in respect of outcomes, and the impact that it is going to have on the wider community in which they live.
>
> 92. I would strongly recommend that the parties re-consider some form of alternative dispute resolution process – which might include further mediation, or some other way of facilitating agreement – before matters in this case move forward and further costs are incurred.[72]

It follows that the courts, with their new *Churchill* powers and the amended ADR rules, will expect parties to not only consider engaging in a second round of mediation but will increasingly also expect the parties to take constructive steps in arranging and participating in a second round of mediation, regardless of whether they have done so in compliance with a relevant protocol. In the context of the recommendations of the CJC Final Report and the GPaP, it means that there will be greater emphasis on the need for disputing parties to seriously consider, engage, and comply with the protocols and to focus their efforts on resolving their disputes at an early stage. The possibility that the court may order a second round of ADR will also help to focus the minds of the parties when preparing for and participating in ADR and on narrowing any issues in dispute, which can then facilitate more effective and efficient judicial case management if proceedings are issued.

5 Way Forward and Conclusions

The GPaP provides a structured and formal procedural framework that has the potential to transform access to justice for small businesses. By setting out three sequential procedural steps, it promotes early cooperation and constructive engagement between the parties, facilitates the early settlement of disputes through ADR, and helps to further, via the joint stocktake report, the principle of proportionality. Where proceedings are issued, it ensures that resolution remains proportionate to the nature, value, and complexity of the dispute and supports the court in more efficient judicial case management. The GPaP's procedural clarity and flexibility make it particularly well-suited to the types of disputes frequently encountered by small businesses, where parties often lack resources and require straightforward and easily accessible ADR processes. Its structure can also be readily adapted to incorporate early information, advice and signposting to ensure that small businesses are prop-

72 Emphasis added.

erly guided and informed of the ways in which they may be able to resolve their disputes before incurring the expense and time of lengthy court proceedings.

The design of the GPaP, including its use of plain, accessible language, means that it can be incorporated into the current efforts to create a digital justice system. Its procedural framework could easily be developed into an online portal capable of gathering relevant data – such as the letter of claim and letter of reply, key documents and the joint stocktake report – and transferring that data seamlessly to the online court process. The Online Civil Money Claims (OCMC)[73] system provides a clear illustration of this potential. Although OCMC enables individuals and businesses to issue, respond to, and manage low-value civil claims online, it currently lacks a pre-action stage. An online GPaP portal could fill this gap by connecting directly with the OCMC system so that information generated at the pre-action stage feeds automatically and directly into OCMC. The OCMC system, with the help of artificial intelligence, can then convert the relevant data into formal statements of case (ie, particulars of claim and defence). This would streamline the procedures, reduce duplication, and save both time and cost for small businesses. At the same time, it would help courts to uphold the principle of proportionality and manage their limited resources more effectively across the civil justice system.

The GPaP meets the OPRC's proposed inclusion framework. The inclusion framework provides a set of principles and guidance designed to ensure that the development and operation of the online procedure rules promulgated by the OPRC promote accessibility, fairness, and effective participation for all users, particularly those who are digitally excluded or vulnerable. The inclusion framework emphasises digital inclusion through user-centred design, plain language, and the collection of data to monitor accessibility outcomes. The GPaP's structure already reflects some of these principles to ensure that all can access and understand the nature and role of the GPaP and procedural expectations and obligations. Digitising the GPaP will also allow further safeguards, guidance, and support to be incorporated within the procedural framework of the GPaP, which will help to promote effective and fair participation by small businesses in pre-action dispute resolution.

The GPaP also meets the objectives of the pre-action model framework in promoting access to justice and enabling claims to be resolved quickly, efficiently and fairly, and at proportionate cost. Digitising the GPaP will also help

73 UK Government, *Make a court claim for money,* https://www.gov.uk/make-court-claim-for-money/make-claim (accessed 27 August 2026).

to facilitate the smooth transfer of data to the online courts. Through effective signposting and structured data exchange, the GPaP can ensure continuity and coherence across the dispute resolution process – from initial engagement and ADR through to court proceedings. However, it should be noted that the pre-action model's reference to the need for the parties to 'consider' ADR, appears to be weaker than the language used in *Churchill*, the amended CPR, the online rules, the CJC Final Report, and indeed the GPaP itself, which emphasises the mandatory need to consider and engage with relevant ADR processes. Unless this language is strengthened in the pre-action model, there is a risk that the momentum towards a culture of proportionate, ADR-focused dispute resolution could be diluted, which could undermine the broader reform efforts to enhance access to justice.

These developments demonstrate the significant potential of the GPaP as a tool for improving early intervention, assistance, and dispute resolution at the pre-action stage. Its structured processes, adaptability, and digital potential allow it to be integrated within the future digital justice system to enhance access to justice for small businesses.

References

Civil Justice Council, *ADR and Civil Justice: CJC ADR Working Group Final Report* (November 2018).

Civil Justice Council, *Compulsory ADR: Report* (June 2021).

Civil Justice Council, *Improving Access to Justice for Consumers and Small Businesses in Collective Claims* (7 May 2010).

Civil Justice Council, *Review of Litigation Funding: Final Report* (June 2025).

Civil Justice Council, *Review of Pre-Action Protocols: Final Report Part I* (August 2023).

Civil Justice Council, *Review of Pre-Action Protocols: Final Report Phase 2* (August 2024).

Civil Justice Council, *Review of the Pre-Action Protocols: Interim Report* (November 2021).

Department of Trade and Industry, *Business Population Estimates 2024* https://www.gov.uk/government/statistics/business-population-estimates-2024 (accessed 27 August 2026).

Enterprise Research Centre, *The State of Small Business Britain 2024: Rising to the Challenge* (Economic and Social Research Council 2024).

Federation of Small Businesses, *Tied-Up* https://www.fsb.org.uk/resources/policy-reports/tied-up-MCYQSHZP7PDRESNN573SGHQLINQU (accessed 27 August 2026).

Federation of Small Businesses, *Written Evidence to the UK Parliament: SME Legal Disputes and Costs* (Parliamentary Committees 2025) https://committees.parliament.uk/writtenevidence/127780/pdf/ (accessed 27 August 2026).
Hutton G, *Business Statistics: Research Briefing* (House of Commons Library, 11 November 2024).
Goldman Sachs, *10,000 Small Businesses UK Programme* (2025) https://www.goldmansachs.com/community-impact/10000-small-businesses/uk?utm_source=chatgpt.com (accessed 27 August 2026).
HM Courts & Tribunals Service, *Modernising Courts and Tribunals: Benefits of Digital Services* (24 March 2025).
HM Government, 'Make a Court Claim for Money' https://www.gov.uk/make-court-claim-for-money/make-claim (accessed 27 August 2026).
Jackson R, *Review of Civil Litigation Costs: Final Report* (Judiciary 14 January 2010).
Law Society of England and Wales, *21st Century Justice: Final Report* (Law Society June 2025).
Legal Services Board, *New Research Reveals the Legal Struggles Facing Small Businesses* (23 May 2022) https://legalservicesboard.org.uk/news/new-research-reveals-the-legal-struggles-facing-small-businesses-lsb-calls-on-the-government-for-a-legal-support-strategy (accessed 27 August 2026).
Legal Services Board, *Small Business Legal Needs: Wave Four Survey 2021* (April 2022).
Legal Services Board, *Legal Support Strategy for Small Businesses – key Asks* (2022) https://legalservicesboard.org.uk/wp-content/uploads/2022/05/Small-Business-Legal-Support-Strategy-key-asks-1.pdf (accessed 27 August 2026).
Ministry of Justice, *Digital Strategy 2025* (8 April 2022).
Murray A, *Business Statistics: Research Briefing* (House of Commons Library, 3 December 2025).
Online Procedure Rule Committee, *Inclusion Framework and Pre-Action Model for the Digital Justice System* (July 2025).
Vos G, 'The Digital Justice System – An Engine for Resolving Disputes' (International Forum on Online Dispute Resolution, Greenwich University, 30 April 2025).
Vos G, 'The Future of Courts: Expert Panel and Discussion' (University College London, Bentham House, 14 May 2024).
Woolf L, *Access to Justice: Final Report* (1996).

CHAPTER 10

Special Purpose Vehicles in German Law: Improving Access to Justice for Small Businesses?

Astrid Stadler

1 Introduction

The situation of small businesses is addressed by EU law in different contexts, such as competition law, financial options, reduction of bureaucracy, and costs, but there is little awareness of small businesses' problems of access to justice.[1] In this regard, consumer protection always seems to take priority, and the definition of consumers normally does not include small businesses.[2] However, small businesses are often in a similar position to consumers when it comes to enforcing their claims. When it comes to individual claims, such as outstanding payments from customers or disputes with suppliers, they often have to decide whether legal enforcement is worth the effort.

In this context, it is important to bear in mind a general development over the last decades in Germany: the number of cases brought before the civil courts, in general, has been declining for years. Before Local Courts (*Amtsgerichte* (AG)), which have jurisdiction up to an amount in controversy of €10,000,[3] the number of cases dropped by 56.9% from 1995 to 2021. Before German District Courts (*Landgerichte* (LG)), the number of incoming cases dropped from 418,807 cases in 1995 to 330,210 cases in 2021, a decline of 21.2%.[4] Legal science and practice can only speculate about the specific reasons for the decline. Some small cases go to consumer conciliation boards, and a considerable number of major commercial disputes are being

1 Nylund, Chapter 1.

2 For an exception under German law, see below 2.2.

3 The amount was raised from €5,000 from January 2026. Bundesministerium der Justiz, *Regierungsentwurf eines Gesetzes zur Änderung des Zuständigkeitsstreitwerts* https://www.bmjv.de/SharedDocs/Downloads/DE/Gesetzgebung/RegE/RegE_Aenderung_Zustaendigkeitsstreitwert.pdf?__blob=publicationFile&v=2 (all accessed 18 August 2026).

4 More details for the period 2015–2023 are provided in the study by Stefan Ekert, Caroline Meller-Hannich and Monika Nöhre, *Erforschung der Ursachen des Rückgangs der Eingangszahlen bei den Zivilgerichten*, Bundesministerium der Justiz, April 2023, https://www.bmjv.de/SharedDocs/Downloads/DE/Fachinformationen/Abschlussbericht_Eingangszahlen_Zivilgerichte.pdf?__blob=publicationFile&v= (accessed 18 August 2026).

 | HTTPS://DOI.ORG/10.1163/9789004779235-011

litigated before arbitration panels.[5] The exact figures of arbitration cases are unknown, as there are no reliable statistics on ad hoc arbitration. In general, the study by Ekert, Meller-Hannich, and Nöhre came to the conclusion that particularly traders seek other solutions, and prevention of conflicts has priority. Various instruments are not only used for this purpose, such as prepayment by contract partners, avoiding conflicts by regulations in general contract terms, but also voluntary concessions to clients once a conflict has arisen. Litigation has become the last resort.[6]

This is particularly true for small businesses. They are under high cost pressure and regularly face particularly fierce competition. They often do not have their own legal department, which means that every legal dispute ties up considerable human resources needed elsewhere. Legal expenses insurance (BTE – before-the-event), which is very common among private households in Germany, is not available to companies, even small ones. Very small businesses in particular have little experience with legal proceedings and are therefore reluctant to go to court. Their situation does not differ much from the situation of consumers. As a consequence, small businesses have developed a different business and conflict culture compared to large companies. Legal proceedings against suppliers and business partners are generally avoided because there is often a high degree of dependency, and court proceedings can jeopardise business relationships. Informal and voluntary solutions to maintain customer satisfaction prevail in dealings with customers, and there is a strategy to avoid disputes. Small businesses, therefore, often file court cases less often than other companies.[7] Nevertheless, there are situations in which small businesses cannot simply ignore the damage they have suffered and need to have access to court.

This chapter highlights the simplifications in law enforcement that the German legislature intended to achieve with the implementation of the Representative Actions Directive[8] (Section 2.2). In practice, however, this new option is rarely used. Therefore, the focus of this chapter is on a particular solution for claims by small businesses that are part of mass damages. This does not refer to minor damage only, but rather – especially in antitrust law – to major damage suffered by a small business. Here, the assignment

5 Ekert et al (n 4) 14–16.

6 Ekert et al (n 4) 90–240, based on interviews with various stakeholders.

7 For Switzerland, see S Herzberg, S Rieder, 'Das Verhältnis von KMU und zivilgerichtlicher Justiz' (2020) 31 LeGes 1.

8 European Parliament and of the Council Directive (EU) 2020/1828 on representative actions for the protection of the collective interests of consumers and repealing Directive 2009/22/EC (Representative Actions Directive) [2020] OJ L104/1.

model offered by specialised litigation companies (special purpose vehicles) has become established in Germany and elsewhere in Europe. It is not specifically tailored to the situation of small businesses, but it serves their interests to a particular degree. The litigation company, as a claims aggregator, plays a central role in this model, acting as the assignee of the claims to be enforced and as the plaintiff. While this model does not encounter any major difficulties in countries such as the Netherlands[9] or the United Kingdom (since the doctrine of champerty and maintenance has been overcome[10]), it is still viewed critically by some courts and authors in Germany today (Section 3).

Strictly speaking, this assignment model is not an instrument of collective redress in the narrow sense. The bundling of many claims in the hands of a single assignee and plaintiff still requires each individual claim to be decided by the court. This is a significant difference from the German implementation of the Representative Actions Directive in the Consumer Rights Enforcement Act (CREA, *Verbraucherrechtedurchsetzungsgesetz* (*VDuG*)).[11]

---

9 The transfer of a claim is considered a transfer of property under Dutch law and includes the right of action; for details see Ilja Tillema, *Entrepreneurial Mass Litigation* (Erasmus University Rotterdam 2019) 265. It is a matter of interpretation whether a full transfer is intended or only a mandate ('lastgeving', Dutch Civil Code Article 7:414). In many cases, Dutch courts have accepted a mandate, eg, Hoge Raad, 26 November 2004 NL:HR:2004:AP9665 (*Haantjes v Damstra*). The assignment model is also an often used construction in the Netherlands, and legal standing of the special purpose vehicle can be based either on an the assignment, or (in case the court considers it invalid) on the assignee's mandate to enforce the claims in the name of the assignors, see Hoge Raad, 27 November 2009 NL:HR:2009:BH2162 (*VEB v WOL*). Dutch Courts have also accepted assignments to which German law was applicable, eg, Rechtbank Den Haag, 17 December 2014 NL:RBDHA:2014:15722; Rechtbank Amsterdam, 10 May 2017 NL:RBAMS:2017:3166. Nevertheless, the assignment model is not particularly significant in practice in the Netherlands, because it is easier to establish a foundation that can bring a representative action for damages under the WAMCA (Dutch Act on Redress of Mass Damages in Collective Action), in force since 1 January 2020.

10 SPVs normally bear all litigation costs, which can be relevant under the 'maintenance and champerty' doctrine. Criminal liability has been abolished for these cases (Criminal Law Act 1967, s 14(2)), but courts have to decide case-by-case whether a financing agreement is valid. It is normally accepted since the legislator has allowed conditional fee arrangements in 1995 as long as the funder does not exercise control over the proceedings; see Tilema (n 5) 197; Simon Middelton and Jason Rowley, *Cook on Cost* (London 2023) paras 10.10–10.15 with further references.

11 Under the CREA in a collective redress action filed by a qualified entity in the interest of non-individualised consumers, the court has to decide only on the liability of the defendant and on the overall collective amount of damages. The defendant must pay the amount of damages into a fund which is administered and distributed by a fund administrator who also decides on the application of consumers to get compensation (CREA Sections 22–38).

2 Litigation-Related Support for Small Businesses in German Law

2.1 Injunctive Relief in Favour of Small Businesses

Apart from individual lawsuits, German procedural law allows trade associations and chambers of industry and commerce to bring injunctive relief actions on behalf of their members.[12] This protection is not specifically tailored to small businesses, but this option is available in principle under competition law, consumer law, and the law governing general terms and conditions. The main focus here is on the possibility of defending themselves against unfair conduct by competitors by preventing certain types of behaviour. However, compared to injunctions sought by consumer protection organisations, these proceedings are relatively rare.

2.2 Collective Redress Actions

Since the implementation of the Representative Actions Directive into German law,[13] consumer associations can also bring so-called redress actions aimed at obtaining damages in the interest of consumers. As a result of the German legislature's implementation of the Directive in a manner that goes beyond the Directive's requirements, consumer associations are not only able to take legal action in the interests of consumers in the traditional sense. CREA Section 1 includes, in its scope of application, micro businesses with fewer than 10 employees and an annual turnover or balance sheet that does not exceed €2 million. They are simply equated with consumers for the purposes of legal enforcement through collective actions. This regulation is the result of practical experience gained from *Dieselgate*. Not only private individuals but also many small craft businesses and companies had purchased manipulated diesel vehicles from VW. At that time, the model declaratory action introduced in 2018 only allowed consumer associations to bring declaratory actions for consumer claims, leaving these small businesses without support.

Although the idea of treating micro businesses and consumers equally in the context of representative actions is a good one, it will probably have limited practical consequences. Consumer associations are unwilling or unable to enforce small businesses' claims. One reason for this is that consumer associ-

12 Injunctions Act Sections 1–2a and 3; Unfair Competition Act (*Gesetz gegen den unlauteren Wettbewerb*) Sections 8–8b.

13 In October 2023, the Consumer Rights Enforcement Act (CREA) came into force. It includes redress actions and model declaratory actions filed by consumer associations in the interest of named or even unknown consumers.

ations are regularly required by their statutes to act solely in the interests of consumers and have no interest in pursuing the claims of small businesses at the association's cost and risk. However, according to the CREA, only consumer organisations are entitled to bring legal action.

Another reason lies, probably, in a legislative error. According to CREA Section 15, an action for redress is only admissible if the consumer claims (including those of micro businesses) affected by the collective action are essentially similar. According to the law, this is the case if the claims are based on the same facts or a series of essentially comparable facts and on essentially the same questions of fact and law. It follows from these cumulative requirements that the claims must be examined on the same legal basis.[14] As a consequence, the claims of consumers and small businesses, as defined in Section 1 CREA, cannot be pooled in the same redress action if the mass harm event is a contract case.[15] Contract rules are significantly different for B2C and B2B situations due to the European rules on consumer protection. Due to this significant difference, the claims are therefore not 'essentially similar' and the association risks having the action dismissed as inadmissible. As a consequence, consumer organisations have already explicitly excluded small businesses from recently filed contract-based redress actions in order not to jeopardise the admissibility of the action.[16]

3 The Assignment Model

In recent years, the so-called assignment model has become established in the German legal services market for enforcing consumer claims, but particularly for antitrust damages claims of businesses.[17] Small businesses are often victims of cartel agreements, but shy away from enforcing their claims for dam-

14 Stefan F Thönissen, 'Schadensersatz in der Verbandsabhilfeklage' (2023) Recht und Schaden (r+s) 749; D Paulus, '§ 15 mn 20' in D Skaudraszun, *Verbraucherrechtedurchsetzungsgesetz* (CH Beck 2024).

15 Felix Maultzsch, 'Das neue Verbraucherrechtedurchsetzungsgesetz – VDuG', (2024) Zeitschrift für Zivilprozess 119, 136.

16 Bundesjustizamt, 'Redress actions by Verbraucherzentrale Bundesverband (vzbv) – Actions vs DAZN Ltd, Vodafone Deutschland GmbH, and ExtraEnergie GmbH' (Verband- und Musterfeststellungsklagenregister 2025) https://www.bundesjustizamt.de/DE/Themen/Verbraucherrechte/VerbandsklageregisterMusterfeststellungsklagenregister/Verbandsklagenregister/Verbandsklagen/Klagen/202501/VRUG_1_2025_node.html (accessed 19 August 2026).

17 For a detailed analysis, see Holger Hiss, *Bündelung von Kartellschadensersatzansprüchen im Lichte des Rechtsdienstleistungsgesetzes* (Nomos 2023).

ages themselves. They want to avoid direct confrontation with their business partner in court and do not have the human resources to conduct these costly proceedings. Contingency fee arrangements with lawyers are available under German law only for small claims up to an amount of €2,000.[18] However, small businesses are quite willing to pay a price for enforcing their sometimes quite high cartel damages claims if they are not involved in the litigation themselves. The business model of claims vehicles or special purpose vehicles (SPVs) meets precisely this need. Even though it is currently mainly applied in antitrust law, it can, in principle, be transferred to other cases. For minor damages, however, it will remain rather unattractive for both the SPV (hardly worth the success fee) and small businesses.

3.1 Licenced Debt Collecting Companies as Claims Aggregators

3.1.1 Formal Requirements for Claims Aggregators and Cost Issues

There are numerous licenced debt collection companies operating on the German market today, many of which also rely on legal technology for their claims-bundling model. The most common business model is based on a fiduciary assignment of the potential claims for damages to be enforced. The debt collection companies buy either claims from consumers affected by the same mass harm event, such as the violation of consumer law, or a delayed or cancelled flight, which leads to claims for compensation under the rules of the EU Air Passenger Rights Regulation.[19] Companies such as Cartel Damages Claims and other SPVs have established themselves in the field of antitrust law, specialising in the enforcement of claims for damages held by companies arising from cartels. The assigned claims are bundled together in a single action, which has several advantages: the joinder of claims enables joint proceedings and a joint taking of evidence. In addition, significant cost advantages arise particularly in cases involving high claims. Court costs and reimbursable attorneys' fees, which depend on the amount in dispute under German rules, are subject to a cap of the amount in controversy of €30 million,[20] making collective action considerably cheaper than individual lawsuits. The assignees

---

18 Act on the Remuneration of Lawyers (*Rechtsanwaltsvergütungsgesetz*) Section 4a para 1.

19 European Parliament and Council Regulation (EC) No 261/2004 establishing common rules on compensation and assistance to passengers in the event of denied boarding and of cancellation or long delay of flights, and repealing Regulation (EEC) No 295/91 [2004] OJ L46/1.

20 Court Costs Act (*Gerichtskostengesetz*) Section 38 para 2; Act on the Remuneration of Lawyers Section 22 para 2.

typically bear the financial risks of the litigation and, in return, agree with the assignors on a success fee between 25% and 35% of the amount of damages obtained.[21] Licenced debt collectors are not subject to the restrictions on contingency fees for lawyers because they are not lawyers in the formal sense.[22] They often use an external litigation financier to cover the costs of the proceedings, including adverse cost orders.

The debt collectors are legal service providers that are often created solely for the enforcement of claims arising from a particular mass harm event. Under the German Legal Service Act, they are required to obtain a special registration as legal service providers.[23] Registration is intended to ensure a certain degree of official supervision and to guarantee the quality of legal services. Legal service providers must demonstrate specialised legal expertise.[24] However, if they take legal action, they must be represented by a lawyer in court.

A fundamental concern about the involvement of such claims aggregators stems from the loser pays principle and the plaintiff's liability for adverse cost orders in the event of the dismissal of the case. If the SPV does not have sufficient capital to reimburse the defendant's costs in the event of the case being lost, this may, according to the case law of German courts, affect the validity of the assignment.[25] There may be a suspicion that an indigent plaintiff is being put forward to the detriment of the defendant. In practice, the problem is currently solved either by a third-party litigation financier guaranteeing reimbursement or by the claims aggregator voluntarily providing security for the costs of the proceedings.

---

21 For details of the assignment based business model, see Astrid Stadler, 'Funding of mass claims in Germany - caught between a rock and a hard place?' in W van Boom (ed), Litigation, costs, funding and behaviour – implications for the law, (Taylor & Francis 2016) 201 – 221; Astrid Stadler, 'Abtretungsmodelle und gewerbliche Prozessfinanzierung bei Masseschäden' (2018) Wirtschaft und Wettbewerb 189; Astrid Stadler, 'Third party funding of mass litigation in Germany Entreprenurial Parties – Curse or blessing?' in Loic Cadiet, B Hess and M Requejo (eds), *Privatizing Dispute Resolution – Trends and Limits* (Nomos 2019) 209–232; Thomas Riehm, 'Effektive Rechtsdurchsetzung durch finanzierte Abtretungsmodelle', (2024) Neue Juristische Wochenschrift 2713; and Thomas A Heiß, 'Massenverfahren und die Zukunft des deutschen Zivilprozesses' (2025) Neue Juristische Wochenschrift 1625.

22 BGH 13 July 2021, II ZR 84/20 (2021) Neue Juristische Wochenschrift, 3046, para 39.

23 Legal Services Act Section 10.

24 Legal Services Act Section 11: '(1) Debt collection services require special expertise in the areas of law relevant to the debt collection activities applied for, in particular civil law, commercial law, securities law, company law, civil procedure law, including enforcement and insolvency law, and costs law.'

25 LG Düsseldorf 17 December 2013 DE:LGD:2013:1217.37O200.09KART.U.00; OLG Düsseldorf 18 February 2015 DE:OLGD:2015:0218.VI.U.KART3.14.00.

3.1.2 Advantages of the Assignment Model for Small Businesses

Although the assignment model involves a not inconsiderable success fee for the assignees, it offers many advantages, particularly for small businesses. Above all, claims aggregation in the hands of a single plaintiff is an effective instrument for improving bargaining power in cartel damages litigation.

Even in follow-on antitrust lawsuits, individual plaintiffs bear a high risk of proving their case in individual lawsuits. Calculating the damage caused by a cartel can be complicated in individual cases and requires expensive expert opinions.[26] Claimants often face considerable upfront costs to prepare for litigation. Individual plaintiffs cannot afford this. Bundling many similar claims against the same defendants not only reduces costs but also increases the bargaining power of the plaintiff in settlement negotiations. Defendants in cartel damages actions are very often large corporations that are represented by specialised lawyers. They spare no expense when it comes to winning against an individual plaintiff because they want to avoid setting a precedent at all costs. The imbalance between individual plaintiffs and the defendants is further exacerbated by the fact that the jointly and severally liable cartel members (German Antitrust Act (*Gesetz gegen Wettbewerbsbeschränkungen*) Section 33d) regularly form a joint defence group, pool their resources, and develop a common defence strategy that is fundamentally aimed at dismissing the action. However, when faced with multiple claims in a single proceeding and a powerful and financially well-funded plaintiff, the strategy often looks different. The chance of a settlement is thus significantly higher than in an individual lawsuit.

Due to the assignment, the assignors are not directly involved in the court proceedings. This avoids direct confrontation with the defendant, who is the assignors' business partner, which is often very important to small businesses. As a result, due to the cost and personnel structure in small businesses, it is

---

26 Franziska Weber, *Der Kartellschaden* (Tübingen Mohr 2021) 40, with special reference to the situation in Germany and the Netherlands in §§ 5 and 6; Holger Hiss, *Bündelung von Kartellschadensersatzansprüchen im Lichte des Rechtsdienstleistungsgesetzes*, (Nomos Baden-Baden 2023) 201; Cento Veljanovski, 'Calculating Cartel Damages' in P Whelan (ed), *Research Handbook on Cartels*, (Edward Elgar 2021) with further references. Recent case law tends to calculate damages based on an estimation by the court in situations in which even experts are not able to provide exact calculations (Civil Procedure Code (Zivilprozessordnung) Section 287). However, depending on the nature of the cartel, expert opinions have not become completely insignificant; see OLG Schleswig, 12 October 2023, 16 U 97/16 (2021) Beck-Rechtsprechung 27784; BGH 9 July 2024, file no KZR 98/20 (2024) Gewerblicher Rechtsschutz und Urheberrecht-Rechtsprechung 26023 ('LKW Kartell IV').

generally cheaper to outsource the litigation risk to a claims aggregator and accept the contingency fee.

3.2 Attacks on the Assignment Model

It is obvious that the defendants in cartel damages actions are fighting the assignment model on all fronts.[27] They have been successful in some lower German courts for a long time because the courts seize every opportunity to get rid of these complex and almost insurmountable proceedings. If the courts follow the defendant's argument that the assignment to the claims aggregator is already null and void, the action can be dismissed as unfounded without having to address the difficult questions of antitrust damages. Such concessions are psychologically understandable because, under the assignment model, the merits of each individual claim must be examined by the court individually. In some antitrust proceedings, this means that several thousand sales transactions must be examined, and the damage incurred must be calculated.[28] Unlike claim vehicles, German courts often lack the necessary resources to do this.

The attacks on the business model of debt collection companies were also motivated by the fact that lawyers increasingly saw themselves facing competition from players operating under different rules. Unlike lawyers, claims aggregators were able to charge contingency fees, which distorted the competitive environment. The attempt by the German legislator to create a level

27 The attacks were supported in legal literature (often based on expert opinions submitted to the court), see, eg, Daniel Valdini, 'Klagen ohne Risiko – Prozessfinanzierung und Inkassodienstleistung aus einer Hand als zulässige Rechtsdienstleistung?' (2017) Der Betriebsberater 1609; Reinhard Greger, 'Das "Rundum-sorglos-Modell": Innovative Rechtsdienstleistung oder Ausverkauf des Rechts?' (2018) Monatschrift des Deutschen Rechts 897; Martin Henssler, 'Prozessfinanzierende Inkassodienstleister – Befreit von den Schranken des anwaltlichen Berufsrechts?' (2019) Neue Juristische Wochenschrift 545.

28 In May 2026, the Federal Court of Justice issued a landmark decision imposing restrictions on the assignment model. In the case, thousands of claims from more than 20 different jurisdictions were in controversy, and the court estimated it would take 38 years to decide the whole case. It concluded that the claimant abused the assignment model and asked for a separation of claims. As a consequence, it remains unclear for future actions how many claims can be bundled. For details, see BGH 12 May 2026, KZR 6/24 (2026) NZKart 314; Astrid Stadler, 'Bundesgerichtshof rules on the assignment model in Financialrights (12 May 2026) *Case Note KZR 6/24*' (2026) Mass Claims Journal 55.

playing field[29] by granting lawyers contingency fees on a very limited basis[30] failed to allay the concerns of the legal profession.

Formally, the objections to the assignment model regularly referred to the requirements for their activities under the Legal Services Act (*Rechtsdienstleistungsgesetz*). It was repeatedly argued that debt collection companies exceeded their licence when they became active in the highly complex area of antitrust law,[31] and that their registration entitled them at best to extrajudicial activities. Another argument alleges a violation of Section 4 of the Legal Services Act, which addresses conflicts of interest on the part of debt collection service providers. Defendants argued that the bundling of many claims from different assignors of different validity makes it impossible to treat everyone equally in settlement negotiations, for example. If the settlement amount provided by the defendant is distributed pro rata, weak claims are often given preferential treatment over 'good' claims. The involvement of an external litigation funder could also lead to a conflict of interest on the part of the assignee, particularly in settlement negotiations. On the one hand, the funder may wish to end the proceedings early for a certain settlement amount as soon as their investment has paid off. The assignors, to whom the claims aggregator is equally contractually bound, on the other hand, expect the proceedings to continue.[32]

The attacks can generally have far-reaching consequences. Since the courts continue to hold, despite massive criticism, that serious violations of the Legal Services Act render the assignment, and not just the underlying agency agreement, null and void,[33] this would lead to the dismissal of the action as unfounded. In the past, this had already led to the lawsuit not

29 Law on the Promotion of Consumer-Friendly Offers in the Legal Services Market (Gesetz zur Förderung verbrauchergerechter Angebote im Rechtsdienstleistungsmarkt), 10 August 2021, Federal Law Gazette I 2021, 3415 (the new act imposed stricter regulations for the registration of legal service providers, but also allowed contingency fee arrangements for lawyers for small claims). For details of the legislator's position, see Draft of the Federal Government, BR-Drs 58/21 (22 January 2021).

30 Act on the Remuneration of Lawyers Section 4a(1).

31 LG Stuttgart, 20 January 2022, case no 30 O 176/19, juris, para 88; LG Mainz, 7 October 2022, case no 9 O 125/20, juris; for similar cases arising from other cartels see LG Hannover, 4 May 2020, case no 18 O 50/16, juris, para 171; LG Hannover, 1 February 2021, case no 18 O 34/17, juris 296; LG Stuttgart, 28 April 2022, case no 30 O 17/18, juris, para 74.

32 For these arguments, see the authors referred to in n 27.

33 German Civil Code (*Bürgerliches Gesetzbuch*) Section 134 together with the provisions of Legal Services Act.

suspending the limitation period because the wrong creditor had brought the action. The antitrust damages claims were therefore finally time-barred.[34]

The Federal Court of Justice (*Bundesgerichtshof*, BGH) has finally rejected these arguments in a number of landmark decisions and confirmed the admissibility of the assignment model. The court confirmed that licenced debt collectors may also enforce cartel damages claims in court and that they need not prove specialised knowledge in antitrust law in their application for registration.[35] It was also held that, in principle, no conflict of interest relevant under Section 4 of the Legal Services Act exists when a debt collector bundles numerous claims by different assignors in a single lawsuit.[36] The court emphasised that the assignors (at least in cartel damages cases) regularly make an informed choice and are aware that not all claims can be treated equally, but would accept possible disadvantages in view of the immense advantages of joint enforcement.[37]

3.3 Necessity of Making the Assignment Model Available Under European Law

3.3.1 Reference for a Preliminary Ruling by the LG Dortmund 2023

The fact that small businesses benefit particularly from the assignment model in combination with litigation financing cannot obscure the fact that this model has generally become an important instrument of private enforcement for all injured parties, particularly in antitrust law. In the *CDC Hydro-*

---

34 Astrid Stadler, 'Die Bündelung von gleichgerichteten Ansprüchen durch Inkassozession' (2014) *Juristenzeitung* 613; LG Dortmund, 13 March 2023, case no 8 O 7/20(Kart) (2023) Beck-Rechtsprechung 5354, para 27. Today, it is a controversial issue whether an action brought on the basis of a void assignment can stop the limitation period from running. OLG Düsseldorf, 10 August 2023, case no 6 U 133/22 (2023) Beck-Rechtsprechung 21320, para 34, denied the question, but other court decisions still require that the 'right' creditor files the action, BGH, 9 December 2010, III ZR 56/10 (2011) Neue Juristische Wochenschrift 2193, para 9; Riehm (n 21).

35 See, BGH 13 July 2021, II ZR 84/20 (2021) Neue Juristische Wochenschrift 3046; BGH 13 June 2022, VIa ZR 418/21 (2022) Neue Juristische Wochenschrift 3350; BGH 5 December 2022, VIa ZR 998/22 (2022) Beck-Rechtsprechung 37853, para 14.

36 BGH 13 June 2022, VIa ZR 418/21 (2022) Neue Juristische Wochenschrift 3350, para 50; BGH, 13 July 2021, II ZR 84/20 (2021) Neue Juristische Wochenschrift 3046 paras 47 and 49; BGH, 5 December 2022, VIa ZR 998/22 (2022) Beck-Rechtsprechung 37853, para 14.

37 This might be different if the assignors are consumers who are not aware of the risks of bundling and third-party funding. A 2021 reform of the Legal Services Act therefore has imposed numerous information duties on legal service providers as a safeguard for consumers, for details see Legal Services Act Sections 13a and 13b.

gen Peroxide case, Advocate General *Jääskinen* already stated in 2014 that a joint action of the victims of a cartel may be the only reasonable way to enforce antitrust claims.[38] On the occasion of the adoption of the Damages Directive,[39] the European Commission also emphasised that the acquisition of potential claims for damages for joint enforcement is lawful and facilitates access to litigation financing.[40]

In 2023, the LG Dortmund referred similar questions to the European Court of Justice for a preliminary ruling.[41] The factual background was a series of cartel damages actions related to timber marketing. The Federal Cartel Office had raised antitrust concerns regarding the marketing of round timber (felled tree trunks in their raw state) by German state forestry agencies and, in some cases, by private forest owners with large areas of land in several German states. The joint marketing of timber could restrict competition by bundling supply and influencing pricing. Sawmills had to accept the prices set by state forestry administrations. Large sawmills were affected, but so were small and medium-sized ones. In the action brought before the LG Dortmund in 2020, the plaintiff, a claims aggregator, claimed damages for antitrust violations on behalf of a total of 32 sawmill companies. The claim for damages arising from the antitrust infringement is based on several hundred thousand individual roundwood purchases made by the assignors.

In a nutshell, the Court came to the conclusion that the bundling of these claims by the plaintiff might violate the Legal Services Act, as the debt collector lacked specific expertise in antitrust law that the court considered essential for standalone cartel damages actions.[42] If this were to be decided, the action would have to be dismissed as unfounded on the merits due to the assignments being null and void. In this respect, however, the Court had doubts as to whether this interpretation of the German Legal Services Act did not constitute a violation of the Damages Directive. According to the directive, anyone who has suffered damage as a result of a cartel is entitled to full compensation, and the directive must be implemented by the Member States

---

38 Case C-352/13 *Cartel Damage Claims (CDC) Hydrogen Peroxide SA v Akzo Nobel NV and Others*, Opinion of Advocate General Jääskinen [2014] EU:C:2014:2443, para 29.

39 European Parliament and Council Directive 2014/104/EU of the European Parliament and of the Council of 26 November 2014 on certain rules governing actions for damages under national law for infringements of the competition law provisions of the Member States and of the European Union (Damages Directive) [2014] OJ L349/1.

40 Commission, 'Communication from the Commission – Guidelines for national courts on how to estimate the share of overcharge which was passed on to the indirect purchasers', C/2019/4899, para 27.

41 LG Dortmund 13 March 2023, case no 8 O 7/20 (Kart) (2023) Beck-Rechtsprechung 5354.

42 Ibid, para 26.

in accordance with the principle of *effet utile*. In this context, the court stated that the assignment model under German law is *de facto* the only sensible way to enforce antitrust claims, as there would otherwise be no possibility of collective redress. A strict interpretation of the legal framework of the assignment model could therefore violate the Directive.

It referred the question to the European Court of Justice as to whether, if an interpretation in conformity with European law is ruled out, the relevant provisions of German law must remain inapplicable, which would mean that the assignments are valid in any event from this point of view and that effective enforcement of the law is possible.

3.3.2 Decision of the European Court of Justice

In its ruling, the ECJ emphasised the great importance of private enforcement in antitrust law, but refrained from making the clear statement the LG Dortmund had hoped for. The Court left open the question whether the collective action based on assignments was the only way to enforce the claims in the specific case and whether there was a threat of a violation of EU law. The ECJ confirmed that the Damages Directive 'must be interpreted as precluding an interpretation of national legislation which has the effect of preventing persons allegedly harmed by an infringement of competition law from assigning their rights to compensation to a provider of legal services so that it may assert them, collectively, in an action for damages'. However, this only applies on the condition that

> – national law does not provide for any other possibility of grouping together the individual claims of those injured persons that would ensure the effectiveness of the exercise of those rights to compensation, and
> – the bringing of an individual action for damages is, having regard to all the circumstances of the case, impossible or excessively difficult for those persons, with the result that they are deprived of their right to effective judicial protection.[43]

It passed the ball back to the referring court, which alone can and must decide whether these conditions are fulfilled.[44] The ECJ considers that the complexity of the antitrust damages alone does not make enforcement by means of

43 Case C-253/23 *ASG 2 Ausgleichsgesellschaft für die Sägeindustrie Nordrhein-Westfalen GmbH v Land Nordrhein-Westfalen* [2025] EU:C:2025:40, para 95.

44 Case C-253, para 84.

individual actions excessively difficult from the outset.[45] Furthermore, if the referring court considers the assignment model to be the only practicable means of enforcing the cartel damages claims, the referring court must examine whether an interpretation of the Legal Services Act in conformity with EU law might not be possible after all.

3.3.3 Consequences of the Decision

It has already been concluded from the judgment that the ECJ considers collective redress at least for antitrust law to be guaranteed by EU law if no effective private enforcement is available otherwise.[46] This is a considerable step forward.

The referring court had essentially already explained the necessity of using the assignment model specifically for a standalone action. The pitfalls of the Legal Services Act lie in the fact that the assignment to the claims aggregator is regularly a fiduciary assignment, and the assignors remain economically interested in the enforcement of the claim because they ultimately receive the proceeds minus the success fee. Not covered by the Legal Services Act and therefore unproblematic would be an assignment of claims by way of 'genuine factoring', a complete and final assignment in which the assignor is fully satisfied with the purchase price paid by the assignee. However, this is not a viable option in view of the special features of antitrust damages. The LG Dortmund emphasised:[47]

> First, there are significant problems with determining the purchase price and accounting for it, because the amount of damages required for this is ultimately unknown in antitrust damages cases and is therefore the core problem in every case. The assignors would therefore have to sell their claims to a third party for a fraction of their nominal value due to significant security discounts and would ultimately give up their prospects of compensation, which is why this is not an effective means of enforcing claims.

It is unlikely that the referring court will back down from this position. In the present case, it must then either deny that there has been a violation of the

---

45 Case C-253, para 86.

46 Christopher Unseld, Annotation to CJEU 28 January 2025, Case C-253/23, Kartellrecht: Notwendigkeit eines kollektiven Rechtsbehelfs im Kartellschadensersatz' (2025) Europäische Zeitschrift für Wirtschaftsrecht, 434, 435.

47 This was also emphasised by LG Dortmund 13 March 2023 DE:LGDO:2023:0313.8O7.20-KART.00, para 33.

Legal Services Act on the basis of an interpretation of its provisions in line with European law or declare the relevant provisions inapplicable as contrary to European law.

4 Conclusions

The assignment model is an important option for small businesses, particularly for the purposes of enforcing their rights in antitrust and competition law. Unlike large companies, small businesses are often unable to enforce their claims in individual proceedings for several reasons. Despite much hostility, the assignment model has ultimately prevailed in Germany both legally and in practice. This significantly improves access to justice for small businesses. Consumers, by contrast, can sue individually with the help of legal expenses insurance or, in simple mass damage cases, join a representative action brought by a consumer association. The options for small businesses, on the other hand, are much more limited for the reasons discussed. Their situation has not yet been adequately addressed by national or European legislators. The solutions developed by the legal services market come at a price (success fees), but at least they fill a gap in certain situations today. Once courts and lawyers have finally accepted the role of debt collectors and their business model, the legal services market will be able to offer flexible solutions for various situations. A basic prerequisite remains that third-party financing is not subject to excessive legislative restrictions in the future.[48]

Bibliography

Ekert S, Meller-Hannich C and Nöhre N, *Erforschung der Ursachen des Rückgangs der Eingangszahlen bei den Zivilgerichten* (Bundesministerium der Justiz April 2023).

Greger R, 'Das "Rundum-sorglos-Modell": Innovative Rechtsdienstleistung oder Ausverkauf des Rechts?' (2018) Monatsschrift des Deutschen Rechts 897.

48 The proposal of the European Parliament for a Directive on Responsible third-party funding of civil litigation from September 2022 (2020/2130(INL)) was met with considerable criticism. Based on a mapping study on third-party funding by the EU Commission the Commission seems to accept that there is currently no need for legislative action. See *Mapping third-party litigation funding in the European Union* (final report, March 2025): https://commission.europa.eu/strategy-and-policy/policies/justice-and-fundamental-rights/civil-justice/civil-and-commercial-law/third-party-litigation-funding-tplf_en (accessed 19 August 2026).

Heiß TA, 'Massenverfahren und die Zukunft des deutschen Zivilprozesses' (2024) Neue Juristische Wochenschrift 1625.

Henssler M, 'Prozessfinanzierende Inkassodienstleister – Befreit von den Schranken des anwaltlichen Berufsrechts?' (2019) Neue Juristische Wochenschrift 545.

Herzberg S and Rieder S, 'Das Verhältnis von KMU und zivilgerichtlicher Justiz' (2020) 31 LeGes 1.

Hiss H, *Bündelung von Kartellschadensersatzansprüchen im Lichte des Rechtsdienstleistungsgesetzes* (Nomos 2023).

Maultzsch F, 'Das neue Verbraucherrechtedurchsetzungsgesetz – VDuG' (2024) Zeitschrift für Zivilprozess 137.

Paulus D, '§ 15 mn 20' in D Skaudraszun (ed), *Verbraucherrechtedurchsetzungsgesetz* (1st edn, CH Beck 2024).

Riehm T, 'Effektive Rechtsdurchsetzung durch finanzierte Abtretungsmodelle' (2024) Neue Juristische Wochenschrift 2713.

Stadler A, 'Abtretungsmodelle und gewerbliche Prozessfinanzierung bei Masseschäden' (2016) Wirtschaft und Wettbewerb 189.

Stadler A, 'Die Bündelung von gleichgerichteten Ansprüchen durch Inkassozession' (2014) JuristenZeitung 613.

Stadler A, 'Funding of Mass Claims in Germany – Caught between a Rock and a Hard Place?' in W van Boom (ed), *Litigation, Costs, Funding and Behaviour – Implications for the Law* (Taylor & Francis 2016).

Stadler A, 'Third Party Funding of Mass Litigation in Germany: Entrepreneurial Parties – Curse or Blessing?' in L Cadiet, B Hess and M Requejo (eds), *Privatising Dispute Resolution – Trends and Limits* (Nomos 2019).

Stadler A., 'Bundesgerichtshof rules on the assignment model in Financialrights (12 May 2026)' (2026) Mass Claims Journal 55.

Thönissen SF, 'Schadensersatz in der Verbandsabhilfeklage' (2023) Recht und Schaden 749.

Tillema I, *Entrepreneurial Mass Litigation* (Erasmus University Rotterdam 2019).

Unseld C, Annotation to CJEU 28 January 2025, Case C-253/23 'Kartellrecht: Notwendigkeit eines kollektiven Rechtsbehelfs im Kartellschadensersatz' (2025) Europäische Zeitschrift für Wirtschaftsrecht 434.

Valdini D, 'Klagen ohne Risiko – Prozessfinanzierung und Inkassodienstleistung aus einer Hand als zulässige Rechtsdienstleistung?' (2017) Der Betriebs-Berater 1609.

Veljanovski C, 'Calculating Cartel Damages' in P Whelan (ed), *Research Handbook on Cartels* (Edward Elgar 2021).

Weber F, *Der Kartellschaden* (Mohr Siebeck 2021).

Index

 | HTTPS://DOI.ORG/10.1163/9789004779235-012